ENGLAND
IN THE AGE OF
DICKENS

Jeremy Black is Professor of History at Exeter University. He is a prolific lecturer and writer, the author of over 100 books. Many concern aspects of eighteenth-century British, European and American political, diplomatic and military history but he has also published on the history of the press, cartography, warfare, culture and on the nature and uses of history itself. He sits on the editorial boards of *History Today*, *International History Review*, *Journal of Military History*, and *Media History*.

Praise for Jeremy Black

George III

'Black's analysis of George III is a welcome addition. [He] ... manages to pepper his trim narrative with lovely frills. The mark of a good short book is its ability to inspire curiosity and further investigation. Black achieves just that.'

Gerard DeGroot, *THE TIMES*

'Black brilliantly demolishes the paranoiac Whig view of George ... The George who emerges is a far more attractive figure than the Whig historians depicted.'

Andrew Roberts, *THE CRITIC*

A Short History of Britain

'A superb account ... Written by one of Britain's leading historians, it draws on an unrivalled knowledge and a wealth of scholarship; at the same time it is a highly readable and engaging. This is history at its best ... If you want to read a single book to understand how the past informs the present, this is it.'

William Gibson, Professor of History, Oxford Brookes University

'An important and much-needed overview and re-appraisal of British history from the Romans to the present ... offered in a lively and compelling manner ... should be read widely by anyone interested in the history of Britain.'

Keith Laybourn, Diamond Jubilee Professor, University of Huddersfield

ENGLAND
IN THE AGE OF
DICKENS
1812–70

JEREMY BLACK

AMBERLEY

For
Richard Humphreys

This edition published 2023

Amberley Publishing
The Hill, Stroud
Gloucestershire, GL5 4EP

www.amberley-books.com

Copyright © Jeremy Black, 2021, 2023

The right of Jeremy Black to be identified as
the Author of this work has been asserted in
accordance with the Copyright, Designs and
Patents Act 1988.

ISBN 978 1 3981 1549 1 (paperback)
ISBN 978 1 3981 0170 8 (ebook)

British Library Cataloguing in Publication Data.
A catalogue record for this book is available
from the British Library.

1 2 3 4 5 6 7 8 9 10

Typesetting by SJmagic DESIGN SERVICES, India.
Printed in India.

CONTENTS

PREFACE

To many, Dickens is the chronicler of Victorian England, and
notably of Victorian London. Understandably so. Largely based
in the capital, Dickens produced amateur dramatics for the
queen, and knew leading lights of the reign, including three prime
ministers: Benjamin Disraeli, William Gladstone and, most of all,
Lord John Russell, a key political figure from the 1830s to the
1860s and the last with considerable mutual sympathy.

Yet, Dickens (1812–70), who was seven years younger than the
queen, died with thirty-one years of the reign (1837–1901) still
to go. Moreover, most of his formative years were spent in earlier
reigns: those of George IV (as king, 1820–30, rather than Prince
Regent), and of William IV (1830–7). Although it might seem
hard to credit, Dickens' life overlapped with that of Jane Austen
(1775–1816), and had hers not been so cruelly cut short by
illness, the overlap would have been longer. For that matter, there
were overlaps with the writers of Romanticism, notably Robert
Southey and William Wordsworth, who were poets laureate from
1813 to 1843 and 1843 to 1850 respectively.

So placing Dickens is less easy than it might appear. He travelled extensively by train and crossed the Atlantic to the United States by steamer. Yet, his life was distant from such late Victorian innovations as the bicycle, the motor car, the telephone, alternating current for electricity, and the cinema. Indeed, the world he depicted appeared somewhat dated in that backdrop, and very much was so.

The context for Dickens' life is that of the early nineteenth century. Moulded by it, he was part of the reaction to its conditions and values; and thus a framer of the Victorian age, rather than its product. This is even more the case if his novels are considered, for, in his last years, Dickens largely abandoned the format in order to focus on his public readings. In November 1865, *Our Mutual Friend*, his last complete novel, was published. The readings were more lucrative, both in terms of the money earned and with regard to the important validation offered Dickens by the applauding audience. Dickens returned to novels at the close, with his atmospheric, but unfinished, *Mystery of Edwin Drood*; but that was an echo of an earlier career.

Moreover, although *Our Mutual Friend* begins with the words 'In these times of ours,' some of his novels, and not only the two historical ones – *A Tale of Two Cities* and *Barnaby Rudge* – were not contemporaneous, but, instead, set in earlier periods. Thus, the action of *Great Expectations* can be dated to 1807–26, while *Little Dorrit* was set when there were no railways: Arthur Clennam comes from Dover to London by coach, and Tip Dorrit from London to Liverpool by boat, rather than train, while, in the introduction, Marshalsea Prison is referred to 'thirty years ago', with the addition, 'It remained there some years afterwards; but it is gone now.'[1] In *David Copperfield*, Murdstone and Grinby's warehouse 'was down in Blackfriars. Modern improvements have altered the place; but it was the last house ...'[2] *The Old Curiosity Shop* is set about 1825; and *Edwin Drood* is set before the railway came to Cloisterham, which is based on Rochester; whereas 'in these days' the railway goes through.[3]

In many respects, Dickens was most comfortable with these earlier days, both in describing reality and in handling the imagination. Thus, he handles travel by coach with a better sensitivity to events and moods than travel by train. Instead, the train is described as an imposition on the landscape.

There are excellent biographies of Dickens, and I recommend in particular that by Claire Tomalin, while Peter Ackroyd's throws brilliant light on Dickens' working methods. This is not such a work. Instead, following on from similar books on Shakespeare and Austen, I consider the backdrop of his age, both in terms of what happened and by reference to his novels. This backdrop not only provided him with the experiences that he turned into gripping copy, but also offered his readers and listeners the experience to appreciate this most dramatic of novelists. He also wrote plays, but they had less success, and only deserve revival as curiosities.

Dickens might appear to be describing and conjuring up a world far distant from that of the present day, but there is much in his work that directly speaks to the latter, not least because he focused on London, unlike Thomas Hardy who concentrated on the rural world and hated modernity. Dickens writes of the pressurised nature of modern urban life, the strains of modernisation – especially in rapidly expanding cities – and disturbing aspects of social vulnerability, and they are all very contemporary. The current focus on identity through gender, race and sexuality may appear to have fewer echoes in his work, but Dickens' concerns with capital, income, social opportunity, and class are more pertinent on a global scale. So also with his view that morality was in large part more significant than formal structures, a view made more relevant by modern distortions of language such that many democracies, for example, are not democratic. Self-validation by the group, a classic feature of modern society, and one facilitated by social media, can be considered with reference to Dickens' comment in *Nicholas Nickleby*:

cases of injustice, and oppression, and tyranny, and the most extravagant bigotry, are in constant occurrence among us every day. It is the custom to trumpet forth much wonder and astonishment at the chief actors therein setting at defiance so completely the opinion of the world; but there is no greater fallacy; it is precisely because they do consult the opinion of their own little world that such things take place at all, and strike the great world dumb with amazement.[4]

I have benefited from the wealth of scholarship available and from the comments on earlier drafts by George Boyce, Duncan Campbell, Bruce Coleman, Eileen Cox, Grayson Ditchfield, Bill Gibson, Will Hay, Peter Spear and Philip Waller. None is responsible for any errors that remain, but all have helped with their comments, and I would like to take this opportunity to record my sadness at the death of George, a friend of over three decades' standing. It is a great pleasure to dedicate this book to Richard Humphreys, a long-time friend who helps provide the reassurance of sensible advice.

I

LONDON: THE STAGE OF ALL

Tiers upon tiers of vessels, scores of masts, labyrinths of tackle, idle sails, splashing oars, gliding row-boats, lumbering barges, sunken piles, with ugly lodgings for the water-rat within their mud-discoloured nooks; church steeples, warehouses, house-roofs, arches, bridges, men and women, children, casks, cranes, boxes, horses, coaches, idlers, and hard-labourers: there they were, all jumbled up together, any summer morning.[1]

Born in Kent, and not in London's Kent suburbs, Dickens was a Londoner only by adoption. Yet, the city fixed his novels as a presence thanks to the strong and lasting grip of his experience there from childhood. These included the travails of young labour, in his case in a factory that made blacking, a paste dye for shoes and stoves. There was also his adult vocation as a busy journalist and editor, his life in a range of rented property, as well as his active commitment to social life in the city, notably that of restaurants and theatres.

There were other places of appeal for Dickens, notably Kent, where he bought Gad's Hill, a residence he had identified in childhood. So also with his journeys to the Continent, particularly to France, but also to Italy and Switzerland. Yet, even though experience of the Continent led Dickens to become disenchanted with London, and while he was delighted to move to Gad's Hill, it was to the city that Dickens turned most frequently, and literally so in his long walks – by modern standards very long walks – in the evening. These were not the strolls of a *boulevardier*, as were to become popular for Parisians, but, rather, as with his presence, speech, acting, and writing, determined, energetic, purposeful walks, pushing himself, his body and his mind, observing and reflecting, sorting ideas and absorbing impressions. He began his pamphlet *Sunday under Three Heads* (1836), a rejoinder to attempts to enforce Sabbatarianism, thus: 'There are few things from which I derive greater pleasure, than walking through some of the principal streets of London on a fine Sunday, in summer, and watching the cheerful faces of the lively groups with which they are thronged.'

His walks built on the pattern of eighteenth-century perambulations, walking for discovery, and the related publications with which Dickens was familiar, notably those by Ned Ward.[2] The Bröntes were also vigorous walkers.

Dickens also had some of his characters walk long distances in London, as was indeed normal, and thereby gain an opportunity to reflect on what they saw. Thus, in *Little Dorrit*, in the person of Arthur Clennam, a positive figure:

As he went along, upon a dreary night, the dim streets by which he went seemed all depositories of oppressive secrets. The deserted counting-houses, with their secrets of books and papers locked up in chests and safes; the banking-houses, with their secrets of strong rooms and walls, the keys of which were in a very few secret pockets and a very few secret breasts; the secrets of all the dispersed grinders in the vast mill, among whom there were doubtless plunderers, forgers, and trust-betrayers of many sorts, whom the light of any day that dawned might reveal; he could have fancied that these things, in hiding, imparted a heaviness to the air.

The shadow thickening and thickening as he approached its source, he thought of the secrets of the lonely church-vaults, where the people who had hoarded and secreted in iron coffers were in their turn similarly hoarded, not yet at rest from doing harm; and then of the secrets of the river, as it rolled its turbid tide between two frowning wildernesses of secrets, extending, thick and dense, for many miles.[3]

So, let us start with the London of Dickens' lifetime. It was the world city, and its image, once happily confined for painters and mapmakers in a single vista, now burst the page unless a distant aerial viewpoint was taken. The variety of London also challenged the novelist. The simple dichotomy of Henry Fielding's era, a century earlier, that of the industrious and moral City versus the luxurious and decadent West End (and Dickens was very familiar with Fielding's novels), still had its value as a device. Thus, in *Martin Chuzzlewit*, Tom Pinch, taking a coach from Salisbury, finds it

… none of your steady-going, yoked coaches, but a swaggering, rakish, dissipated London coach; up all night, and lying by all day, and leading a devil of a life. It cared no more for Salisbury than if it had been a hamlet. It rattled noisily through the best streets, defied the Cathedral, took the worst corners sharpest, went cutting in everywhere, making everything get out of its way; and spun along the open country-road, blowing a lively defiance out of its key-bugle.[4]

Reference is also made to the boldness of a 'London knock'. Mr Chuckster, a notary's clerk, patronises the pleasant Garlands at lunch in *The Old Curiosity Shop*:

Mr Chuckster exerted his utmost abilities to enchant his entertainers, and impress them with a conviction of the mental superiority of those who dwelt in town; with which view he led the discourse to the small scandal of the day, in which he was justly considered by his friends to shine prodigiously. Thus, he was in a condition to relate the exact circumstances of the difference between the Marquis of Mizzler and Lord Bobby, which it appeared originated in a disputed bottle of champagne, and not in a pigeon-pie, as erroneously reported in the newspapers ...

It goes on like so, at length, with Dickens thus making fun of the concerns, irrelevance and unreality of metropolitan 'polite society', as well as of newspapers.

However, there was so much more to report of the capital. Indeed, London's rapid development, including the 'bran-new house in a bran-new quarter' in which the socially ambitious Veneerings live in *Our Mutual Friend,*⁵ challenged conventional beliefs that certain areas were inhabited only by particular types of people; as, instead, it became necessary to define new neighbourhoods, and to redefine established ones. Thus, in Anthony Trollope's *The Way We Live Now* (1874–5), Adolphus Longestaffe, the snobbish squire who was very different to the Veneerings, favours 'the old streets lying between Piccadilly and Oxford Street ... Queen's Gate and the quarters around were, according to Mr Longestaffe, devoted to opulent tradesmen. Even Belgrave Square, though its aristocratic properties must be admitted, still smelled of the mortar,' the last a phrase that captured an ability to suggest circumstances through the senses.

Dickens' knowledge and understanding of London, both high and low, had served him well in his youthful *Scenes of London Life from Sketches by Boz* in which London was subject as much as stage. The book's illustrations, by George Cruikshank, included troubling scenes of the public life of the streets: in *Monmouth Street* children played in the gutter. Given the limited sanitation of the period, this was a serious health hazard, but the point was really the menace and low life of the notorious St Giles' 'rookery' or slum.

Dickens' account was different from that of a successful predecessor of the early 1820s, *Life in London; or the Day and Night Scenes of Jerry Hawthorn, Esq., and his elegant friend,*

Corinthian Tom, accompanied by Bob Logic, the Oxonian, in their Rambles and Sprees through the Metropolis, although it influenced him. This was a very successful shilling monthly, launched in 1821; the author was Pierce Egan the Elder, the illustrator was Isaac Robert Cruickshank,[6] and George IV accepted the dedication. Like Dickens in many of his novels, Egan provided alternate scenes of high and low life with lively dialogue. In 1828, Egan produced his *Finish to the Adventures of Tom, Jerry and Logic*. In a fashion that Dickens was to emulate, Tom falls victim to chance, breaking his neck at a steeplechase, while Jerry returns to the country, marries his early sweetheart and becomes a generous landlord. The original had been a celebration of London life, and Egan wrote the sequel as a concession to the moralistic outrage that his original treatment had aroused. Egan pioneered serial publication, blazing a trail for Dickens, while his work also proved very effective on the stage.

As a result of his perambulations, as well as his frequent changes of address, Dickens himself had a very clear idea of London's neighbourhoods. His sense of locality, and of how it was fixed by society, were facetiously presented in the description of Cadogan Place in *Nicholas Nickleby*:

Cadogan Place is the one slight bond that joins two great extremes; it is the connecting link between the aristocratic pavements of Belgrave Square, and the barbarism of Chelsea. It is in Sloane Street, but not of it. The people in Cadogan Place look down upon Sloane Street, and think Brompton low. They affect fashion too, and wonder where the New Road is. Not that they claim to be on precisely the same footing as the high folks of Belgrave Square and Grosvenor Place, but that they stand, with reference to them, rather in the light of those illegitimate children of the great who are content to boast of their connections, although their connections disavow them. Wearing as much as they can of the airs and semblances of loftiest rank, the people of Cadogan Place have the realities of middle station. It is the conductor which communicates to the inhabitants of regions beyond its limit, the shock of pride of birth and rank, which it has not within itself, but derives from a fountainhead beyond; or, like the ligament which unites the Siamese twins, it contains something of the life and essence of two distinct bodies, and yet belongs to neither ... this doubtful ground ...[7]

There were also much worse areas in London, such as the 'Saint Mark's District' in Bermondsey, which Dickens visited in 1853:

intensely poor ... Hickman's Folly ... which looks like the last hopeless climax of everything poor and filthy ... odious sheds for horses, and donkeys, and vagrants, and rubbish ... wooden houses like horrible old packing cases full of fever for a countless number of years ... a wan child ... a starved old white horse ... and I ... stared at one another in silence for some five minutes as if we were so many figures in a dismal allegory.[8]

The sense of gradation between neighbourhoods, a sense of which Londoners were acutely conscious, was captured in *Our Mutual Friend*, as Eugene and Mortimer leave a dinner at the Veneerings' and roll 'down' by carriage:

by the Monument, and by the Tower, and by the Docks; down to Ratcliffe, and by Rotherhithe; down by where accumulated scum of humanity seemed to be washed from higher grounds, like so much moral sewage.[9]

At the same time, alongside differences between areas, there were those within them, to which Dickens referred in *Dombey and Son*. As Charles Booth's maps of London poverty were to reveal clearly later in the century, there were many streets of poverty close to those of comfort.

Across his work, Dickens captured London as the grim 'modern Babylon' of Micawber's description in *David Copperfield*,[10] a place presented by Shelley in *Peter Bell the Third* (1819): 'Hell is a city much like London – A populous and a smoky city.' Dickens took from Wordsworth the idea of London and urbanisation as worrying, if not evil. In *The Old Curiosity Shop*, flight from London is a major theme and London pursues the escapees. Dickens was also opposed to London churches, for example in *Dombey and Son*, whereas he found rural ones lovely and holy. Dickens was particularly critical of London in 1849, at the time of his anger with the behaviour of the crowd at a public execution. In the 1860s, he gave a physical sense of siege by complaining about 'a black shrill city ... a beleaguered city, invested by the great Marsh Forces of Essex and Kent'.[11] Visiting Paris, which he came to do frequently, made Dickens less keen on London.

London definitely provided a harsh environment for life, but it was also one of vigour, an element Dickens repeatedly captured alongside the grimness: 'Life and death went hand in hand; wealth and poverty stood side by side; repletion and starvation laid them down together.'[12] In 1814, when the parks were opened to the people as part of a national jubilee held to celebrate victory over, and thus peace with, France, Charles Lamb complained to Wordsworth:

> all that was countrified in the parks is all but obliterated ... booths and drinking places go all around it [Hyde Park] ... the stench of liquors, bad tobacco, dirty people and provisions, conquers the air and we are stifled and suffocated in Hyde Park.[13]

There was certainly no shortage of people in London. Its population of 958,863 in 1801, the year of the first national census, had nearly doubled by 1831. As urban numbers grew, so population density rose, leading to serious overcrowding, and particularly so for the poor. In part, this rise in numbers during Dickens' lifetime was due to natural growth, but migration, notably within the British Isles but also from overseas, was also significant. Employment was the great magnet, including for domestic service, as the better-off parts of London were a vast employer of servants, the majority of whom were women.

More generally, southern England, indeed a workless St Albans in *Bleak House*,[14] the West Country and East Anglia, were the prime sources of migrants to London. Thus, in his journey to the capital, Dickens was part of a broader pattern of movement. The wonder of his discovery of the city was captured in *David Copperfield*:

> What an amazing place London was to me when I saw it in the distance, and how I believed all the adventures of all my favourite heroes to be constantly enacting and re-enacting there, and how I vaguely made it out in my own mind to be fuller of wonders and wickedness than all the cities of the earth, I need not stop here to relate.[15]

But there was much else. By modern standards, average death rates were brutally high. Those of London were not that exceptional for big cities at the time, and rates were already dropping from the peaks in the previous century. Yet, however described, and in a way thereby eased, most memorably and repeatedly in *Dombey and Son* in terms of the sea and the river going thither,[16] death was ever-present in Dickens' novels. His life was to be scarred by unexpected early death, including the son possibly born from his relationship with Ellen Ternan.

Nevertheless, earlier marriage, in part as a result of economic opportunity, but also due to strict conventions about pre-marital sex, meant more children, for Dickens as for others. This birth rate helped to outstrip deaths, and thus contributed to London having a largely young population, which, in turn, affected the fertility level. Dickens very much captured this situation. When Oliver Twist arrives in London in the company of the Artful Dodger, he finds in the wretched area 'a good many small shops, but the only stock in trade appeared to be heaps of children ... crawling in and out at the doors, or screaming from the inside'.[17] As he knew from personal experience, however, both of his siblings and of his children, large families did not necessarily bring happiness. Growing up as one of eight children in a poor area of London with his mother dying young, my own father very much had this view. In the early nineteenth century, with resources under pressure, children could be used as a form of cheap labour, as Dickens in effect was when he was sent to the blacking factory. However, the shame of that provides more of a dynamic for the lives of Dickens and David Copperfield, rather than a consideration of how those born, as it were, to such labour experienced it.

Dickens observed of his married daughter, Kate, that she and her husband 'have no family as yet, and (if they would take my word for the fact) are better without one'.[18] Yet, Dickens objected strongly to criticism by political economists and moralists who argued that the poor should not have children. Filer in *The Chimes*, an instructive work that, however, being a Christmas story, receives insufficient attention, takes this view, declaring against

> the ignorance of the first principles of political economy on the part of these people; their improvidence; their wickedness ... A man may live to be as old as Methuselah, and may labour all his life for the benefit of such people as those; and may heap up facts on figures, facts on figures, facts on figures, mountains high and dry; and he can no more hope persuade 'em that they have no right or business to be married, than he can hope to persuade 'em that they have no earthly right or business to be born. And *that* we know they haven't. We reduced it to a mathematical certainty long ago.

London's capacity, in its 'roaring streets',[19] as the great absorber of the nation meant that it was best placed to cope with those seen as unusual in any regard as well as those who faced difficulties in their home environment. This absorption was not so much a matter of inclusiveness, although that existed in particular neighbourhoods. Instead, there was the possibility, in the city's vastness, to find those with similar backgrounds, commitments and interests, thereby creating a virtual community as well as a renewed identity for the individuals concerned. One aspect of the city's character, an aspect made much of by Dickens, was the opportunity it provided for what was regarded as oddness, at least in mannerisms.

London's capacity for absorption was also shown in criminal purposes and pursuits, and at many levels. These included those escaping the countryside whom Fagin sought to recruit in *Oliver Twist*. There were also, as in Arthur Conan Doyle's Sherlock Holmes stories, individuals passing themselves off as others in order to escape the law, such as returned transportees from Australia, as in *Great Expectations*, or for fraudulent purposes, as with Tigg Montague in *Martin Chuzzlewit*. The latter employed Nadgett as a confidential inquirer:

> he carried contradictory cards, in some of which he called himself a coal-merchant, in others a wine-merchant, in others a commission-agent, in others a collector, in others an accountant ... he belonged to a class; a race peculiar to the City; who are secrets as profound to one another, as they are to the rest of mankind.[20]

Bucket plays a comparable, although far more honourable, detecting role in *Bleak House*, where, again, there is disguise to face, in what is very much presented as a society in flux:

> false names, false hair, false titles, false jewellery, and false histories ... howsoever bad the devil can be in fustian or smock-frock ... he is a more designing, callous and intolerable devil when he sticks a pin in his shirt-front, calls himself a gentleman, backs a card or colour, plays a game or so of billiards, and knows a little about bills and promissory notes, than in any other form he wears.[21]

Like their counterparts elsewhere, migrants to London were disproportionately young, indeed mainly in their twenties. There were also variations as far as the parts of London were concerned, something that any Londoner would know. Rural migrants tended to avoid London's inner city, where three-quarters of residents were London-born, and many others were Irish. Migrants were also part of a highly fluid demographic situation: mobility between residences within London, and into and out of London, was highest among casual labourers, whose job security was lowest. Moreover, among migrants, turnover in residences was high. At any rate, a large part of the working-class populace occupied the same housing for only a few months. Rent was a heavy burden and pressure from landlords a difficult reality, as in *Little Dorrit*. Landlords' agents were, as presented by Dickens, a menacing presence. For different reasons, in part due to a growing family but also to the general preference for rent over purchase, Dickens moved frequently.

London's growth ensured that the countryside was swallowed up by new suburban developments. John Walker's map of 1830 recorded villages such as Dulwich and Haringey in the countryside, but the situation changed rapidly. Although Ford Madox Brown's Hampstead was still surrounded by suburban greenery when he painted it in *English Autumn Afternoon* (1852–4), it had been fully rural thirty years earlier, when the poet John Keats had lived there. John Ruskin was struck by the same change. In 1970, Robert, 5th Marquess of Salisbury, recalled: 'When my father [James, 1861–1947] was a child, he would ride by the side of his mother's carriage from Hatfield to London. It was utterly unspoiled until one got to Swiss Cottage.'[22]

As a residential city, London expanded more to the west than to the east as far as the middle class, with their lower-density housing, was concerned; but the poor focused on the east. Entrepreneurial large-scale builders, notably Thomas Cubitt, who erected Belgrave and Lowndes Squares in Chelsea and adapted Tavistock House for Dickens in 1851, played a key role in London's expansion. However, most housebuilding was small-scale, and a very large number of builders were involved. The huge building trade suffered badly from the boom-to-bust nature of housebuilding. In response to the expansion of the city, the Commons Preservation Society was founded in 1865. The very scale of the city is made oppressive by Dickens in *Little Dorrit*:

'Nothing to see but streets, streets, streets. Nothing to breathe but streets, streets, streets.'[23] The streets, of course, provided housing.

There were visionary ideas for London's future, notably by John Claudius Loudon, a Scottish-born landscape-gardener who produced the *Gardener's Magazine*. His *Hints on Breathing Places for the Metropolis, and for Country Towns and Villages, on fixed Principles* (1829) indicated the extent to which London's expansion was leading to fresh thinking by at least a few. Loudon proposed

> surrounding London, as it already exists, with a zone of open country, at the distance of say one mile, or one mile and a half, from what may be considered the centre, say from St Paul's. This zone of country may be half a mile broad, and may contain ... part of Hyde Park, the Regent's Park, Islington, Bethnal Green, the Commercial Docks, Camberwell, Lambeth, and Pimlico; and it may be succeeded by a zone of town one mile broad, containing Kensington, Bayswater, Paddington, Kentish Town, Clapton, Limehouse, Deptford, Clapham, and Chelsea; and thus the metropolis may be extended in alternative mile zones of buildings with half mile zones of country or gardens, till one of the zones touched the sea.

The reality, instead, was of development related to transport routes and driven by entrepreneurial builders, a situation that was more generally the case with the urbanisation of the period.[24] London's growth, however, was qualitative as well as quantitative. It eventually resulted in a major change in the housing stock for the bulk of the public, one that can make Dickensian scenes set in an earlier London hard to visualise. By the 1860s, the terraced streets we know today were being built, and, by the 1870s, a standard version of working-class housing was the two-up-two-down 'through terrace', with its access at both front and rear, solid construction and adequate ventilation, and sometimes a small garden or back yard. The traditional terraced house reflected the rise in average real wages in the 1850s and 1860s as the economic boom of industrialisation brought widespread prosperity, including consumer influence over markets to those previously lacking it, a situation not discussed in Dickens' novels.

These houses were a great improvement on the back-to-back, the lodging house and the damp cellar in which all too many had lived, and that Dickens described at length. In part, this was because terraced houses were built at a time of prosperity and rising construction standards, when covered sewerage systems and adequately piped clean water were being included in new residences – albeit with issues about quality, notably with sewerage. With their separate rooms, these houses enabled greater definition of the spheres of domestic activity, from chatting or reading to eating or sleeping, all of which had major implications for family behaviour and gender roles, as well as for a sense of privacy. Dickens was particularly good on these points.

Terraced houses were usually built on straight streets. The move toward straighter streets owed much to the growing volume of horse-drawn and wheeled traffic, poorly suited for right angles, and the traffic was also helped by better road surfacing. This street pattern replaced an earlier style of layout frequently described in terms of a warren, the 'labyrinth of dismal courts and blind alleys, called Entries' that Dickens frequently wrote about for London, described in Coketown (Preston in *Hard Times*), and found in Liverpool in 1860.[25] This earlier style had been difficult to keep clean or to keep light because it contained so many self-enclosed alleyways, closes or courts. In contrast, the straight streets of terraced houses, equally apportioned, and relatively spaciously laid out, were easier to light and to provide with supplies of gas, water, electricity and drainage. This was true not only of areas as a whole, but also of individual properties.

Government action was important in this change. The removal of the Brick Tax in 1850 encouraged the large-scale utilisation of bricks in construction, and their use, as opposed to wood or plaster, helped keep damp at bay. Already in *The Old Curiosity Shop*, Richard Swiveller had dreamed 'that his first act of power was to lay waste the market-garden of Mr Cheggs and turn it into a brick-field',[26] a startling image of the destructiveness of change. Less dramatically, the end of the Wallpaper Tax in 1861 affected the interior of houses.

Nevertheless, many of the urban poor and the casually employed still lived in the one-roomed dwellings, tenements, back-to-backs, rookeries and courts so ferociously and frequently described or mentioned by Dickens. Their walls frequently ran with damp, sanitation was often primitive, lighting was limited, and poorly swept chimneys contributed to the fug in many homes. As Dickens emphasised, health was greatly affected as a consequence. To a degree that was later to attract comment from George Bernard Shaw, prominent and wealthy individuals derived income from areas of poor housing. These included the Cecil family, from whom Robert, 3rd Marquess of Salisbury, MP from 1853 until he entered the House of Lords in 1868, was to become Prime Minister in 1885.

Dickens delivered one of his most devastating condemnations in *Dombey and Son*, a condemnation as part of a longer discussion of what it was to be natural, a topic that troubled Dickens:

> ... follow the good clergyman or doctor, who, with his life imperilled at every breath he draws, goes down into their dens, lying within the echoes of our carriage wheels and daily tread upon the pavement-stones. Look round upon the world of odious sights – millions of immortal creatures have no other world on earth ... Breathe the polluted air, foul with every impurity that is poisonous to health and life; and have every sense, conferred upon our race for its delight and happiness, offended, sickened and disgusted, and made a channel by which misery and death alone can enter.[27]

The growth that was most apparent to contemporaries was that of riverine London. Dickens captured this growth with his frequent references, both real and symbolic, to the Thames. In

Great Expectations, Pip travels down the Thames and its 'tiers of shipping':

> Here, were the Leith, Aberdeen and Glasgow steamers, loading and unloading goods ... here, were colliers by the score and score ... Here ... was tomorrow's steamer for Rotterdam ... and here tomorrow's for Hamburg ... again among the tiers of shipping ... hammers going in ship-builders' yards.[28]

The Thames at London, indeed, was a phenomenally busy port. In 1827, London received 1.9 million tons of coal, mostly from colliers (boats) sent from Newcastle and Sunderland; in 1855 4.2 million tons (3 million by sea); and in 1879, 6.6 million, although rail was by then more important as the means of supply. In *The Old Curiosity Shop*, Daniel Quilp, the villainous moneylender, rentier, shipbreaker and smuggler, falls into the Thames near his wharf and drowns. The novel provides Dickens with an opportunity to give an account of riverine bustle, one that, as with humans, he characteristically focused at first on lesser craft:

> A fleet of barges were coming lazily on, some sideways, some head first, some stern first; all in a wrong-headed, dogged, obstinate way, bumping up against the larger craft, running under the bows of steamboats, getting into every kind of nook and corner where they had no business, and being crunched on all sides like so many walnut-shells; while each with its pair of long sweeps struggling and splashing in the water looked like some lumbering fish in pain. In some of the vessels at anchor all hands were busily engaged in coiling ropes, spreading out sails to dry, taking in or discharging their cargoes; in others no life was visible but two or three tarry boys, and perhaps a barking dog running to and fro upon the deck or scrambling up to look over the side and bark the louder for the view. Coming slowly on through the forests of masts was a great steam ship, beating the water in short impatient strokes with her heavy paddles as though she wanted room to breathe, and advancing in her huge bulk like a sea monster among the

minnows of the Thames. On either side were long black tiers of colliers; between them vessels slowly working out of harbour with sails glistening in the sun, and creaking noise on board, re-echoed from a hundred quarters. The water and all upon it was in active motion, dancing and buoyant and bubbling up; while the old grey Tower and piles of building on the shore, with many a church-spire shooting up between, looked coldly on, and seemed to disdain their chafing, restless neighbours.[29]

This sense of the London church as cold was a frequent one with Dickens.

In *Our Mutual Friend*, the Thames yields coal, wood, a basket used to shelter a baby, and bodies for scavengers. Dickens captured the hardness of the river to a degree that many neglected. It was a place of accidents and suicides. Indeed, Quilp's death is inaccurately recorded as a suicide. David Copperfield prevents the 'fallen' Martha Endell from throwing herself into the river.[30]

Work on the river and in the London docks was generally poorly paid and casual. Many cargoes were moved by hand, and employment levels fluctuated greatly with trade, as most hiring was on a daily basis, and remained so until de-casualisation in the 1860s. There were frequent injuries. The situation encouraged a hard-working environment in the docks and was to lead to bitter labour disputes.

Dickens in part presented an older world on the river. Vessels would moor in the Thames, their cargoes transferred to small, unpowered barges, known as lighters, which would take the goods to the wharves. Before steam tugs began to be used to tow the lighters, they were manoeuvred using only long oars, known as 'sweeps', and by taking advantage of the tides and winds, a highly skilled job that required considerable knowledge of the 'set' of the tides.

Yet, as the century progressed, and shipping increased in size and volume, new docks became ever larger and were built further downstream. This was a process akin to industrialisation.

Following on from earlier docks that were closer to the City, notably London Dock (1801), the East India Docks (1805), Surrey Commercial Docks (1807), and St Katharine Docks (1828), the Royal Victoria Dock of 1855, the first of the 'Royal' docks, was able to cater for the large steamships of the day, and could handle massive quantities of goods. The major expansion of dockyards reduced congestion on the Thames, making it easier to control trade, and to cut the large-scale pilfering from open wharves (many of the new docks were surrounded by high walls for this very purpose). This expansion also responded to the needs of the larger iron merchantmen and, later, those dealing in steel. Thus, in a way that Dickens did not really capture, and that would not have lent itself to his interest in individuals, the river system developed in response to the changes in the nature of shipping, revealing a dynamism seen in other aspects of the city's infrastructure and economy. The pilfering was a part of the alternative economy he understood so well and which he often wrote about, notably in terms of the use of the second-hand, both pilfered and not.

The Thames, however, was less important than hitherto for shipbuilding. The switch from timber was important, as Britain had major competitive advantages for ships built of iron and powered by coal. However, although iron shipbuilding at Millwall and Blackwall on the Thames flourished in the mid-century, with Isambard Kingdom Brunel's mighty *Great Eastern*, 'the Great Leviathan', launched from Millwall in 1858, the new geography of the industry focused instead on the Clyde, the Tyne and the Wear, all of which were closer to coal and iron. Dickens saw the *Great Eastern* when he visited the Mersey.

The docks provided the basis in London for a mass of industrial activity, not least as they came to be integrated into the railway system. Imports such as sugar, timber and tobacco were processed. The specialisation seen with individual wharves, such as Canary Wharf for ships from the Canary Isles, reflected the granulated nature of London's localities. This was a nature that Dickens, with his walks, fully appreciated; although he tended to subordinate this granulation to his focus on individuals and their homes. The description of the Chuzzlewit emporium and of Mrs Todgers' boarding house captures this dimension.

The coal unloaded in the docks fed energy to the city, although, as Dickens noted, the coal pervaded the city's environment, making it 'gritty', giving St Paul's a black dome, and providing Barnard's Inn with 'a frouzy mourning of soot and smoke'. In Staples Inn, 'a few smoky sparrows twitter in smoky trees', and this defeat of nature by London's smoke is a frequent theme in the novels. The choking fog in London makes Edwin Drood's eyes smart like pepper.[31] 'A penitential garb of soot' cloaks London when Arthur Clennam returns.[32] Dickens notes that 'winter's suns in the city are very feeble indeed'.[33] He also found the 'coal smoke' of Newcastle oppressive.[34] The alternative, however, to coal fires was usually to be in a 'shivering machine', which was David Copperfield's experience of school and, indeed, the situation in the city churches.

A separate source of pollution was smoke from the many factories, for example in Lambeth, from which the effluvium affected the Houses of Parliament. Coal was an encouragement for industry, including gasworks; and the availability of coal, coke and gas focused the location of industries using their products, such as tar distilleries and sulphuric acid factories. Silvertown (named after a rubber factory founded by S.W. Silver in 1852) and West Ham became major centres of the chemical industry. Notwithstanding the far-reaching industrialisation of northern England in the Industrial Revolution, London remained the largest centre of manufacturing throughout Dickens' lifetime. This left echoes in novels such as Albert Smith's *The Struggles and Adventures of Christopher Tadpole* (1848), with its description of the many riverside factories in Vauxhall. There was extensive industrial activity across much of London, but some centres, for instance West Ham and the Wandle Valley (Wandsworth), were particularly significant. David Copperfield follows Martha Endell along the marshy riverside of the Thames from Westminster south, alongside 'the great blank Prison', Millbank Penitentiary:

'The clash and glare of sundry fiery Works upon the river-side, arose by night to disturb everything except the heavy and unbroken smoke that poured out of their chimneys.'[35]

Relatively few of London's businesses employed large numbers of workers, although the breweries and distilleries did: drink, indeed, was a major industry in London, which was a factor in the opposition to temperance. Most of London's factories were, in practice, 'sweatshops', notably (but not only) in East London, and especially near the docks. Advanced technology could still play a role with these 'sweatshops' and in some of the engineering workshops. Small concerns prevailed, workshops rather than factories, and 86 per cent of London's employers in 1851 had fewer than ten employees. This was the case with most of the establishments Dickens wrote about, and accentuated the significance of personal links. Coketown in *Hard Times* was his major engagement with a large labour force, and even then he left unclear what the factories in the story produced.

Industry overlapped with the service economy in a range of jobs such as baking and millinery. The variety of the service economy – from domestic service to banking, a variety captured by Dickens, ensured very different wages, but many jobs had the insecurity and low wages of casual labour. Nevertheless, the combination of this service sector with manufacturing provided London with a greater economic resilience than that of economic centres that were heavily dependent on one particular sector. The nation's wealth, indeed, focused on London, and its bankers and merchants deployed it around the world. Dickens in *Dombey and Son* offered an account of 'the Bank of England with its vaults of gold and silver', 'the rich East India House, teeming with suggestions of precious stuffs and stones' and items of the romantic imagination, and 'outfitting warehouses ready to pack off anybody anywhere, fully equipped in half an hour'.[36]

Urban life, meanwhile, was being transformed by new transport methods and patterns. George Shillibeer introduced to London in 1829 the Paris system of omnibuses. In turn, in 1856, the London General Omnibus Company was founded, and omnibuses became a key element in the transport system. Trams – horse-drawn buses operated on rails – appeared in 1869. Individuals who had hitherto travelled largely by foot now took the tram. Whereas many members of City Masonic lodges in the 1840s had lived in Clerkenwell or Seven Dials, their successors of the 1870s increasingly lived in more distant Walthamstow or Wandsworth. Dickens was a particularly adroit observer of the expansion and of its disruptive consequences. In particular, as he noted in *Dombey and Son*, identity is lost:

> The neighbourhood ... has as little of the country to recommend it as it has of the town. It is neither of the town or country. The former, like the giant in his travelling boots, has made a stride and passed it, and has set his brick-and-mortar heel a long way in advance, but the intermediate space between the giant's feet, as yet, is only blighted country, and not town ... a few tall chimneys belching smoke all day and night ... the brick-fields and the lanes where turf is cut, and where the fences tumble down, and where the dusty nettles grow, and where a scrap or two of hedge may yet be seen.[37]

In *Our Mutual Friend*, Reginald Wilfer, a poor clerk, a group often mentioned by Dickens, goes home at the end of his work in the city to

> ... the Holloway region north of London, and then divided from it by fields and trees. Between Battle Bridge and that part of the Holloway district in which he dwelt, was a tract of suburban Sahara, where tiles and bricks were burnt, bones were boiled, carpets were beat, rubbish was shot, dogs were fought, and dust was heaped by contractors.[38]

Walworth, where, in *Great Expectations*, Wemmick lives in a 'little wooden cottage in the midst of plots of garden', is described by Dickens as 'a collection of back lanes, ditches, and little gardens'.[39] London's ability to cover up an older world that, nevertheless, continued to have a ghostly presence was captured in *The Haunted Man*, Dickens' 1848 Christmas book:

His dwelling was so solitary and vault-like, – an old, retired part of an ancient endowment for students, once a brave edifice, planted in an open place, but now the obsolete whim of forgotten architects, smoke-age-and-weather-darkened, squeezed on every side by the overgrowing of the great city, and choked, like an old well, with stones and bricks; its small quadrangles, lying down in very pits formed by the streets and buildings, which, in course of time, had been constructed above its heavy chimney stacks.[40]

The shaping of the expanding city was an issue. The architect James Pennethorne proposed in the 1830s that a major thoroughfare be built from the far east of London to the far west, but his and other of his plans were deemed too ambitious and costly by the government, although they were the basis for New Oxford Street, Endell Street, Cranbourn Street and Commercial Street. Acts of Parliament were necessary to implement new schemes, such as that of 1846 for the extension of Commercial Street to Shoreditch. It was only the establishment of the Metropolitan Board of Works in 1855 that provided a body able to push through new road schemes, such as Victoria Street and Charing Cross Road, and, indeed, the board was to take up some of Pennethorne's earlier ideas, including Garrick and Southwark Streets. However, Pennethorne's plans, especially those for bold streets, were generally only executed in part. There was no equivalent to Baron Haussmann's town-clearing and roadbuilding in Paris for Napoleon III, in large part because of a lack of comparable government power and determination.

Nevertheless, ambitious and expensive new structures were built in grand style in London, including Holborn Viaduct (1869), which carried the road to the City over Farringdon Street and the culverted River Fleet, and which was built of elaborate cast iron and adorned with statues. New buildings, moreover, played a key role in the regularisation of commerce. The massive Coal Exchange with its mighty rotunda was built on Lower Thames Street, close to the river, in 1847–9, followed by Billingsgate

Market in 1850–3, and Smithfield Meat Market in 1867–8. The last also reflected the pressure for sanitary reform, as the new market was built on the site of the live cattle market, which had been moved to Islington in 1855 by the City Corporation in response to demands for cleanliness. Dickens had described the hubbub of this earlier Smithfield in *Oliver Twist*:

> ... The ground was covered, nearly ankle-deep, with filth and mire ... the whistling of drovers, the barking of dogs, the bellowing and plunging of oxen, the bleating of sheep, the grunting and squeaking of pigs; the cries of hawkers, the shouts, oaths, and quarrelling on all sides; the ringing of bells and roar of voices, that issued from every public-house; the crowding, pushing, driving, beating, whooping, and yelling; the hideous and discordant din that resounded from every corner of the market.[41]

In *Great Expectations*, the 'shameful place' is 'all asmear with filth and fat and blood and foam'.[42] Visitors had a similar response, Thomas Maslen writing in 1843:

> Of all the horrid abominations with which London has been cursed, there is not one that can come up to that disgusting place, West Smithfield Market, for cruelty, filth, effluvia, pestilence, impiety, horrid language, danger, disgusting and shuddering sights, and every obnoxious item that can be imagined.

The cruelty referred to the treatment of animals. There was no comparable discussion by Dickens of the new Smithfield, but then he died soon after it opened.

Covent Garden Market was very different to Smithfield, although, in *The Old Curiosity Shop*, Dickens captured the unattractive aspect of the use of women there:

> Covent Garden Market at sunrise too, in the spring or summer, when the fragrance of sweet flowers is in the air, overpowering even the unwholesome streams of last night's debauchery, and

driving the dusky thrush, whose cage has hung outside a garret window all night long, half mad with joy! Poor bird! the only neighbouring thing at all akin to the other little captives, some of whom, shrinking from the hot hands of drunken purchasers, lie drooping on the path already, while others, soddened by close contact, await the time when they shall be watered and freshened up to please more sober company, and make old clerks who pass them on their road to business, wonder what has filled their breasts with visions of the country.

A wistful note, and one, possibly making reference to wistful fecundity, looking toward the positive presentation of a Shropshire village later in the novel.[43]

Executions, the hanging that Fagin is shown as deservedly awaiting at the end of *Oliver Twist*, were another instance of the life played out in public, and Dickens went to see them despite 'the beastly nature of the scene'.[44] Angered by levity from the large crowd attending a 'general entertainment' in 1849, Dickens pressed for executions to be conducted in private within prisons. This happened in 1868 after the House of Lords had earlier rejected a recommendation to that end by a Commons Select Committee in 1856. Dickens' view, in turn, was decried by some as advocating a form of secret assassination; while Dickens himself was sceptical about the chance of ending capital punishment by means of pressure exerted through public meetings, in light of 'the enormous crimes which have been committed within the last year or two, and are fresh, unhappily, in the public memory'.[45]

The overlap between Dickens' experience of London and his writing, both novels and journalism, was apparent and an aspect of the extent to which his writing was a matter of his responses. And not only for Dickens among novelists. London-born Wilkie Collins, who was a regular contributor to his friend Dickens' *Household Words*, used London as a spectral setting for the first appearance of Anne Catherick, the woman in white, in his impressive novel of that name published in 1859–60.

Moreover, the press provided much relevant material. In 1849–50, the *Morning Chronicle* printed Henry Mayhew's accounts of the London poor.

Whether rich or poor, everyone was threatened by the environmental situation. Fast-expanding London proved a breeding ground for disease, a situation accentuated by the appalling character of sanitation. Another source of infection came from overcrowded cemeteries, which remained a problem in inner London until the 1850s, whereas Paris had closed its central cemetery the previous century. Moreover, this was a problem identified by reformers. Dickens was opposed to traditional burial practices, notably graves close to where people lived. This was a particular problem in poor areas of London, a theme touched on in *Nicholas Nickleby*. In *Bleak House*, Dickens added a critical social tone:

> ... bears off the body of our dear brother here departed, to a hemmed-in churchyard, pestiferous and obscene, whence malignant diseases are communicated to the bodies of our dear brothers and sisters who have not departed; while our dear brothers and sisters who hang about official backstairs – would to Heaven they *had* departed! – are very complacent and agreeable. Into a beastly scrap of ground which a Turk would reject as a savage abomination, and a Caffre would shudder at, they bring our dear brother here departed, to receive Christian burial ... with every villainy of life in action close on death, and every poisonous element of death in action close on life – here, they lower our dear brother down a foot or two: here, sow him in corruption, to be raised in corruption: an avenging ghost at many a sick bedside: a shameful testimony to future ages, how civilisation and barbarism walked this boastful island together ... the iron gate, on which the poisoned air deposits its witch-ointment slimy to the touch![46]

The vigour of the writing helps explain why the swearing 'Gothic' version of the novel as a play offered in 2019 by the David Glass Ensemble failed. Vigorous swearing is no substitute for the moral force of Dickens' measured vitriol. Later in *Bleak House*, Dickens refers to 'vermin parasites' in the houses.[47]

The sewer system was particularly deficient, as large amounts of waste were discharged into the Thames without treatment, and upriver of water sources. In 1828, William Heath dedicated to the London water companies his masterly caricature 'Monster Soup commonly called Thames Water', an illustration of the filth and toxic life in the river. In law, the sewers were intended for the run-off of rainwater, and household waste was supposed to be collected in subterranean cesspools from which it was to be removed by local rakers who would sell it as manure to farmers. This system, however, collapsed as a result of the rising population and of the development and adoption of the flushing toilet, which washed effluent into the sewers with great efficiency. In July 1842, Dickens, indeed, pressed the house agent in Broadstairs to provide a house for rent with a 'water closet'. Seven years later, Dickens was bothered by the sewage from the hostel he was helping run, as it ran into 'the open air and undoubtedly poisoning the atmosphere about the house'.[48]

More generally, the water companies chose to ignore the degree to which they were providing contaminated water. Dickens was scathing in 1849 about 'that preposterous jumble of imbecility and rottenness', the Metropolitan Commission of Sewers.[49] *Bleak House* was particularly pertinent for cholera, as with the search for Jo:

> Mr Snagsby passes along the middle of a villainous street, undrained, unventilated, deep in black mud and corrupt water – though the roads are dry elsewhere – and reeking with such smells and sights that he, who has lived in London all his life, can scarce believe his senses. Branching from this street and its heaps of ruins, are other streets and courts so infamous that Mr Snagsby sickens in body and mind, and feels as if he were going, every moment deeper down, into the infernal gulf.[50]

Repeating the situation with the Black Death of bubonic plague of 1346–8, the spread of cholera from Asia was especially fatal.

A bacterial infection transmitted largely by water infected by the excreta of victims, cholera struck first in the 1830s. The capital was hard-hit, with major outbreaks in 1831–2, 1848–9, 1853–4 and 1866, over 17,000 Londoners dying of cholera in 1848–9, 10,000 in 1854 and 6,000 in 1866. The poor suffered worse, largely due to overcrowding and inadequate sanitary arrangements.

In turn, the death or illness of breadwinners wrecked family economies, producing or exacerbating misery, while children lacking one or both parents are a frequent topic for Dickens, and at all levels of society. Dickens reflected in 1844: 'There are old fairy-tales about men being changed into stones; but the men *I* know are changed into Gravestones, with terrible rapidity and reality.'[51] He was also aware that his accounts of the illness and/or death of children, notably Paul Dombey and Little Nell, brought solace to at least some grieving parents.[52]

It was in London that Dr John Snow, a leading anaesthetist who was noted as an advocate of chloroform, was able to carry out the research that enabled him to conclude, in his *On the Mode and Communication of Cholera* (1849), that the disease was transmitted not via 'miasma' or bad air, as was generally believed, but through drinking water contaminated by sewage, a problem that highlighted the state of the Thames. This research was supplemented, in a second edition published in 1855, by an analysis of the 1853–4 epidemic, and it led to the closure of the public water pump in Broad Street in Soho, where a sewer was found to be leaking into the well. After this closure, the number of new cases of cholera fell. Snow also showed that the majority of the victims had drunk water provided by the Southwark and Vauxhall Company, which extracted water from near sewer outflows. Snow is still celebrated in the name of a pub, the John Snow, in what has been renamed Broadwick Street; a replica of the street pump has been sited nearby.

Cholera was not the only killer. Typhus frequently spread from prisons such as Newgate to the wider population. Dysentery, diarrhoea, diphtheria, whooping cough, scarlet fever, measles and enteric fever were all major problems, although, thanks in part to vaccination, smallpox declined. Epidemics, which provided Dickens with opportunities to write about the diseased character of London circumstances, encouraged debate over the causes of mortality. Arguments that the social environment played a key role in the deadliness of these epidemics, and that the situation could thus be improved, drew on statistical research. The status of such research rose with the foundation of the Statistical Society of London in 1834. Its original leading lights included Charles Babbage (a friend of Dickens), Thomas Malthus and William Whewell, all of whom had played a role, in 1833, in founding a statistical section of the British Association for the Advancement of Science.

Referred to by Dickens as 'a deadly sewer',[53] the section of the Thames between London and Hungerford bridges was described by Michael Faraday, a prominent scientist, in the *Times* in 1855, as a 'fermenting sewer', a description that was accurate in both parts. A more vivid comment was provided by the striking *Punch* cartoon 'Father Thames Introducing his Offspring to the Fair City of London', of 3 July 1858, a response to the 'Great Stink' of that summer. In this facetious design for a fresco for the new Houses of Parliament, to replace those burned down in an accident in 1834, a filthy Thames, polluted by factories, sewage and steamships, presented figures representing diphtheria, scrofula and cholera to London. These children match the terrible conditions described by Dickens, in both print and correspondence.

The decision to tackle public health essentially through engineering projects directed by administrators ensured that alternative responses, such as measures to alleviate poverty, were side-tracked, although most were scarcely practical. The focus was on sewerage systems and clean water, and not on securing the supply of food and work or income at levels sufficient to lessen the impact of disease. Dickens was aware that the latter was necessary. Moreover, in a later preface to the *Pickwick Papers*, Dickens was to hope that eventually it would be understood 'that the universal diffusion of common means of decency and health is as much the right of the poorest of the poor, as it is indispensable to the safety of the rich, and of the state'. He could appreciate this linkage across society; and that gave much of his work its power and resonance.

The administration of the 1834 Poor Law system faced issues in London, not least because much of central London and of the large semi-suburban parishes were not under the Act as they had their own local Acts for poor relief which were not affected by the 1834 Act. There were, however, numerous scandals over medical care and living conditions, scandals that made readers highly receptive to Dickens' accounts and that helped drive Dickens to his work. As a result of these scandals, of a desire, in the context of continuing mass support for Whig principles,[54] to reduce the degree of autonomy, to spread the burden of high poor rates in poorer parishes of Poor Law Unions to wealthier ones, and of the mid-1860s economic downturn, the Metropolitan Poor Law Act passed in 1867 led to the establishment in London of large new Poor Law hospitals and asylums.

Henry Mayhew, in *London Labour and the London Poor* (1861–2), estimated that 10,000 of London's lodging houses were of the lowest sort, by which he meant places in which criminals and prostitutes resided. Although in part becoming dated in his assessment of the situation due to changes in the provision of poor relief, Dickens had an acute sense of the impact of hardship on personality, and thereby, he repeatedly argued, on society as a whole. Moreover, his presentation of the poor was less critical than that of Charles Booth; although Booth, in his *Life and Labour of The People of London* (1889–1903), also explained the problems posed by harsh labour conditions and a lack of social welfare.

In contrast, in Whitechapel in 1865, William Booth and his wife Catherine, who were primarily concerned with spiritual destitution rather than material hardship, launched the 'Christian Mission to the Heathen of our Own Country' focused on spiritual salvation, and thirteen years later this became the Salvation Army. The plight of poor children moved crusading philanthropists such as Thomas Barnardo who, in response to the widespread orphaning in the wake of the 1866 cholera epidemic, in 1867 founded the East End Juvenile Mission, the basis of what later became 'Dr Barnardo's Homes'. Similarly inspired, the Reverend Thomas Stephenson established near Waterloo Road a refuge for destitute children in 1869, which was to be the basis of the National Children's Home.

The motives of crusading philanthropists, whose focus was very much on the East End of London, have been queried in recent decades, but, however much philanthropy could serve the interests of spiritual well-being, curiosity and even personal aggrandisement, there was a drive both to offer relieving improvement and, in understanding the plight of the poor, to provide a more nuanced appreciation of the social environment. Yet, the moral panics about the plight of the poor that crusading philanthropy and journalism inspired were, to a degree, replicated by unease about the willingness of philanthropists to compromise class and gender assumptions and roles in their charitable work.

The travails of London that Dickens dealt with were not always so deadly, however. The poor quality of the food available in London shops and hotels was also an issue for all. In 'Refreshments for Travellers', the Grazinglands, a Midlands couple, go to London to transact some business at the Bank of England, only to find a dire pastry cook, with 'a beetle-haunted kitchen', and the alternative appalling and expensive lunch at Jairing's hotel, one characterised moreover by condescension from the staff.

In addition, Dickens, in revelling in the language of the street, did not lose sight of London's humour.[55] He captured the extent to which, despite the extent of controlling reform, which included the end of public theatre, in the shape of Bartholomew Fair and Greenwich Fair in 1855 and 1857 respectively, there was also an expansion of elements of public informality, indeed of the performance of London. Street markets and music halls were aspects of this informal vitality.[56] The spectacle could be unattractive. In 1851, there were anti-Catholic riots in London at a time of concern about 'Papal Aggression' in the shape of the reintroduction of the Catholic hierarchy into Britain. In 1859–60, the strength of anti-Catholic views was shown in the anti-Ritualist demonstrations held in St George's-in-the-East in Wapping. In addition, local schoolboys were paid to pelt with eggs the curate, who was a notorious Ritualist. This was a tamer version of the zeal for cruel humour seen at public executions, a situation that moved Dickens to anger.

At the same time, albeit now in policed streets and public spaces, the policing an important theme in *Our Mutual Friend*, there was a continuance of the popular vitality that Dickens knew so well and appreciated more than most writers. It is ironic that this writer about London was depicted on the back of the £10 note, introduced in 1993, alongside, as the illustration of his work, another such instance of popular vitality in the shape of the village cricket match from *The Pickwick Papers*. Other rural matches were mentioned in *Martin Chuzzlewit* and *The Old Curiosity Shop*, while Mr Dick in *David Copperfield* likes cricket. In *Great Expectations*, there is a reference to wicketkeeping, Joe's hat falling from the mantelpiece and being caught.[57] That is an aspect of the impression of ruralism that was so significant for the presentation of English culture in the twentieth century. That, however, was not the prime setting, theme or tone in Dickens' work, which was usually metropolitan in its focus and sense of place.

2

THE CONDITION OF THE PEOPLE

The keeping of strict faith with all classes of the public, and the reception of them with the utmost courtesy, are the first considerations impressed upon all people entrusted with any part of the management of my own Readings.

Dickens, 2 February 1866[1]

The England of the Industrial Revolution was one of growing aggregate wealth, but harsh individual conditions. Indeed, the heavy pressure that the nature of the economy placed on the bulk of the population is indicated by the decline in the average height of army recruits in the second quarter of the nineteenth century. More specifically, working conditions in individual industries were often unpleasant and hazardous, with numerous fatalities, especially in mining, building and fishing, as well as injuries more generally from accidents and the strains arising from the work. Industries in which women worked were also hazardous. For instance, the manufacture of matches from yellow phosphorous contributed to jaundice, psoriasis, chronic diarrhoea and phosphorus-rotted jaw. In *The Chimes*, Meg's eyes are strained by her sewing for long hours by candlelight, as was indeed the case for many. Moreover, unlike the cotton textile trade, many industries were slow to experience technological transformation, with the result that general living standards only rose noticeably from the mid-century.

Legislation might bring improvement, but the situation, both in those cases and elsewhere, remained very difficult. In particular, the Factory Acts regulating conditions of employment in the textile industry still left work there both long and arduous. The 1833 Act established a factory inspectorate and prevented the employment of under-nines; but nine- and ten-year-olds could still work eight-hour days (which by 1836 would also apply to those under thirteen), and eleven- to seventeen-year-olds twelve hours. The 1844 Act cut the hours of under-thirteens to six and a half hours, and of eighteen-year-olds and all women to twelve; those of 1847 and 1850 reduced the hours of women and under-eighteens to ten hours.

Nevertheless, there was opposition to such legislation, for example by Lord Brougham, a former prominent Whig reformer, whom Dickens mocked in *The Chimes* as Sir Joseph Bowley, 'the Poor Man's Friend', who is presented as an unctuous hypocrite. Moreover, working conditions, in the textile industry and others, continued to be harsh, especially for those paid on a low piece-rate basis, such as many of the workers in tailoring. This situation led to criticism, as in Thomas Hood's poem 'The Song of the Shirt' (1843), and Charles Kingsley's novel *Alton Locke: Tailor and Poet* (1850); the latter a call for sanitary reform and Christian Socialism, but not for radical activism. In *Hard Times*, Bounderby described 'the work in our mills': 'It's the pleasantest work there is, and it's the lightest work there is, and it's the best-paid work there is ... we couldn't improve the mills themselves, unless we laid down Turkey carpets on the floors.'[2] Reality, as Dickens' readers knew, was totally different. Indeed, in 1847–8, a severe depression led to wage cuts, an attempt to reverse which was the reason for the Preston textile weavers' strike in 1853–4, which was the basis for *Hard Times*.[3]

The situation was even worse for those who were more 'marginal' to the economy. Bereavement, accident and illness helped take many into this category, but so did birth and death. Henry Stuart, who reported on East Anglian poor relief in 1834, found three main groups of inmates in the often miserable parish workhouses: the old and infirm, orphaned and illegitimate children, and unmarried pregnant women; the last was a group treated particularly harshly, and far more so than the men responsible for their pregnancies.

Passed in 1834, the Poor Law Amendment Act introduced national guidelines, in place of the former more varied parish-based system. The Workhouse Test Act of 1723 encouraged parishes to found workhouses in order to provide the poor with work and accommodation, but too few were founded to deal with the problem, especially as the population rose from the mid-century. In the late eighteenth century, workhouses, although encouraged by the Relief of the Poor Act of 1782 (Gilbert's Act), remained less important than 'outdoor relief': offering assistance, and sometimes work, to the poor in their own homes. Such a system is administered, if that is not too kind a word, by Mr Bumble, the overbearing and callous parish beadle in *Oliver Twist*, who gives away bread and cheese with considerable reluctance: 'The great principle of out-of-door relief, is, to give the paupers exactly what they don't want; and then they get tired of coming.'[4] In practice, the novel shows both outdoor relief and workhouses to be as appalling as Bumble. There were certainly serious deficiencies with both systems.

Under the Speenhamland system of outdoor relief, introduced in 1795 and named after the parish best known for adopting it, although it was never universally applied, both the unemployed and wage labourers received payments reflecting the price of bread and the size of their family. Payments to families were made to the man, in keeping with the male-centred nature of society and, specifically, the role of the man as head of the household. Thus, the 1834 legislation brought major change. Overseen by the Poor Law Commissioners in London, the uniform workhouse system that the legislation sought to create was deliberately not generous to its inmates for fear that this would both discourage people from working and impose too high a burden on ratepayers. Outdoor relief was abolished for the able-bodied. Instead, they were obliged to enter the workhouse, where they were to endure conditions no better than could be expected outside, in order to deter all bar the very destitute from being 'a charge' on that community. Bastardy, and indigent marriage and parenthood, were to be discouraged.

In general, expenditure on the workhouses was severely controlled, discipline was harsh, and the stigma attached to dependent poverty grew. Thus, in Wimborne in Dorset, workhouse beds had to be shared, meat was only provided once a week, there were no vegetables other than potatoes until 1849, men and women were segregated, and unmarried mothers had to wear distinctive clothes. Revealed in 1845, the Andover workhouse scandal indicated an abusive and corrupt master of the workhouse and totally inadequate rations. In response, the House of Commons set up a committee in 1846 that revealed serious mismanagement in the oversight of the Act. The Huddersfield workhouse scandal followed in 1848. In *Oliver Twist*, a novel very much written in the shadow of the introduction of the New Poor Law, and successfully so as far as the readership was concerned, Dickens referred to the children as 'juvenile offenders against the poor-laws'. He also took the opportunity to mock prevailing ideas, in the shape of Bumble, who rejects the ideas of more charitable complaining jurors: '"They haven't no more philosophy nor political economy about 'em than that," said the beadle, snapping his fingers contemptuously.'[5] The workhouse was in the fictional town of Mudfog, which was based on Chatham.

There was some active popular opposition to the workhouses. That at Gainsborough in Lincolnshire was destroyed while it was being built in 1837, and there were also disturbances elsewhere, for example at Todmorden in Yorkshire. For many years, it was the sole English Poor Law Union area without a workhouse.

Opposition there owed much to John Fielden, a wealthy cotton manufacturer and radical MP. More generally, far from there being a total shift to the workhouses, a degree of outdoor relief continued in many places.

In his journalism, Dickens criticised the legislation, not least its Benthamite utilitarianism and the role of the commissioners. His opinion of the application of the New Poor Law led him to attack it as a whole, but Dickens also took the view that the attitudes of those administering regulations could damn the system. In *The Chimes*, Alderman Cute, a 'famous man for the common people ... Never out of temper with them!', is revealed as harsh, opposed to the poor and determined to enforce a social code that is similar to how Dickens sees the New Poor Law. Cute addresses Meg:

> You are going to be married you say ... Very unbecoming and indelicate in one of your sex! But never mind that. After you are married, you'll quarrel with your husband, and come to be a distressed wife. You may think not: but you will, because I tell you so. Now I give you fair warning, that I have made up my mind to Put distressed wives Down ... Perhaps your husband will die young (most likely) and leave you with a baby. Then you'll be turned out of doors, and wander up and down the streets. Now don't wander near me, my dear, for I am resolved to Put all wandering mothers Down.

And so on for other categories of the poor.

The Chimes also included a reference to Mary Furley, a poor and desperate woman who, in 1844, tried to drown herself and her child in the Thames. The child died, the rescued Mary was sentenced to death for infanticide, and Dickens took part in the furore that led to a commutation of her sentence to transportation. Mary suffered from both institutional neglect in Whitechapel workhouse and, once she had left it, from low pay and theft. Suicide is only narrowly averted in *The Chimes*.

Dickens was opposed more to the nature of the administration of the Poor Law than to the particular regulations themselves, but the latter are also castigated in the shape of their impact. In *Our Mutual Friend*, Betty Higden, with 'fright and abhorrence' on her face, is terrified of the workhouse:

> Kill me sooner than take me there. Throw this pretty child under cart-horses' feet and a loaded wagon, sooner than take him there. Come to us and find us all a-dying, and set a light to us all where we lie, and let us all blaze away with the house into a heap of cinders, sooner than move a corpse of us there! ... the worn-out people that do come down to that, get driven from post to pillar and pillar to post, a-purpose to tire them out ... they grow heartsick of it.[6]

Dickens used this to criticise the 'Lords and Gentlemen and Honourable Boards'. Later in the novel, Betty refers to 'the poor old people that they brick up in the Unions, as you may sometimes see when they let 'em out of the four walls to have a warm in the sun'.[7] The 'Unions' are the workhouses of the Poor Law which were established and organised in the Poor Law Union areas.

In *The Uncommercial Traveller* (1860), Dickens noted another issue: the major problem for provision posed by the sharply differing nature of municipal problems and wealth. At the same time, the poor beggars who assail Carker in France in *Dombey and Son*[8] are in part an acknowledgement of the value of the alternative system of institutional care, and Dickens was keen to see the workhouses as part of the solution of social provision. In August 1842, he wrote: 'I have a new protégé, in the person of a wretched deaf and dumb boy whom I found upon the sands the other day, half dead, and have got (for the present) into the [Poor Law] union infirmary ... A most deplorable case.'[9]

In his writing, Dickens trod the fine line. Treating the poor as responsible for their predicament and plight is callous, as he understood. At the same time, emphasising structures and bad circumstances, as he was apt to do, risks robbing them of agency, dignity and indeed personality. Dickens sought to counter that tendency, but also urged improvement. In 1866, he supported the Association for the Improvement of the Infirmaries of London Workhouses, commenting:

> Few anomalies in the land are so horrible to me as the unchecked existence of many shameful sickwards for paupers, side by side with a constantly recurring expression of conventional wonder that the poor should creep into corners to die rather than fester and rot in such infamous places.[10]

This was well-deserved criticism. Dickens was also aware of the limitations of conventional philanthropy, as with Charity Pecksniff 'making impracticable nightcaps for the poor',[11] which is an aspect of the platitudinous nature of much care and of the more particular inadequacies of the unctuous Pecksniffs.

There was a significant gender dimension to social attitude, conditions and oversight. Social assumptions and conventions pressed far harder on women than on men. Thus, women, not men, were blamed for the spread of venereal disease. Under the Contagious Diseases Acts (1864, 1866, 1869), passed because of concern about the health of the armed forces, women suspected of being prostitutes, and not the men who also might have spread disease, were subjected to physical examination and detention, if infected, in garrison towns and ports. Prostitution was also common in port cities. In Liverpool, the second English port city after London, and the most significant for trans-Atlantic trade, where 30,000 sailors were ashore at any one time, there was a major rise in prostitution from about 300 brothels in 1836 to 538 in 1846, while in 1857 there were at least 200 regular prostitutes under the age of twelve in the city.

More generally, urban, industrial society served women little better than rural society had done. Women were affected by social and environmental challenges similar to those confronting men, but they also faced additional problems. Like most men, most women had to cope with gruelling labour and debilitating diseases, but their legal position was worse. This was a reflection of a culture that awarded control and respect to men, and repeatedly left little role for female merit or achievement, or belittled them, a theme frequently seen with Dickens. The restrictive nature of the work available to women and the confining implications of family and social life together defined existence for the vast majority of women.

Moreover, some women were badly treated, as with the repeatedly beaten wife in the tale told to the Pickwickians by a Kent clergyman. In *Great Expectations*, the evil Compeyson frequently kicks his wife, Sally; while, in *David Copperfield*, Betsey Trotwood was believed to have been beaten by her husband. Drummle ill-treats Estella, and also ill-treats a horse. The youthful tinker whom David encounters has a woman with a black eye, and David sees him knock her down onto the hard road so that her face bleeds. There is no romanticisation of the 'trampers', and this contrasts with David's sentimental imagining of the 'cheerful companionship' of hop-pickers that comes immediately before.[12]

A significant proportion of the working classes lived together out of wedlock, as did some of the middle class.[13] Social and economic pressures helped to encourage poor women towards co-habiting or marriage and also, whether or not they married, towards employment. Co-habitation or marriage offered most women a form of precarious stability. In contrast, the marital prospects of unmarried mothers were low, with the significant exception of widows with children of a first marriage, particularly if they possessed some property. As a result, single women often resorted to abortion, which was treated as a crime and was hazardous to health. Moreover, unmarried mothers frequently became prostitutes, or, in a generally censorious society, were treated as such. The absence of an effective social welfare system, and the low wages paid to most women, ensured that prostitution, either full- or part-time, was the fate of many. Part-time prostitution was generally related to economic conditions.

The bleakness of the situation was enhanced by the practice of law and administration, both established and new. Thus, as under the 'Old Poor Law', the Poor Law Amendment Act of 1834 placed the financial responsibility for illegitimate children solely on their mothers. The plight of prostitutes was a theme in Dickens' charitable work and writing, and notably in *Oliver Twist*:

> ... women: some with the last lingering tinge of their early freshness, almost fading as you looked: others with every mark and stamp of their sex utterly beaten out, and presenting but one loathsome blank of profligacy and crime: some mere girls, others but young women, and none past the prime of life: formed the darkest and saddest portion of this dreary picture.[14]

Women often did very arduous jobs, such as coal-carrying in the mines. Moreover, in 1851, 229,000 women were employed in agriculture. Referring to Kate Nickleby, en route from the City to work in a dressmaker and shop in the West End at 7.45 a.m., Dickens wrote of

> ... many sickly girls, whose business, like that of the poor worm, is to produce, with patient toil, the finery that bedecks the thoughtless and luxurious, traverse our street, making towards the scene of their daily labour, and catching, as if by stealth, in their hurried walk, the only gasp of wholesome air and glimpse of sunlight which cheers their monotonous existence during the long train of hours that makes a working day ... their unhealthy looks and feeble gait.

Her trying and tiring work that day finished at 9 p.m.[15]

At the same time, domestic service was a major category of employment, with women outnumbering men in it. Many tasks, such as cleaning and drying clothes, involved much effort. It was possible in the hierarchy of service to gain promotion, but, in general, domestic service was unskilled and not a career. Wages were poor, and pay was largely in kind as board and lodging, which made life very hard for those who wished to marry and leave service. The working conditions were generally better and less hazardous than in the factories, where repetitive work for many hours was expected, while women usually received the low-status, low-pay jobs.

At the same time, hierarchy and deference were very pronounced for servants. Anthony Trollope presented, in *He Knew He Was Right* (1868–9), the snobbish, religious, reactionary spinster Jemima Stanbury who

> ... kept three maid-servants ... But it was not every young woman who could live with her. A rigidity as to hours, as to religious exercises, and as to dress, was exacted, under which many poor girls altogether broke down; but they who could stand this rigidity came to know that their places were very valuable.

So also with the far wealthier Sir Leicester Dedlock in Dickens' *Bleak House*:

> He supposes all his dependents to be utterly bereft of individual characters, intentions, or opinions, and is persuaded that he was born to supersede the necessity of their having any. If he were to make a discovery to the contrary, he would be simply stunned – would never recover himself, most likely, except to gasp and die.[16]

In the 'Gothick Horror' view of society, servant girls ended up as prostitutes and then committed suicide in the Thames. Alongside this was the reality of those who had worked for years and saved up their modest wages as a nest egg, which was easier to do after the foundation of the Post Office Savings Bank in 1861. These women were seen as highly desirable as wives, not least as they brought a sort of dowry with them.

A good employer, Dickens was nevertheless worried about male servants purloining his vintage champagne,[17] and was upset in 1866, and again in 1867, when there were thefts of money from him. In *Barnaby Rudge*, Sir John's valet takes his cash when he is dead, but Sir John is a villain. Dickens could let off steam about staff, as in 1834, when, staying in Furnival's Inn, he complained about the lack of work done there on a Sunday, including the provision of dinner:

> I have had an explosion with nineteen out of the twenty Laundresses in the Inn already, and can't get 'done for.' Some Methodistical ruffian has been among 'em, and they have got the cant about 'profaning the Sabbath' – and violating that commandment which embraces within its scope not only the stranger within the gates, but cattle of every description, including Laundresses.[18]

The general notion of gender equality was one of respect for separate functions, development and spheres, and the definition of the distinctive nature of the ideal female condition was one that, by modern standards, certainly did not entail equality. At the same time, women were often very important in business, whether on their own or as key members of family businesses. Thus, study of the situation in the north-west of England indicates that the role of women and their importance in wills, as both wives and daughters, were important aspects of the fostering of the family economy for the next generation.[19]

Dickens' account, however, was more mixed, as in his description of the repeated neglect of Florence Dombey by her father in terms of capitalism:

> what was a girl to Dombey and Son! In the capital of the House's name and dignity, such a child was merely a piece of base coin that couldn't be invested – a bad boy – nothing more.[20]

At the same time, the wish of Mr Boffin to leave all his wealth to his wife is expressed clearly when he gives instructions for his will.

Alongside their major part in the workforce, women's special role was widely defined, however, as that of home and family, and was used to justify their exclusion from other spheres. To a certain extent, such issues were meaningless for most women, because their economic conditions, and the nature of medical knowledge and attention, ensured that their circumstances were bleak. A particular consequence was the frequent suicides of young women, as reported by the 'Uncommercial Traveller' from Wapping, or the haggard, sickly woman making opium pipes at the start of *Edwin Drood*: 'What visions can *she* have? ... Visions of many butchers' shops, and public-houses, and much credit?'[21]

There were other forms of bleakness. In 1840, Dickens served on a coroner's jury considering the death of the baby of Eliza Burgess, a domestic servant, whom, it was decided, deserved trial for concealment of birth, not murder. Dickens wrote:

> Whether it was the poor baby, or its poor mother, or the coffin, or my fellow-jurymen, or what not, I can't say, but last night I had a most violent attack of sickness and indigestion which not only prevented me from sleeping, but even from lying down. Accordingly Kate and I sat up through the dreary watches.[22]

The death of Fanny Robin in Hardy's *Far from the Madding Crowd* provides a comparison.

Alongside this bleakness, however, were medical improvements, as with the use from November 1847 of chloroform as an anaesthetic in childbirth. Dickens proved happy to ignore prejudice against it by many doctors, and, in February 1849, chloroform was employed to help his wife have a painless delivery. Queen Victoria's use of chloroform for childbirth gave its introduction a great boost.

A potentially important change was the institution of divorce proceedings in 1857. Before that Act, divorce, as pointed out in *Hard Times*, required a private Act of Parliament. This was a very difficult process, only open to the wealthy, or via a separation achieved through the ecclesiastical courts, once covered by Dickens as a reporter, which did not allow remarriage. Even after the Act, divorce still remained costly, and therefore not a possibility for the poor. As a result, former practices of 'self-divorce' continued, including the 'wifesales' described by Thomas

Hardy, while co-habitation was another option, although offering most women no economic security.

Women suffered because marital desertions were generally a matter of men leaving, with the women bearing the burden of supporting the children: poverty made some men heedless of the Victorian cult of the family and patriarchy. Thomas Newcome, Rector of Shenley in Hertfordshire and a JP, recorded in 1822: 'Two Girls – Sunday Scholars formerly – who came before me without feeling or shame (but such little measure as I could inject it into them) to swear Bastards to Ridge parish ... I detail the above as "Signs of the Times."'² The cult of the family was strengthened by the belief that the home was the key to maintaining morality.

Courtship and marriage were scarcely easy processes. Bella Wilfer, a congenital whiner, complains about being presented for matrimony 'like a dozen of spoons, with everything cut and dried beforehand, like orange chips'. Also in *Our Mutual Friend*, Sophronia Akershem marries for money, only to discover that there is none; a fraud she has also pulled on her husband, in what is a comic irony that captures the pervasive practice of deceit. She then warns against another marriage: 'It is a partnership affair, a money speculation. She has no strength of will or character to help herself, and she is on the brink of being sold into wretchedness for life.'²³

The arrogant attitude of men to women, whether wives, daughters, lovers, or others (although less often mothers), was frequently captured by Dickens, and rightly harshly criticised. Jonas Chuzzlewit sets out to crush the spirits of his wife, Merry Pecksniff, and strikes her, while her sanctimonious father, with his 'placid leer', sees himself as the protector whom Mary Chuzzlewit needs. His proposal is described as that of 'an affectionate boa-constrictor'.²⁴ So also with Rosa Bud being, as it were, willed in matrimony to Edwin Drood, with whom she has nothing in common, and Mr Sapsea proposing to Miss Brobity in *Edwin Drood*:

... she did me the honour to be so overshadowed with a species of Awe, as to be able to articulate only the two words, 'O Thou!'

meaning myself. Her limpid blue eyes were fixed upon me, her semi-transparent hands were clasped together, pallor over-spread her aquiline features, and, though encouraged to proceed, she never did proceed a word further. I disposed of the parallel establishment by private contract, and we became as nearly one as could be expected under the circumstances. But she never could, and she never did, find a phrase satisfactory to her perhaps-too-favourable estimate of my intellect. To the very last (feeble action of liver), she addressed me in the same unfinished terms.

In a joke, Dickens has the more clear-thinking and younger Jasper say, 'Ah!' and nearly add, 'men!'[25]

More dramatically, Kate Nickleby repeatedly stands up against the abusive behaviour of Sir Mulberry Hawk, who is revealed as a vile and ultimately deadly parasite on the aristocracy, and as part of the contamination of life and manners that stems from hangers on. Sir Mulberry is not of the aristocracy, but he is a baronet (a hereditary knighthood), and thus a figure in hereditary society, as well as a dissolute and worthless rogue. That he will not accept a challenge to a duel from Nicholas Nickleby demonstrates the competing notions of honour that are at stake, as well as affirming his caddish manner and arrogant personality.

Dickens observes, 'If ever the rights of women, and all that kind of things, are properly attended to, it will be through her powerful intellect.'[26] Yet meanwhile, successive extensions of the franchise did not bring the vote to women in national elections, although, from the late 1860s, they were being given the vote for various local authorities. However, women were socially less dependent than is generally assumed, and more so than their legal situation might suggest.

Turning to both women and men, charity could temper hardship. However, for the recipients, charity often entailed deference, if not subordination. Andrew Reed's charity, established in 1813 for the education of orphans, led to the foundation of schools, first at Clapton and then at Watford. Subscribers to the charity were awarded votes, as in *The Chimes*, and widows had to lobby them to gain entry for their offspring. Indeed, Mr Dombey had the right to nominate a child to be taught by the Charitable Grinders. This proves a terrible fate for the boy in question. Dombey's philanthropy is also an appalling mixture of condescension and utilitarianism:

'I am far from being friendly,' pursued Mr Dombey, 'to what is called by persons of levelling sentiments, general education. But it is necessary that the inferior classes should continue to be taught to know their position, and to conduct themselves properly. So far I approve of schools.'[27]

Dickens, in contrast, was fascinated by the 'interesting and curious ... working of children's minds'.[28] Parliament made the first grants towards education in 1833, but the Newcastle Commission of 1858 showed that only one in eight children aged five to twelve was receiving education at any one time. However, it was well known, and admitted, that a much higher proportion had some schooling for periods (sometimes interrupted) between those ages. The suggestion, therefore, that most children were completely unschooled before the effects of Forster's Education Act of 1870 is wrong; although levels of schooling did vary between classes and between different parts of society. On the whole, they were higher in urban society.

Dickens provided a clear linkage between living conditions and work, notably so in *Hard Times*:

It was a town of red brick, or of brick that would have been red if the smoke and ashes had allowed it; but as matters stood it was a town unnatural red and black like the painted face of a savage. It was a town of machinery and tall chimneys, out of which interminable serpents of smoke trailed themselves for ever and ever, and never got uncoiled. It had a black canal in it, and a river that ran purple with ill-smelling dye, and vast piles of buildings full of windows where there was a rattling and trembling all day long, and where the piston of the steam-engine worked monotonously up and own, like the head of an elephant in a state of melancholy madness. It contained several large streets all very like one another, and many small streets still more like one another, inhabited by people equally like one another, who all want in and out at the same hours, with the same sound upon the pavements, to do the same work, and to whom every day was the same as yesterday and tomorrow, and every year the counterpart of the last and the next.[29]

Pollution was a seemingly intractable problem. In his *A Morning's Walk from London to Kew* (1817), Sir Richard Phillips commented, 'It must in a future age be ... difficult to believe that the Londoners could have resided in the dense atmosphere of coal-smoke.' Indeed, an increase in respiratory diseases in London in part countered the health benefits stemming from action against smallpox and, later, cholera.

Air pollution contributed greatly to the fogs that frequently shrouded London. These fogs played a role in the details of life there, as well as a key and lasting role in the image of the city. This was famously so at the beginning of *Bleak House*. In the oft-reproduced engraving 'Over London by Rail', in Gustave Doré and Blanchard Jerrold's *London: a Pilgrimage* (1872), the houses are shrouded in smoke and overshadowed by the railway arches, and people are reduced to minor figures. Dickens tried to return these figures to significance.

This was a world away from the rural small town depicted in the *Pickwick Papers* with Muggleton, or the image of Wiltshire's rural beauty in *Martin Chuzzlewit*,[30] but then the latter was not exactly the world of the Tolpuddle Martyrs of 1834, with its rural tension in Dorset, repeatedly the setting for Hardy's novels, reaching the point of instability. Dickens could not cover everything, nor did he seek to do so. He might stride across rural England on his walks, and praise walking rather than carriages, as well as providing a fine account of a carriage journey across southern England.[31] Nevertheless, rural England was not generally his subject nor setting. Instead, Dickens' axis was that of society and the individual, and he counterpointed the two across a range of backgrounds among which London was very much to the fore.

At the same time as he focused on the particular plight of the poor, Dickens, who fundamentally adopted the perspective of a moralist, was repeatedly at pains to indicate that flaws and problems spanned society. Indeed, that was part of the pattern of his plots and the structure of the society they illuminated:

> Were this miserable mother, and this miserable daughter, only the reduction to their lowest grade of certain social vices sometimes prevailing higher up? In this round world of many circles within circles, do we make a weary journey from the high grade to the low to find at last that they lie close together, that the two extremes touch, and that our journey's end is but our starting-place? Allowing for great difference of stuff and texture, was the pattern of this woof repeated among gentle blood at all?[32]

He shows that it is. Alongside his anger, the cruelty of society was thrown in by Dickens almost casually as in his discussion of the Chelsea Ladies' Seminary:

> The several duties of instruction in this establishment were thus discharged. English grammar, composition, geography, and the use of the dumb-bells, by Miss Melissa Wackles; writing, arithmetic, dancing, music, and general fascination, by Miss Sophy Wackles; the art of needle-work, marking, and samplery, by Miss Jane Wackles; corporal punishment, fasting, and other tortures and terrors, by Mrs Wackles ... an excellent but rather venomous old lady of three-score.[33]

Dickens' sense of similarities across society was captured, a view inherently highly unwelcome to the élite, at the beginning of *Our Mutual Friend* when Eugene remarks of the police station: 'Not *much* worse than Lady Tippins.'[34] At the same time, such facetiousness about the police was only readily safe for the élite, and thus the remark also revealed difference. Nevertheless, the essential similarities of humanity make the treatment by the 'élite' of their 'inferiors' far more reprehensible. Thus, Veneering instructs 'his driver to charge at the Public in the streets, like the life-guards at Waterloo',[35] a remark at once menacing and ridiculous, that might have led readers to think of the Peterloo massacre in 1819.

Dickens is keen to emphasise a deeper justice. The judge condemning Magwitch and others is, like them, passing on, with absolute equality, 'to the greater Judgment that knoweth all things and cannot err'.[36] Dickens is also sarcastic about the source of honours and the nature of snobbery, as in his account of Mrs Pocket, daughter of a knight who felt he should have been made a baronet and had therefore

> tacked himself on to the nobles of the earth ... I believe he had been knighted himself for storming the English grammar at the point of the pen, in a desperate address engrossed on vellum, on the occasion of the laying of the first stone of some building or other, and for handing some Royal Personage either the trowel or the mortar ... he had directed Mrs Pocket to be brought up from her cradle as one who in the nature of things must marry a title, and who was to be guarded from the acquisition of plebeian domestic knowledge ... She had grown up highly ornamental, but perfectly helpless and useless.[37]

A more vicious social snobbery in that novel enables Compeyson, the villain of the piece, to receive a much lighter sentence than Magwitch; the episode revealing the lack of justice in the law, which is a repeated point for Dickens.[38]

At the same time, Dickens scarcely offered an account of two competing social orders. Instead, as in *Oliver Twist*, there were gradations of oppression. Noah Claypole, a charity boy, is despised by the local shop-boys:

> But, now that fortune had cast in his way a nameless orphan [Oliver], at whom even the meanest could point the finger of scorn,

he retorted on him with interest. This affords charming food for contemplation. It shows us what a beautiful thing human nature sometimes is; and how impartially the same amiable qualities are developed in the finest lord and the dirtiest charity-boy.[39]

At every level, Dickens was concerned about childhood lost, and the false values involved. This was the case both for major characters and for those who play a walk-on role. The eldest pupil of Ruth Pinch was 'a premature little woman of thirteen years old, who had already arrived at such a pitch of whalebone and education that she had nothing girlish about her: which was a source of great rejoicing to all her relations and friends'.[40] The cruelty of adults toward children is revealed anew. Cruelty to animals was also a feature of English society.

There was in Dickens the sentimentality and pathos of much of the culture and values of the period. Understandably, both were at full display with the death of children, as with the tomb of Ellen Jane and Marianne Robinson in Lichfield Cathedral: 'Their affectionate mother in fond remembrance of their heaven-loved innocence consigns their resemblances to this sanctuary in humble gratitude for the glorious assurance that of such is the kingdom of God.' Yet, with Dickens, there was a far harder edge, one that focused on the cruelty of adults, and of society as a whole.

A somewhat less negative account about England and social conditions can be offered by referring to those in other countries of the time and by drawing attention to the impact of the economic problems and crises of the period. Inherently unstable, the economy was made more so by the need for a long recovery after the prolonged warfare from 1793 to 1815. Indeed, Dickens was a post-war figure who did not really understand the impact of the war. The major expansion of the money supply and rampant inflation of the war years was succeeded and tamed by a long period of hard money and deflation, one exacerbated first by the resumption of the gold standard, and then by Sir Robert Peel's unduly admired Bank Charter Act of 1844 which restricted note issue. The effects of the latter, which had to be suspended regularly, were alleviated only with the discovery of gold in both Australia and California in 1849. The latter boosted the money supply permitted by the gold standard and facilitated the mid-Victorian boom from about 1850. In other words, there were far more problems for society than those posed by real-life Mr Bumbles.

3

THE WORLD OF STEAM

Wonderful thing, steam, sir.

Dickens, 'The River', *Evening Chronicle*, 6 June 1835

The latest is best ... not to believe in the nineteenth century, one might as well disbelieve that a child grows into a man ... without that Faith in Time what anchor have we in any secular speculation.

This remark, in 1857, by the painter William Bell Scott (1811–90), was exemplified in his painting *The Nineteenth Century, Iron and Coal* (1861), which was set in the vibrant industrial city of Newcastle. His canvas sought to capture, as Scott stated, 'everything of the common labour, life and applied science of the day'. The nobility of labour was to the fore, as Scott depicted workers at Robert Stephenson's engineering works, one of the largest manufacturers of railway engines in the world, as well as an Armstrong artillery piece which was made on the Tyne, the steam of modern communications, and telegraph wires. This was culture displaying power, the power of the world's leading economy. It rested on coal; or 'antediluvian forest' as Dickens, indicating his knowledge, pointed out.[1]

The dramatic onset of the Age of Steam had been present to everybody with the transformation brought by the railway, and to England first in the world. The horse ceased to define the possibilities of land travel. As a result, unprecedented speeds of travel became possible, and then commonplace. The new sounds and sights contributed to a powerful sense of change, which was overwhelmingly seen by commentators as progress. The *St James's Chronicle* of 30 March 1847 was far from alone in considering the impact of rail travel on the human body. It was widely believed that it brought on labour for pregnant women.[2] In January 1847, Dickens used the comparison of 'Railroad speed', and that February he had the good luck to catch the express train at Folkestone for London, the journey only taking two hours and twenty minutes,[3] although in part by cutting down on intermediate stops, such as Cloisterham (Rochester), as mentioned in *Edwin Drood*.

The railway, as railroads along which horse-drawn wagons moved coal, existed before the locomotive (moving) steam engine. However, the development of the locomotive provided the key technology for the rail revolution, and industrialisation supplied the necessary demand, capital and skills. The belief in the beneficial impact of the train was captured in Dickens' *The Uncommercial Traveller*. The traveller was pressed by the landlord of the Dolphin's Head to sign a petition for a branch line: 'I bound myself to the modest statement that universal traffic, happiness, prosperity, and civilisation, together with unbounded national triumph in competition with the foreigner, would infallibly flow from the Branch.' In *Middlemarch*, George Eliot has Caleb Garth, the wisest and finest character in the book, remark, 'Now my lads, you can't hinder the railroad: it will be made whether you like it or not.'

In Dickens' melancholic story 'Our School', however, the train was less benign. Revisiting the scene of his education, he found the memory violated: 'A great trunk-line had swallowed the playground, sliced away the schoolroom, and pared off the corner of the house.' Dickens was able to capture many aspects of the human drama of rail. Although he benefited from it, he did not worship technology.

Change proved rapid and dramatic, and it all occurred during Dickens' lifetime. Services from London reached Birmingham in 1838 (with part of the line opened in 1837 to facilitate travel to London for Victoria's coronation), Southampton in 1840, Exeter in 1844, Norwich in 1845, Ipswich and Bury St Edmunds in 1846, Plymouth in 1847, and Truro in 1859. Tunnels were blasted through hills, like the Kilsby tunnel (1834–8) between London and Birmingham. Between 1830 and 1868, about 30,000 bridges were built in Britain, a very clear demonstration of the process of linkage. The cost was formidable. The London to Brighton line opened in 1841, including the spur to Shoreham, alone cost £2,569,359.

On 29 August 1850, in one of the public displays of ceremony that the era greatly loved, Victoria opened the Royal Border Bridge over the River Tweed at Berwick. Designed by Robert Stephenson (1803–59), one of the greatest engineers of the day, this viaduct of twenty-eight arches cost £253,000, and is still impressive today, the height of the bridge and the curve of the approach providing a fine vista. This was a man-made vista, as those of Victoria's reign increasingly were, and notably so with the railway. The bridge provided the last railway link between London and Edinburgh, one that enabled Victoria readily to go to Balmoral, her place in the Scottish Highlands, whereas George IV had gone to Edinburgh by sea. Robert was to be buried in Westminster Abbey, a recognition of the importance of engineering.

The setting of most of the novels, however, is before the time of trains, or soon after their arrival; and this situation affected the options for the characters Dickens deployed. Thus, in *Bleak House*, Mrs Rouncewell and Mrs Bagnet leave Lincolnshire for London by carriage:

Railroads shall soon traverse all this country, and with a rattle and a glare the engine and train shall shoot like a meteor over the wide night-landscape, turning the moon paler; but, as yet, such things are non-existent in these parts, though not wholly unexpected. Preparations are afoot, measurements are made, ground is staked out. Bridges are begun, and their not yet united piers desolately look at one another over roads and streams, like brick and mortar couples with an obstacle to their union; fragments of embankments are thrown up, and left as precipices ... everything looks chaotic, and abandoned in full hopelessness.[4]

The railway reached Lincoln in 1846, but much of the large county was not served until later.

The process by which the rail system expanded was controversial, as noted in *Edwin Drood*, where Cloisterham lacked a railway and Mr Sapsea had said there never would, or should, be one:

And yet, marvellous to consider, it has come to pass, in these days, that Express Trains don't think Cloisterham worth stopping at, but yell and whirl through it on their larger errands, casting the dust off their wheels as a testimony against its insignificance. Some remote fragment of Main Line to somewhere else, there was, which was going to ruin the Money Market if it failed, and Church and State if it succeeded, and (of course), the Constitution, whether or no; but even that had already so unsettled Cloisterham traffic, that the traffic, deserting the high road, came sneaking in from an unprecedented part of the country by a back stable-way.[5]

There was massive destruction involved in the building of stations and lines, with trains proving the strong 'iron monster'.[6] Dickens discussed this destruction in his account of north London. Camden Town and nearby areas were transformed by the building of Euston, King's Cross and St Pancras stations, and their extensive supporting marshalling yards and lines. This was the biggest concentration of major stations and railway facilities in London and the country. In *Dombey and Son*, Camden Town is the epicentre of change:

> The first shock of a great earthquake had ... rent the whole neighbourhood to its centre ... Houses were knocked down; streets broken through and stopped ... Everywhere were bridges that led nowhere ... mounds of ashes blocked up rights of way, and wholly changed the law and custom of the neighbourhood ... the yet unfinished and unopened Railroad was in progress, and, from the very core of all this dire disorder, trailed smoothly away, upon its mighty course of civilisation and improvement.[7]

Alongside spectacle and class distinction, railways also provided material for the language, as with Dickens' 'the course of true love is not a railway'.[8] In *Great Expectations*, 'Joe's education, like steam, was yet in its infancy.'[9]

At the same time, the nature of the new network posed problems. Dickens found this in January 1862 when travelling from Leamington Spa to Cheltenham via Birmingham, where he was 'stranded' for an hour. He discussed this in terms of 'cross-Railway-travelling'.[10] It remains the case today. This situation was also true of contemporary France.

More seriously, there were accidents, notably the Staplehurst one affecting the Folkestone express in 1865, an accident, due to mistimed plate repairs, in which ten were killed and fourteen seriously injured, although not Dickens, who helped tend the wounded. This was death in the midst of life and not the prepared death that Victorians commonly discussed. The accident, about which he wrote powerfully,[11] noting the role of chance,[12] led Dickens to become more nervous about travelling, and he disliked the rocking on carriages which led him to advise against the Leicester to London express in 1867.[13] Yet, family and friends also suffered from accidents on the road, including horses bolting, which affected Dickens' wife, and wheels coming off carriages, which injured Charles Fechter in 1865.

The scale of rail construction and operations helped ensure the development of the relevant skills. As with other branches of industrial capitalism, the rail system required large numbers of trained (and motivated) employees able to provide the technical and administrative skills required. Experienced and skilful manpower made projects more predictable, errors less common, and investment safer. Engineering education developed. At the same time, Dickens, characteristically, was well aware that the railways relied on continual hard work, and that they affected the health of the workers. Thus Mr Toodle is a stoker: '"The ashes sometimes gets in here" – touching his chest – "and makes a man speak gruff, as at the present time".'[14]

The organisational sophistication of railways was particularly impressive, both in terms of creating a system and, also, more obviously, of managing the works, trains, freight and passengers. Indeed, in 1848, Dickens referred to someone 'in the midst of enormous Druidical altars of other peoples' luggage, at Euston Square'.[15] Management to a timetable was a potent practice, both for the railways themselves, and for the economy as a whole. The Railway Clearing House, established in 1842, led to standard rates and apportioned through revenues, ensuring that the apparent systemic confusion commented on by Dickens was in practice not a full description of the system.

Yet, activity attracted fraud, notably with George Hudson, the 'Railway King', whose speculative schemes caused the financial crisis that hit the railways in 1849. Two years earlier, Dickens had referred to him as 'the Giant Humbug of this time, and not a pleasant illustration of our English Virtues'.[16] With the prominent exception of the Duke of Wellington, most of society cut Hudson after his bankruptcy and did not continue to visit him.

Dickens followed up the Staplehurst crash by writing: 'Every day of my life, I think more and more what an ill-governed country this is, and what a pass our political system has got to. How has this enormous Railway No-System grown up without guidance, and now its abuses are so represented in Parliament by Directors, Contractors, Scrip Jobbers, and so forth, that no

Minister dare touch it.'[17] Birmingham and London remained cities uncomfortably divided between railway companies and their respective stations.

In practice, however, there was regulation, not least 'Parliamentary trains', those operated to comply with the Railway Regulation Act of 1844 obliging train companies to provide inexpensive rail transport for the less affluent:

> The provision of at least one train a day each way at a speed of not less than twelve miles an hour including stops, which were to be made at all stations, and of carriages protected from the weather and provided with seats; for all which luxuries not more than a penny a mile might be charged.

Commuting into London and its 'swarm of life'[18] rapidly developed, as an extensive network spread over nearby areas. Rail services from London Bridge reached Deptford in 1836 and Greenwich in 1838, while the London to Croydon line opened in 1839, followed by lines to Margate in 1846, and to Southend in 1856. By then, the tolls on turnpikes no longer appeared viable and, in 1857, the Toll Reform Committee recommended their abolition on all tolls within 6 miles of Charing Cross. Their abolition rapidly followed.

The major rail lines also had a great impact on what became London suburbia, opening up areas for development. Thus, in 1838, the line to Southampton reached what is now Surbiton, leading to the building of housing estates around the station. Alongside increased specialisation of function, as well as the clearance of rookeries (slums), suburbanisation played a big part in the decline of population in the central areas, not least the City, from the 1850s onwards.

Change extended to what became the Underground or Tube. In 1862, William Gladstone, the Chancellor of the Exchequer, joined the directors of the Metropolitan Railway on the first run over the full length of their new underground railway. This linked Paddington, the terminus for trains from the West Country, south

Wales and the south-west Midlands to Farringdon in the City. The Underground had to fit into the existing cityscape and the new geography of the railway stations.

Urban street patterns also focused on the new railway stations. The major ones, such as Isambard Kingdom Brunel's Paddington and Gilbert Scott and W. H. Barlow's St Pancras, were designed as masterpieces of iron and glass, in effect more lasting versions of the Crystal Palace built for the Great Exhibition in 1851. The stations each also had large railway hotels, such as the Great Western Royal Hotel at Paddington, opened in 1854. In a piece of 1860 decrying 'Refreshments for Travellers', Dickens had an interesting reflection on the new impersonality of society with reference to

> the great station hotel ... Where we have no individuality ... We can get on very well indeed at such a place, but still not perfectly well; and this may be, because the place is largely wholesale, and there is a lingering personal retail interest within us that asks to be satisfied.

This was very different to the situation described in Dickens' novels which offered relatively little on the train and, instead, were in large part located in the stagecoach era.

In place of 'the mail-coaches which were whirling out of town' in *Oliver Twist*, and knocking people down in *Little Dorrit*,[19] the train transformed postal services, which were organised, as before, from London. In 1840, instead of the earlier system of calculating the cost for each individual piece of post, a new relatively inexpensive uniform charging system was introduced, and, to that end, the Penny Black, the world's first postage stamp, was released. The number of letters delivered in the United Kingdom rose from 82.5 million in 1839 to 411 million in 1853. As a result of trains and steamships, it became possible at a distance to receive a reply on the same day on which letters were sent, thus contributing to a postal culture of speeded-up and reliable correspondence. This was an important adjunct to literary forms, such as the plots in detective novels. The Post Office established the Post Office Savings Bank in 1861, and took part in the nationalisation of telegraphs in 1870. The combination of the train, the time, and the post led to Dickens referring to 'Train-time', while the recovery of the railroads from winter disruption resulted in him writing that he supposed the post had 'asserted itself triumphantly'.[20]

Whereas stagecoaches were usually bumpy, crowded and poorly lit, the first two themes in Dickens' writing, trains were more convenient for reading in, and it became a normal activity for their passengers. Networks of railway bookstores helped create, as well as satisfy, a new market. These bookstores revolutionised the sale of books. In 1848, the first of what was to be the network of W.H. Smith railway bookstalls was opened at Euston Station. Smith went on to gain a monopoly and to become a prominent Conservative politician.

The new mass-produced train timetables provided opportunities for publishers, but they posed problems of comprehension, both of the display of complex information in them, and for those whose literacy was limited. Samuel Wilberforce, Bishop of Oxford (1845–69) and Winchester (1869–73), one of the great public speakers of the age, and a noted critic of Darwin, joked that the book beginning with B that every bishop read was Bradshaw's, the railway timetable. Dickens also referred to Bradshaw.[21]

The railways needed a standard time for their timetables, in order to lessen the risk of collisions and to make connections possible, thus ensuring that railways and timetables could operate as part of a system. This characteristic was important to effectiveness and profitability. In place of the previous variations of time in England from east to west, with the sun, for example, overhead at Bristol ten minutes behind London, the railways adopted the Greenwich Observatory standard as 'railway time'. In 1840, the Great Western Railway, that to the west of England, became the first railway to adopt London time, and by 1847 most British rail companies had followed suit. From its offices on the

Strand in London, the Electric Telegraph Company communicated Greenwich Time from 1852, the entire process reflecting the centrality of London. More generally, the fixing of time and time-based practices were very important in changing the nature of the world of work.

Clocks were kept accurate by the electric telegraph that was erected along railway lines largely to that end. The electric telegraph was patented in Britain in 1837, with an electromagnet utilised to transmit and receive electric signals. The telegraph was initially used by private companies to transmit information about trains. However, the original railway lines came first, and the use of the telegraph, a later technology, was initially established by trial and error, not least as it was important to decide how best to register signals, with a choice between visual and acoustic methods, and manual or automatic ones. Seeing, in Paris in January 1856, the play *Rentrée à Paris*, Dickens was 'moved and excited by the telegraph part of it': an electric telegraph office was depicted.

Time, industrialisation and automation were linked. When Dickens was born in 1812, the low level of clock and watch ownership encouraged reliance on the position of the sun, as well as on tower clocks on churches and town buildings, and on church bells. In turn, machine-made clocks offered greater predictability and lower prices than handmade ones. Mechanisation permitted the manufacture of clocks in batches, thus gaining economies of scale. More precise pinions, the fine teeth in a mechanical watch that transmit energy from the spring to the hands, increased the accuracy of watches. Specifications in timekeeping improved, and uniformity was ensured by the use of measuring equipment.

The sense of time and space changed as a result of the train, which offered a potent symbol of the human capacity to use new knowledge to remodel the environment and to create totally new sensations and links. Thus, the train was a means of modernisation and a source, symbol and site of a new sensibility that was active in space and time.

The opening up of the telegraph for public use led to a marked expansion in usage and in reference to the system. As a separate facilitator of speed, but also a pressure toward it, the telegraph vastly speeded up the communication of news, and thus expectations of prompt news, which helps explain the use of 'Mercury' in the title of newspapers. The birth of Queen Victoria's second son, Alfred, in 1844 provided the content of the first press telegram sent from Windsor to London: it made it possible for the *Times* to print the news in an edition that went to press forty minutes after the birth.

The impact of the train itself, however, could be swallowed in the new industrial landscape. In Coketown, which was based on Preston, an important railway town on the westerly route to Scotland, 'the Express whirled in full sight of the Fairy Palace over the arches near: little felt amid the jarring of the machinery, and scarcely heard above its crash and rattle'.[22] Nevertheless, in the nearby countryside, the impression was stronger: 'The seizure of the station with a fit of trembling, gradually deepening to a complaint of the heart, announced the train. Fire and steam, and smoke, and red light, a hiss; a crash, a bell, and a shriek.'[23]

Thanks in part to the train, local trends were eclipsed by metropolitan fashions. Railways meant the rapid circulation of news, notably of London newspapers across the country. They also provided news items, and of many types. For example, there was consideration of appropriate conduct on the new form of transport, notably between men and women. Indeed, publications as a whole, in offering commentary on social conventions, provided a means to help mould them.

Details of the planned new rail links offered much copy for newspapers, for example for the Worcester and Oxford railway in the *Birmingham Herald* of 4 August 1836. Shareholder meetings were discussed, while railway timetables were printed. The general attitude was that of praise for new links tempered by criticism of schemes deemed inappropriate. The *Staffordshire Advertiser* of 14 October 1848 reported the opening of the Crewe branch of the North Staffordshire Railway, 'which will give the district an outlet to Liverpool, Chester and Holyhead as well as for the present to Manchester and the North'. The spread of rail brought out the 'boosterism' of the press, its willingness to praise particular local causes.

Railways also saw the presentation in a new form of existing social and economic distinctions. There were three classes for passengers, with very different conditions and fare. On the London to Brighton line, the third-class carriages lacked roofs until 1852, and, thereby, were exposed to the weather and to the hot ash from the engine. Return fares on the line in 1845 were:

Class	1st	2nd	3rd
Cost in shillings (old money)	21	9	5
Cost (modern equivalents)	£1.10p	45p	25p

Roads, in comparison, became less important than railways. Nevertheless, the railway system could not have worked without an effective road network, with people and goods moving accordingly to and from stations. Moreover, not everywhere had railway stations. The remarkable turnpike system preceded the railways and facilitated it. There was improvement alongside the trains, not least with road surfaces and bridge-building, such as the suspension bridge across the River Tees at Thorlton opened in 1831, and the bridges across the Thames. The 1862 Highways Act enabled the combination of parishes into highway districts in order to improve the roads. Indeed, nineteenth-century Britain saw an increasing use of horses, mainly for road transport and travel.

Steam was seen in the coastal passenger services patronised by Dickens, such as between London and Margate, and his 1834 journey from London to Leith as a newspaper reporter, as well as by the cross-Channel trips he frequently took. In staying on the Isle of Wight in 1849, Dickens was able to advise visitors to take the train from Waterloo to Gosport, and then a steamer to Ryde. This was an instance of the way in which England had become far more accessible from London. Separately, the role of steamships ensured that the concern with wind direction, seen for example in 'the wind's in the east', the catchphrase of John Jarndyce in *Bleak House*, became less relevant for shipping. Steamships did not end the importance of the winds, although it was reduced. Steamships, however, could still be wrecked by storms, and the period saw significant efforts to improve weather prediction mainly for shipping purposes. Given Dickens' early life, it is not surprising that both the river and the sea play a major role in his fiction. Although the Thames and the North Sea were in part conquered by steam, they remained potent settings and metaphors in his work.

Steam, which was used in London by breweries – a long-established industry – for pumping liquids, also drove the new industries, and notably so in the north. Bradford in Yorkshire became the global centre of worsted production and exchange, with factory horsepower in the city rising 718 per cent between 1810 and 1830, and the population climbing from 16,012 in 1810 to 103,778 in 1850. Mechanisation brought profit, larger factories, and a wave of immigrants. Innovation was continual in Bradford as elsewhere. The mechanisation of yarn spinning was followed in 1826, despite riots by hostile workers, by the spread of machine production into worsted weaving. By 1850, the work formerly done in Bradford by thousands of handloom weavers working in the countryside was performed by 17,642 automatic looms contained in factories and mass-producing women's dress fabrics.

Dickens visited industrial areas, and employed his experience in his work, for example the road between Birmingham and the major industrial city of Wolverhampton on which he travelled in 1840 and used later that year in *The Old Curiosity Shop*. Already in that novel, he had described the arrival in Birmingham by canal and the disorientation that the city caused to Little Nell:

The water had become thicker and dirtier ... the paths of coal-ash and huts of staring brick, marked the vicinity of some great manufacturing town ... Now, the clustered roofs, and piles of buildings trembling with the working of engines, and dimly resounding with their shrieks and throbbings; the tall chimneys vomiting forth a black vapour, which hung in a dense ill-favoured cloud above the housetops and filled the air with gloom; the clank of hammers beating upon iron, the roar of busy streets and noisy crowds, gradually augmenting until all the various sounds blended into one and none was distinguishable for itself, announced the termination of their journey ... The child and her grandfather ... stood amid its din and tumult, and in the pouring rain, as strange, bewildered, and confused, as if they had lived a thousand years before, and were raised from the dead and placed there by a miracle.[24]

Birmingham indeed presents 'a mountain heap of misery, the very sight of which increased their hopelessness and suffering'.[25] 'The keeper of the fire', who is rewarded in the last chapter for kindness to Nell, reflects similar ideas about Birmingham.[26] The Black Country is described as dominated by the 'black vomit' from the furnaces 'shutting out the face of day', and at night as a dystopia:

night, when the smoke was changed to fire; when every chimney spirited up its flame; and places, that had been dark vaults all day, now shone red-hot, with figures moving to and fro within their blazing jaws, and calling to one another with hoarse cries – night, when the noise of every strange machine was aggravated by the darkness; when the people near them looked wilder and more savage; when bands of unemployed labourers paraded in the roads, or clustered by torchlight round their leaders, who told them in stern language of their wrongs, and urged them on to frightful cries and threats; when maddened men, armed with sword and firebrand, spurning the tears and prayers of women who would restrain them, rushed forth on errands of terror and destruction, to work no ruin half so surely as their own – night, when carts came rumbling by, filled with rude coffins (for contagious disease and death had been busy with the living crops); when orphans cried,

and distracted women shrieked and followed in their wake – night,
when some called for bread, and some for drink to drown their
cares ... night, which, unlike the night that Heaven sends on earth,
brought with it no peace, nor quiet, nor signs of blessed sleep.[27]

No wonder the Shropshire village where Nell ends up is
presented, in comparison, as a beautiful refuge. Indeed the novel
is much influenced by Wordsworthian pastoralism and by the
Gothic Revival. Dickens later moved away from both, so the
work hardly represents typical Dickens, although the latter is
a problematic concept, not least as Dickens changed his mind
on various matters as he aged. The description of the village is
one reason why some scholars have contrasted Dickens with a
pessimistic Thomas Hardy, who offered a harsh view of rural life.

The description of worker discontent in *The Old Curiosity
Shop* given above is hysterical, and underlines the moral, rather
than political nature of Dickens' radicalism. In practice, Dickens
sought to engage with the working population in the Midlands,
seeking in a public reading for the proposed Birmingham and
Midland Institute in 1853 'to have a large audience of working
people'. His wish for them to be admitted free was not fulfilled,
but the tickets were priced low.[28]

In *Bleak House*, George Rouncewell, whom Dickens makes a
sympathetic observer, visits

... the iron country ... coalpits and ashes, high chimneys and
red bricks, blighted verdure, scorching fires, and a heavy never-
lightening cloud of smoke, become the features of the scenery ...
the black canal bridge of a busy town, with a clang of iron in it ...
an iron taste, an iron smell, and a Babel of iron sounds.[29]

Dickens also took images from industry, as with the riverside
walk of Edwin Drood and Rosa Bud in a non-industrial setting:

Among the mighty store of wonderful chains that are for ever
forging, day and night, in the vast iron-works of the time and

circumstance, there was one chain forged in the moment of that small conclusion, riveted to the foundations of heaven and earth, and gifted with invincible force to hold and drag.[30]

In contrast to the West Midlands, areas without coal, such as East Anglia and the West Country, suffered de-industrialisation or did not develop industries; although other factors were also important. There were also exceptions such as Tiverton and Barnstaple in Devon, where machine-made lace manufacture was established. By 1830, 1,000 people were being employed by John Boden in the latter, and, largely as a result, the population of the town rose from 5,079 in 1821 to 7,902 in 1841. However, the lifestyle and densely inhabited working-class neighbourhoods that developed in Barnstaple and Tiverton were more typical of northern than southern England. The relative economic and demographic importance of the key industrial zones, the north and the Midlands, rose as that of the south and east fell. In the north, the population of Liverpool increased from 83,050 in 1801 to 375,955 in 1851, and that of County Durham by 34.7 per cent in 1861–71.

Factories became of greater importance. In *Isabella* (1820), John Keats referred to

... many a weary hand did swelt
In torched mines and noisy factories.

Much work was increasingly part of a mechanised process and notably from the 1850s, a period of a major increase in industrial production. Thus, Owen and Uglow's stocking factory in Tewkesbury employed 600 workmen and 150 women in 1860, the company benefiting from inventing and patenting the reinforcing of the underfoot and heels of stockings.

The supply of coal was also a key element of transportation, notably by rail, canal and coastal shipping. Wilkins Micawber considered an entry into 'the Medway Coal Trade', only to discover that he did not have the requisite capital.[31] This was an observation delivered in *David Copperfield*, an essentially light novel, and without the heavy remarks about money breeding money that would be expected in, for example, *Our Mutual Friend*.

Newspapers were also affected by steam technology, which speeded up printing. Introduced by the *Times* in 1814, this allowed the paper to go to press later, and thus to contain more recent news than its competitors, and moreover to cut wage bills. The railways also played a key role in newspaper circulation and distribution.

Steam exemplified technology, a word used in 1828 by Jacob Bigelow to describe the application of scientific knowledge to industry. The following year, Thomas Carlyle, whom Dickens read – notably on the French Revolution – and was influenced by, coined the word industrialism. Economies of scale brought much greater profit, as well as creating new hierarchies of organisation. Alongside steam power, these economies of scale contributed greatly to the marked rise in the amount of goods and services produced and consumed by the average person, which, in addition to what was gained from overseas commercial expansion, helped overcome earlier resource constraints on living standards.

The social transformation possible through steam power was positively discussed in *Bleak House* in the person of a son of Mrs Rouncewell, the housekeeper at Sir Leicester Dedlock's seat of Chesney Wold. Mrs Rouncewell wanted him to become steward,

> ... but he took, when he was a schoolboy, to constructing steam-engines out of saucepans, and setting birds to draw their own water, with the least possible amount of labour; so assisting them with artful contrivance of hydraulic pressure, that a thirsty canary had only, in a literal sense, to put his shoulder to the wheel, and the job was done. This propensity gave Mrs Rouncewell great uneasiness. She felt it, with a mother's anguish, to be a move in the Wat Tyler direction: well knowing that Sir Leicester had that general impression of an aptitude for any art to which smoke and a

tall chimney might be considered essential. But the doomed young rebel (otherwise a mild youth, and very persevering), showing no sign of grace ... constructing a model of a power-loom.

Sir Leicester said, 'The iron country farther north is, I suppose, the congenial direction for a boy with these tendencies.' The boy succeeds, making his fortune and being invited to stand for Parliament. He has a son who is significantly called Watt, and who disrupts Sir Leicester's precious, horribly snobbish, and totally misplaced, sense of equanimity.[32]

Steam also revolutionised circulation and flow, and for Dickens these were the antitheses to the stagnation and stoppage that, both literally and metaphorically, harmed individuals and society. In his use of metaphors, there was a clear antithesis, one given moral force not least with the linkage of stoppage and stagnation to secrecy and crime. At the same time, men of energy and business, such as Carker in *Dombey and Son*, could be evil. Moreover, the good, such as the old-fashioned Solomon Gills in *Little Dorrit*, with his very dated stock and his rarely visited nautical instrument-maker's shop, could be hit hard by change: 'Competition, competition – new invention, new invention – alteration, alteration – the world's gone past me.'[33] Dickens makes clear the moral strength of the household but does not disguise the redundancy of the shop.

This was a world in which everything was commodified, as with dust in *Our Mutual Friend*, and indeed money, so that Montague's dinner 'was as good a one as money (or credit, no matter which) could produce'.[34] The qualification nicely expressed the lack of any true foundation for the dinner. In a more sinister fashion, Ephraim Flintwinch 'the lunatic-keeper ... speculated unsuccessfully in lunatics, he got into difficulty about over-roasting a patient to bring him to reason'. Of Ralph Nickleby, 'this promising lad commenced usurer on a limited scale at school; putting out at good interest a small capital of slate-pencil and marbles, and gradually extending his operations until they aspired to the copper coinage of this realm, in which he speculated to considerable advantages'. He follows this career as a crooked adult.[35] Moreover, alongside the official economy came the parallel economy, as with Saffron Hill in London in *Oliver Twist*, 'the emporium of petty larceny',[36] which, indeed, it was.

Bankruptcy, real or metaphorical, is an ever-present aspect of the world of Dickens' characters, is important to his plots, and can encompass the good and the bad, the official economy and its unofficial parallel. In Dickens' work, bankruptcy is a risk for major characters as well as minor ones, for example Nicholas Nickleby Senior. In financial terms, bankruptcy serves as the snake in a snakes-and-ladders board (but scarcely board-game) of a society in which risk and reputation are intertwined, and wealth and status are very unclear and highly uncertain. This is a major theme in Dicken's' work, including his last full-length novel, *Our Mutual Friend*. A standard plot device for Dickens and others, that of a problematic inheritance and a questionable will, provides only part of a system of 'mis-value', with all the misunderstandings, deliberate and otherwise, that flow from that. The Lammles and Bella Wilfer provide different instances of this situation, one that Dickens repeatedly uses to test the values of so many of his characters.

Dickens also offered a contrasting set of values, as in the voice of the virtuous Tom Pinch reproaching his sister's employer:

As to your suspicion and distrust of her: even of her word: if she is not above their reach, you have no right to employ her ... If you imagine that the payment of an annual sum of money gives it to you, you immensely exaggerate its power and value. Your money is the least part of your bargain in such a case. You may be punctual in that to half a second on the clock, and yet be Bankrupt.[37]

4

CRIME AND THE PRESS

They cut his throat from ear to ear,
His brains they battered in,
His name was Mr William Weare,
He dwelt in Lyon's Inn.

Anonymous contemporary verses on the
'Gill's Hill murder' of 1823

Pressures for reform in part drew on the long-standing sense of London as corrupt and corrupting. This image was reiterated in melodrama, which was the theme of much of Dickens' writings, whether for the stage or for the page. He had a lifelong interest in journalism which extended to marrying, in 1836, Catherine Hogarth, the daughter of the editor of the *Evening Chronicle*.

In part, the depiction of London was influenced by wider national and international archetypes. Thus, the plot of *London by Night* (1843), a work attributed to Charles Selby, was based on Eugène Sue's *Les Mystères de Paris* (1842–3). Foreign depravity, which Dickens noted in the case of 'what we often said of the canker at the root of all that Paris life',[1] could be linked to London's cosmopolitanism. Thus, in William Travers's *London by Night* (1868), a wicked French madame inveigled unsuspecting British virgins into her brothel in a plot that combined xenophobia with the frisson of London as the centre for debauchery. Both themes were to be taken forward in the dramatic presentation of Chinese opium dens in Dockland. Dickens visited a den in Shadwell in 1869 to gain material for the opening scene in *Edwin Drood*. Dickens makes Mademoiselle Hortense, a French maid, a manipulative, evil figure in *Bleak House*, indeed 'a Devil'.[2] So also with Rigaud, a more central character to the plot of *Little Dorrit*, and a deeply sinister and dangerous one.

In practice, most crime was home-grown, as with the Gill's Hill murder, on which much of the press focused in 1823: William Weare, a London gambler, was murdered there at the behest of John Thurtell, a well-connected, but somewhat shady, amateur boxer to whom he was in debt. There was also extensive coverage of the murder in chapbooks and ballads. Commenting on this case in its editorial of 6 November 1823, the *Birmingham Chronicle* was shocked to note the existence in London of 'a fraternity ... for the express purpose of robbery and murder'.

London as violent and sinful was a message reiterated across the country, preparing the way for the reception of Dickens' novels. Thus, *Drewry's Staffordshire Gazette* of 2 August 1827 provided details of a London poisoning, while the *Sherborne Mercury* of 10 January 1837 devoted over a column to an item headlined 'Atrocious Murder in Ratcliff Highway: Examination of the Murderer'. This was followed by another item headlined 'The Edgeware Road Murder'. The impact of such reporting was seen in *Martin Chuzzlewit* when Tom Pinch arrives in London from Salisbury:

> He was particularly anxious, among other notorious localities, to have those streets pointed out to him which were appropriated to the slaughter of countrymen; and was quite disappointed to find, after half-an-hour's walking, that he hadn't had his pocket picked.

But on John Westlock's inventing a pickpocket for his gratification, and pointing out a highly respectable stranger as one of that fraternity, he was much delighted.

In London, Tom did not in the event fall into 'the dens of any of those preparers of cannibalistic pastry, who are represented in many standard country legends as doing a lively retail business in the Metropolis'.[3]

Dickens noted the frequent display of murder in the press. Accounts of 'dreadful murders were on show' when newspaper was used to cover furniture in *Dombey and Son*,[4] which was an instructive image of such stories as waste paper. In *All The Year Round*, Dickens was concerned about the large number of accounts of murders,[5] although, as today, murder was probably a tiny percentage of crime, but attracted much media attention alongside that of Dickens. In *Our Mutual Friend*:

> ... the Harmon Murder – as it came to be popularly called – went up and down, and ebbed and flowed, now in the country, now among palaces, now among hovels, now among lords and ladies and gentlefolks, now among labourers and hammerers and ballast-heavers.[6]

An atmosphere of excitable fear ensured that Bella and Lavinia Wilfer suspect John Rokesmith as a murderer in the same novel; while Betty Higden, who loves a newspaper, likes to hear Sloppy read it aloud: 'He do the Police in different voices,'[7] a memorable phrase used by T. S. Eliot in *The Waste Land* (1922); indeed he considered entitling the poem with the Dickens' quotation.

In *Great Expectations*, Mr Wopsle read the newspaper aloud at the Three Jolly Bargemen: 'A highly popular murder had been committed, and Mr Wopsle was imbrued in blood to the eyebrows. He gloated over every abhorrent adjective in the description, and identified himself with every witness at the Inquest' imitating their expressions. A stranger, the impressive but disconcerting lawyer Jaggers, then points out the principle of innocent until proven guilty.[8] Near the close of *Oliver Twist*, 'to-night's paper says that Fagin's 'took' although it has to be asked, 'Is it true, or a lie?'[9] Sir Mulberry Hawk promises a murder to read of in the press.[10] Jonas Chuzzlewit reads a newspaper when ordering the delivery of poison.

Dickens provides a broader contextualisation of press panics about crime. In *The Chimes*, which is characterised by Dickens' satire on political economy, Toby Veck, a poor old man, finds the newspapers

> ... full of obserwations [*sic*] ... I like to know the news as well as any man ... but it almost goes against the grain with me to read a paper now. It frightens me, almost. I don't know what we poor people are coming to ... We seem to do dreadful things; we seem to give a deal of trouble; we are always being complained of and guarded against. One way or another, we fill the paper.

The press certainly frequently contributed to London's growing importance as a centre for crime and punishment, a feature seen in Dickens' writing. This centrality was not only a matter of London's reputation and the press. In addition, London's policemen were sent to the provinces to investigate crimes, while the London courts tried defendants for crimes committed elsewhere. Dickens himself visited Stanfield Hall, the site of a recent dramatic double murder, during his East Anglian trip in January 1849. He was understandably unimpressed with the police work at the scene.[11]

Dickens' support for capital punishment, but not public executions, led him into the public domain, as with his letters to the *Times* on 13 and 17 November 1849. The issue obliged Dickens to consider the nature of change, and, with that, of secrecy. Replying to criticism, he wrote:

> Will you consider whether all the improvements in prisons and punishments that have been made within the last twenty years, have, or have not, been all productive of 'mystery'? I can remember

very well, when the silent system was objected to as mysterious, and opposed to the genius of English Society. Yet there is no question that it has been a great benefit. The Prison Vans are mysterious vehicles, but surely they are better than the old system of marching prisoners through the streets chained to a long chain, like the galley slaves in Don Quixote. Is there no mystery about transportation, and our manner of sending men away to Norfolk Island or elsewhere? None in abandoning the use of a man's name, and knowing him only by a number? Is not the whole improved and altered system from beginning to end a mystery?

Dickens felt that in the eighteenth century, when there were whippings before spectators and no mystery about execution, the situation was undesirable and crime was serious.[12] The problem of deterrence troubled him, not only with regard to criminals but also to the impact on society of deterrent practices.

Interest in crime was national as well as local, and encouraged the printing of items from other newspapers. The *Taunton Courier* of 6 February 1828 carried an account from the *Bath Journal* under the heading 'The Murder in Marlborough Buildings, Bath – Confession of the Murderer'. The *Courier*, a London evening paper, on 18 September 1832 carried a story headlined 'Shocking Murder', with the *Bolton Chronicle* as the source. An editorial in *Trewman's Exeter Flying Post* of 3 January 1856, calling for the establishment of a county police, noted correctly that 'scarcely a week passes without our paper containing the record of numerous thefts, of a more or less aggravated character'. In *David Copperfield*, John Maldon languidly and callously observes, 'There's a long statement in the papers about a murder. But somebody is always being murdered.'[13]

Crime reports were purchased from courtroom reporters, with murder and lurid adultery trial reports those of greatest value. The reporters were freelancers, as was the pattern across much of the press. The accounts in newspapers proved an important source for the public understanding of criminality and the response, notably the legal system. They were matched by books, such as the much-thumbed frightening and moralistic history of the lives and trials of great criminals that Fagin gives Oliver Twist. Such books sold well.

Accident reports were a variant on crime stories, again with drama but with less moralising. The *St James's Chronicle* of 1 April 1845 reported on a serious fire at Doncaster, and the issue of 16 November 1847 on a shipwreck. Commenting on people being blown into the Surrey Canal, Dickens, in 'Refreshments for Travellers', ironically asked whether they did so to get into the newspapers.

The Sunday newspapers, the success of which, in small part, reflected the churches' failure to act as a means of spreading opinion, made crime the basis of their success, and, in doing so, profited from the developments in advertising in the early nineteenth century. Many of the articles were well calculated for the placards that were fixed to mail coaches and also put up around newspaper offices. These placards made use of large-typeface advertising.

Dickens was unconvinced about the accuracy of much newspaper reporting, a view repeatedly supported by erroneous reporting on his life. Commenting on the eagerness of the Sunday papers for news about the Dombeys after Edith fled, Perch from Dombey's office sanctimoniously notes that, in the King's Arms, he happened 'last week, to let a little observation fall there, and next morning, which was Sunday, I see it worked up in print in a most surprising manner'. However, the self-important Perch is then revealed to misrepresent totally what he does hear.[14] This passage is a humorous, as well as clear, indictment of newspaper sources. So also with the bullying magistrate Mr Fang, who is depicted as very different to the newspaper editorial commending him.[15] However, there is no criticism in Dickens' novels of the contents and methods of the London press comparable to the vitriol he directed at the New York press in *Martin Chuzzlewit*, a vitriol based on his response to the attacks he had received from them, not least as a consequence of the copyright issue.[16]

The London Sunday papers enjoyed a burst of expansion in the 1840s, a decade that very much saw the development of Dickens' writing, as well as, in 1846, eighteen days in which he was briefly editor of the newly established *Daily News*. The foundation of *Lloyd's Weekly London Newspaper* (later shortened to *Lloyd's Weekly News*) in 1842 was followed by the *News of the World* (1843), the *Weekly Times* (1847), and *Reynolds's Weekly Newspaper* (1850). Each was successful in coining the high murder rate. These Sundays benefited from the high cost of taking a more regular newspaper, from the increasing definition of Sunday as leisure time, indeed *the* leisure time, in the more regulated urban environment and economic system that was developing, and from their clear and deliberate association with more accessible and exciting news.

Like Dickens' journalism, the Sundays indicated the growing specialisation of the press. This process reflected a more developed society, the desire and ability of those who controlled and composed the world of printing and publishing to create and respond to opportunities, and the increasing sense, in sphere after sphere, that it was necessary, or at least desirable, to have a particular periodical to note changes, discuss options and activities, and act as a means of coherence.

To indicate the range of the press, a range matching that of culture (discussed in chapter 7), the number of religious newspapers also rose markedly from the late 1820s. With their confessions, often lurid tales of sin, redemption and retribution, pious deaths, and elements of the supernatural, all also facets of Dickens' work, many religious papers were accessible. They provided a readily grasped content, notably an exciting series of individual morality tales that paralleled crime literature and newspaper reporting. While the newspapers looked back to eighteenth-century predecessors, these tales also all in a way drew in part on tropes of the Gothic novel, not least those of virtue under threat and evil as a real presence.

The religious press overlapped with other religious publications, including sermons, poetry and novels. Indeed, sermons probably sold more than novels and poetry until the 1850s, and Charles Spurgeon (1834–92), the magnetic Baptist preacher, possibly sold more sermons than the works of any individual novelist. The religious press also overlapped with the more general world of individual and collective worship, one in which sermons were important. Dickens' 'Story of the Goblins who stole a Sexton' (1867) very much captured the ideas of punishment and redemption, but gave the goblins a partly humorous as well as moral character.

Alongside parallels and overlaps between types of newspapers and between individual titles, there were also contrasts, not least in reading markets, reliance on advertisements, and (differently) politics. The reformist papers included the long-standing *Leeds Mercury*, the *Bristol Mercury*, the *Newcastle Courant*, and the newly launched *Sheffield Independent* (1819) and *Manchester Guardian* (1821), all of which gave calls for moral improvement a pointedly political content and energy, at both local and national levels.

Political and economic opinions, indeed, were developed and expressed through newspapers. Pressure for greater parliamentary representation helped shape the contours of local political activism, and there was a conflation of political opinion and newspaper campaigning. Helping to locate Dickens, this process was aided by the active political role of many newspaper figures, and their central place in public political consciousness within their communities. The role of the reform press included the articulation of a self-conscious middle class.

In contrast, and as part of the process, the opponents of reform were stigmatised as a redundant *ancien régime* caste. An anti-establishment critique became more powerful, largely as a consequence of the protracted nature of the electoral reform crisis in the early 1830s, which led to the Great, or, as it became, First Reform Act of 1832. This crisis, at once national and local, high political and electoral, resulted in sustained excitement. Newspapers were obliged to take sides in this situation. Thus, Edward Barnes used the *Leeds Mercury* in

1830 to promote the successful candidacy of Henry Brougham, a rather radical Whig, for the key constituency of Yorkshire. In 1832, during major riots in the city linked to pressure for parliamentary reform, the windows of the Tory *Nottingham Journal* were broken.

At the same time, illustrating the degree to which the Whigs were outflanked by radicals, a series of unstamped radical papers produced by bold and energetic publishers, such as Richard Carlile, who spent many years in prison, launched sweeping attacks on the establishment and called for action on behalf of the working class. Some of the unstamped newspapers, moreover, pioneered new commercial techniques and styles, and their success threatened established newspapers. John Arthur Roebuck, a radical MP and opponent of the Stamp Duties, as well as of the extremism of much of the unstamped press, issued thirty-six unstamped weekly *Pamphlets for the People* in 1835–6, in order to encourage popular debate and pressure for change.

Leaving aside its radical counterparts, the stamped press was divided over politics. At the outset of Dickens' career, the *Morning Chronicle* backed the Whigs and the *Times* the Tories. The *Morning Chronicle* gave Dickens his key start. A Whig paper in its origins, and remaining firm to this position, it came second to the *Times* in daily sales. The *Times*, which came to criticise the Whig government over the Poor Law Amendment Act of 1834, supported the Tory government of Sir Robert Peel of 1841–6, which was attacked by the *Morning Chronicle*, a paper long noted for its parliamentary reporting, which also printed Henry Mayhew's accounts of the London poor in 1849–50. The *Times* was critical of Dickens' works.

In the 1830s and 1840s, Dickens, a reformer, was an eager protagonist of Whig views in his novels and in the press. He has Mr Bumble, the atrocious parish beadle in *Oliver Twist*, complain about the reporting of poor relief by 'owdacious newspapers',[17] in other words Whig ones. Drawing on his experience as a parliamentary reporter, Dickens was sardonic about MPs, as with Mr Gregsbury and his 'tolerable command of sentences with no meaning in them'. His oratory was that of mundane and somewhat vacuous patriotism:

> ... whether I look merely at home, or ... contemplate the boundless prospect of conquest and possession – achieved by British perseverance and British valour – which is outspread before me, I clasp my hands, and turning my eyes to the broad expanse above my head, exclaim, 'Thank Heaven, I am a Briton!'

And Gregsbury had sent the newspapers a complacent and deceitful letter about his parliamentary actions.[18]

In July 1842, Dickens wrote to Lady Holland, a noted Whig, urging the need to fight 'the battle staunchly, and to the death' over the press, adding that he was strongly inclined to establish a new evening paper for the Whigs and seeking Whig financial support to that end. The Whigs, however, rejected the idea. Dickens commented, later in the month, that he was well acquainted with the management of the press, and also claiming that newspaper writers ignored the 'questions which interest the people, and concern their business and bosoms most'.[19] Dickens himself dined at Holland House with the Whig leaders on 22 July. He also saw Brougham, who had been dropped from the Whig establishment and cabinet after 1834 as unreliable, and not a team player, after which he moved Tory-wards, which was linked to Dickens coming to criticise him.

The 1830s had really seen the abandonment of the attempt by government to subvert and control the London press by financial subsidies, a practice that was common until the 1820s. The growth of independent opinion, as well as greater parliamentary scrutiny of expenditure, convinced ministries of the inefficacy of this method, which became worth neither the money nor the risk. Instead, politicians continued to play the press by other means, not least feeding individual newspapers official news, as Palmerston repeatedly did. This became the most effective way of influencing press coverage. Editors were very grateful if politicians and ministers helped them to scoop rivals.

Alongside rivalry over party politics, a more general sense of new opportunities was insistent in the press. Many items relating to improvements were clearly inserted as paid-for. Yet, over some issues, the opinions of the publishers were clear, while, in others, their willingness to insert particular items suggest their interest in propounding specific views. The press reflected most clearly the opinions and interests of the middling order. Paternalism grounded in moral behaviour and religious attitudes, rather than economic dominance, was the justification of the social policy required for the well-ordered society that was presented by the press as a necessary moral goal; just as the presence of newspapers in coffeehouses and other meeting places was part of the furniture of this sphere. Christian welfare, not egalitarianism, was the goal. Moreover, as well as fostering feelings of regional identity, the provincial press helped to create a national awareness of public politics, so that issues resonated through the political community, with newspapers presenting themselves as taking part in national education, including in politics. Equally, newspaper commentary suggests as much a sense of a desperate prodding of apathetic opinion and hostile interests, as it does any control of priorities for debate and action by a broad, united and mobilised middle class. In addition, there were many newspapers, for example in Shoreditch, dealing with very local news. Some were politically influential.

Meanwhile, newspapers, like novelists, declared their determination to serve all markets. This was a conventional approach that matched commercial goals. Thus, on 7 January 1854, the first issue of the *Staffordshire Sentinel* announced that it would 'be a paper for all classes – fitted for the politician, the social reformer and the family circle'. Dickens very frequently made reference in his writing to characters reading newspapers. In *Our Mutual Friend*, the elderly Abbey Potterson, the masterful owner and manager of a working-class bar, is shown as reading the newspaper, as are the well-connected Twemblow and Podsnap at work, while Betty Higden would sometimes hear a newspaper read out. Becoming a 'Housewife ... another branch of study claimed the attention of Mrs John Rokesmith for a regular period every day. This was the mastering of the newspaper, so that she might be close up with John on general topics when John came home.'

Waiting is a frequent reason for turning to newspapers. In *Great Expectations*, the waiting Mike is reading one. In *Oliver Twist*, one of the two magistrates who decide not to allocate Oliver as an apprentice to the chimney sweep reads a newspaper, as well as Bumble, Sowerberry and the parish clerk while waiting for the clergyman to preside at the pauper funeral, Bumble after dinner when he reaches London, and Barney at the counter in the *Three Cripples*.[20] In *Martin Chuzzlewit*, the porter thinks Pecksniff 'the Paper, and wondered why you didn't shove yourself through the grating as usual'; while Merry Pecksniff 'yawned over yesterday's newspaper', and Jonas Chuzzlewit also reads yesterday's.[21] In *Bleak House*, Esther Summerson is given a paper to read while waiting at Kenge and Carboy's, the lawyers, and 'scraps of newspapers, all referring to Coroners' Inquests', are found among the effects of Nemo. At a very different social level, Sir Leicester Dedlock reads and comments on the newspaper. Edward Dorrit daily goes to 'the coffee-house to read the paper', while Ralph Nickleby finds the advertisement for Squeers's Academy in a newspaper. The advertisement is placed in the *Times*, '*Morning Post*, *Chronicle*, *Herald*, and *Advertiser*'. The hungover Lord Frederick Verisopht and Sir Mulberry Hawk lie around listlessly with newspapers 'strewn about the room'.[22] Scrooge 'read all the newspapers' during his solitary tavern dinner. Waiting to place his order 'for a pint of claret' in a London hotel, Nicholas Nickleby picks up a newspaper to read 'and was in truth half-dozing'. Subsequently, the injured Mulberry Hawk is read to while recovering, and the first action of Madeline Bray's father, on receiving some money, is to obtain a newspaper.[23]

In a long-standing practice, the tone of the press was lightened by the frequent publication of jokes, humorous stories, verses and epigrams. Variety was a key theme, and a means to make newspapers more interesting to a range of readers. Illustrations were increasingly important to this variety. From 1832 to 1845, Charles Knight produced the *Penny Magazine*, a weekly that was the first lavishly illustrated publication to be offered to the working class. He adapted the printing machinery to produce more illustrations. Dickens' journalism became part of that variety, but the serial publication of fiction posed particular problems. This was particularly so for weeklies, a 'specially trying mode of publication ... how patiently and expressly the thing has to be planned for presentation in these fragments, and yet for afterwards fusing together as an uninterrupted whole'.[24] *Punch* and the *Illustrated London News*, both products of the 1840s, showed the attraction of pictures. Initially reformist in tone, they both became much more conservative later.

There was a significant growth, as well as variety, in the market. The total sale of stamped papers – those paying stamp duty, and therefore legal – rose from 14 million in 1780 to 31 million in 1835, and 85 million in 1851, a rate of rise that was far greater than that of the population. There was a rising literacy level that in part reflected an increased desire on the part of the working class for literacy, but the proportion of literates purchasing newspapers was relatively low. Indeed, the per capita readership of newspapers did not begin to rise significantly until the later 1830s. Rising sales helped fund investment including an expansion of regular reporting staff and the move to steam-powered production.

The social location of the newspaper-reading public was restricted not only by the specific 'taxes on knowledge' and the consequent cost of papers, but also by the general social context. In this, both illiteracy and poverty were important. Yet, within these parameters, there was, as with fiction, much reader choice. Furthermore, aside from competition between newspapers, the press as a whole was challenged by magazines, almanacs and chapbooks. The development of an extensive readership for the sensational, represented by stories in the Sunday press, offered a strong indication of a reader demand that could be satisfied by other means.

Reflecting a rise in the prominence of editors, original editorial commentary became common. Many newspapers ceased to be, as many originally had been, a means to use spare printing capacity and to probe market opportunities. They became, instead, more central to the activities of the concerns producing them. Meanwhile, proprietors and editors joined more influential and socially prominent circles.

Nevertheless, the newspaper correspondents were in a more ambiguous social position. So also to a degree with novelists, although Bulwer Lytton and, differently and far less by choice, Dickens displayed an ability to move with ease in exalted social circles. Writers themselves had long moved between journalism and fiction, Henry Fielding being a prime example. In the nineteenth century, social questions, notably the 'Condition of England' issues, could be addressed in both fiction and the press. Each, in turn, helped to shape the other, not least as the serialisation of fiction became far more pronounced from 1836. Moreover, the growth of the readership of each created contexts within which the other was approached and understood. There were important overlaps, not least the syndication of fiction in newspapers. Dickens more directly benefited from the interchange in 1851. His *Household Narrative*, a monthly supplement to *Household Words*, was prosecuted for not paying the newspaper stamp. The Inland Revenue argued that any publication containing news was taxable, but lost the case.

The press, as a whole, sought the reform of its own position. The Association for the Promotion of the Repeal of the Taxes of Knowledge, founded in 1849 by Richard Cobden and other radicals, however, found that the Whig ministry of Lord John Russell (1846–52) lacked a working majority for repeal and, anyway, was concerned about the challenge from Chartism, which had a press of its own. As a result, the taxation on advertisements did not end until 1853, the newspaper stamp duty until 1855, and the paper duties until 1861. Gladstone played a key role in ending the taxes. The end of these duties led to a massive expansion in the press.

Print had the authority of a culture that put the emphasis on reason and the pursuit of the rational through the written word. The press has been presented as a way in which the middle class pushed through its views, against both the élite and the working classes. Maybe so. But the specifics of the moment were too important not to dominate press content. The net effect of the press was certainly to foster democratisation. This process was seen in a matter from which Dickens was to profit with his public readings, namely the carrying of notices of public meetings. Opposition to slavery was a major cause of such meetings. On 3 September 1853, *Bell's Weekly Messenger* announced, 'On Monday Mr W. Brown delivered a lecture on American slavery before a large and respectable audience at the Lecture Hall.' This was very much the press as trumpeter for, and beneficiary of, the world of public politics.

Dickens also saw the press as a necessary counter to the misuse of power, and, in the tradition of William Cobbett, he responded harshly to criticism of newspapers by politicians. In 1867, Dickens attacked Jonathan Gathorne-Hardy, the President of the Poor Law Board, who had condemned the press for writing 'sensationally' against the mismanagement of London workhouses. Dickens' comments proved the basis for an article in *All The Year Round* on 2 March 1867. The symbiosis of press and politics was differently shown when Gregsbury outlined to Nicholas Nickleby the cramming duties of an MP's secretary, a job Nicholas speedily decides he cannot take. Reflecting its role in national life and politics, the press plays a major role in these duties:

> My secretary would have to make himself master of the foreign policy of the world, as it is mirrored in the newspapers; to run his eyes over all accounts of public meetings, all leading articles, and accounts of the proceedings of public bodies; and to make notes of anything which it appeared to him might be made a point of, in any little speech upon the question of some petition lying on the table, or anything of that kind ... Then it would be necessary for

him to make himself acquainted, from day to day, with newspaper paragraphs on passing events; such as 'Mysterious disappearance, and supposed suicide of a pot-boy,' or anything of that sort, upon which I might found a question to the Secretary of State for the Home Department. Then, he would have to copy the question, and as much as I remembered of the answer (including a little compliment about independence and good sense); and to send the manuscript in a frank to the local paper, with perhaps half a dozen lines of leader, to the effect, that I was always to be found in my place in Parliament, and never shrunk from the responsible and arduous duties, and so forth.[25]

5

GOVERNMENT

Forth rushed, from Envy sprung and Self-Conceit,
A Power misnamed the Spirit of Reform,
And through the astonished Island swept in storm,
Threatening to lay all Orders at her feet
That crossed her way.

> William Wordsworth, *Protest Against the Ballot* (1838)

Not one of Wordsworth's masterpieces, his poem reflected the
extent of the conversion to conservatism that was to help him
gain a Civil List pension in 1842, and to become Poet Laureate in
1843, in succession to Robert Southey. Both of these recognitions
for Wordsworth were made under the Tory government of
Sir Robert Peel. Wordsworth's poem underlined the hostility and
fear that reform aroused in many circles. Indeed, he continued in
this work by urging St George, a totemic national figure and also
one resonant of the recent military glory won at the expense of
France, to stop the introduction of the ballot as it threatened to
spawn a 'pest' worse than the dragon he had slain.

Despite Wordsworth, or, rather, at a different level of activity, the trend was certainly toward reform. Government was active and busy, albeit with many weaknesses. It was capable, as Dickens did not really recognise in his fiction, of improving its own processes, as well as of using them to effect change. The correspondence of the Home Office was listed and indexed from 1841, while the Treasury and Foreign Office gained major buildings in 1863. Government, indeed, more generally was seen as a way to prevent disputes and to release the potential of society, the latter the very opposite of Dickens' presentation of the fictitious do-nothing Circumlocution Office in *Little Dorrit*. For example, the creation under the Tithe Commutation Act of 1836 of a system to establish the ownership of tithes, and to assess their value so as to make commutation possible, was necessary because tithes, and disputes over them, were regarded as anachronistic, a limitation on agricultural improvements and a cause of anti-clericalism. Officials acted to process the information. So also with the Inclosure Commissioners. From 1840, a series of Acts were passed enabling tenants for life to borrow money to improve the property, and thus encourage investment and action, and unlock wealth. The supervision of the loans was usually the responsibility of the commissioners, who had to determine the likely value of the improvements that would result from the loans. As Dickens noted, in his case referring to the Poor Law, commissioners were becoming more powerful. They were also more common: the Poor Law, Board of Trade, Post Office, and Board of Health, all had commissioners.

A key element of change was presented by public health, and notably so in London. In *Household Words* on 7 October 1854, Dickens attacked a situation in which workers had to live in 'polluted dens'. The City of London, which remained resolute in defence of its autonomy, and the surrounding parishes, was not affected by the Municipal Corporations Act. However, legislation specific to London was passed in order to deal with the legacy of a large number of often competing local authorities lacking in consistent goals and coherent policy discussion and implementation. A particular problem was posed by the role of parishes as a basis for administration in London outside the City. Although they might have been sub-divided for ecclesiastical purposes, these parishes were significant governmental units deploying considerable staffs and budgets. Unlike the City as a whole, they were not answerable to a mayor or corporation, but, instead, to a parish vestry. Key to this were the vestrymen who, from 1855, in a blow to long-standing oligarchical tendencies decried by Dickens, were elected by an annual meeting. Already in 1831, Hobhouse's Act had brought the start of vestry reform (and democratisation). The Act was very much aimed at the London select vestries and, though permissive, did lead to the reform of several important ones.

The vestry system provided a strong sense of locality, a sense that was the subtext to much of Dickens' fiction, as in the short story 'The Election for Beadle' (1835). This sense of locality was not really equal to the challenge of rising population numbers and also lacked coherence at the level of the city as a whole. Dickens remarked:

> As to Saint Pancras Parish, the only interest I have ever regarded it with, is comprehended in the fact that I consider its vestrymen, paving boards, and other squabbling and jobbing luminaries, a public nuisance, the abolition of which unto the end of time is highly desirable.[1]

The view of public health as a disaster – an accurate assessment – made the existing system of government outside the City seem redundant. Based upon parishes, but complicated by various precincts, liberties, boards and commissions, this was a system of local autonomy and independence, and not of co-operation; a system that was reactive rather than proactive; and one unsuited to deal with the major growth of London's population. The City's system of wards also appeared inadequate, as indeed it was. Although defended on the grounds of the value of self-government, these systems were no longer regarded by national government as valid.

The standard account of London's development assumes that a lack of central authority for the city held back progress, notably having a delaying effect on cleaning things up and providing for better conditions. In practice, however, such authorities themselves posed administrative and political problems.

The Metropolitan Commission for Sewers was established in 1847 by the Whig government at the behest of the ambitious public servant Edwin Chadwick, in part by abolishing six of London's seven commissions of sewers; only that for the City survived. The vestries opposed this restriction of local autonomy. As a result of the existence of the commission, London was excluded from the need to establish a Board of Health in the legislation passed the following year, an exclusion that also reflected the City's determination to maintain its autonomy. Nevertheless, Chadwick used the Board of Health to campaign for reform in London, creating in the process contention over centralisation which was vigorously resisted by the vestries. Dickens supported him and was dismayed in 1854 when the board was not prolonged and Chadwick was replaced as its president by the hostile Sir Benjamin Hall, a supporter of local interests.[2] Yet, with a characteristic inconsistency, Dickens variously complained about centralisation and its target, the vestries. In *Hard Times*, he referred to 'the great public-office Millennium, when Commissioners should reign upon earth'.[3]

In reaction to Chadwick, the Metropolis Local Management Act of 1855 established the Metropolitan Board of Works, its members selected by the major local authorities. A powerful board was a necessary response not only to the problems facing London, but also to the increased scale of the private provision of services. Thus, in 1857, the gas companies moved from competition to an agreement on local monopolies. The Metropolitan Board of Works was the only real restraint on such activities. Although the Metropolis Local Management Act clarified governance at the level of London as a whole, it was only a partial reform and left the vestries in place. However, the Act standardised the way the vestries were elected and the qualifications for membership, as well as consolidating a number of smaller vestries into 'District Boards'.

Looked at differently, the legislation was a response to the failure of Chadwick's drive for centralised government of London on the model of the Metropolitan Police Acts. Instead, in the longer term, the opposition of local authorities, and the variety and independence of opinions they represented, had fallen foul of the pressure for improvement, and, more particularly, of ratepayer opinion and the drive for more broad-based representative government. Two different models of reform had clashed and the political one, of ratepayer democracy, had prevailed over the statist one; at least in the context of the 1850s, a period defined by middle-class liberalism. This tension was to be key in the subsequent history of London. Ratepayer interests lay behind such critical remarks by Dickens as, from 'Doctor Marigold's Prescriptions' in *All the Year Round*: 'Here's a pair of razors that'll shave you closer than the Board of Guardians.'

Local accountability was put under pressure from outside control, including central governmental direction, as with the Metropolis Poor Law Amendment Act of 1867, which established the Metropolitan Common Poor Fund. This granted the Poor Law Board the power to nominate guardians to London Poor Law Boards, and also to redistribute the cost of pauperism among the Poor Law Unions. That rectified a flaw Dickens had castigated, that of the areas with the largest number of the poor having the least resources. Much of the argument over reforming measures lay between compulsion and enabling measures, the latter leaving the initiative with the local authorities. Enabling or permissive legislation was used on a considerable scale by some of the provincial cities, so that local municipal provision ran ahead of any national one. This distinction was at the heart of many controversies of the period. So also with areas that were reluctant to move at the same pace.

As a result of the 'Great Stink', Parliament in 1858 had extended the powers of the Metropolitan Board of Works. The First Commissioner of Works, Benjamin Hall, had Big Ben named after him. From 1859, under the direction of the determined and effective Joseph Bazalgette, Chief Engineer to the Metropolitan Commission of Sewers (a body established in 1847), an effective drainage system was finally constructed, although it was not totally complete until 1875. The intercepting sewers took sewage from earlier pipes that had drained into the Thames, and transported it, instead, to new downstream works and storage tanks from which the effluent could be pumped into the river when the tide was flowing into the North Sea. A large number of steam pumping stations provided the power. Still visible, the big one at Abbey Mills near West Ham, built in 1865–8, was an astonishing instance of the determination to disguise function, with the station's role concealed under Moorish towers and a Slavic dome. In part, there was an element of secrecy, but not that of a Dickensian conspiracy: the storm relief system used London's rivers other than the Thames, completing the process by which these other rivers had been directed underground. This concealment of the rivers made their use for this sewage system acceptable. Most of Bazalgette's work was finished in Dickens' lifetime, and he was impressed by what he saw. In 1865, Dickens observed:

> ... a great embankment rising high and dry out of the Thames on the Middlesex shore from Westminster Bridge to Blackfriars. A really fine work, and really getting on. Moreover, a great system of drainage. Another really fine work, and likewise really getting on.[4]

Bazalgette also designed a few of the new Thames bridges himself. Initially, the Metropolitan Board of Works had a restricted role – sewerage, drainage, roads, bridges, public spaces – but this changed gradually over time. Although Whitehall sought to exercise control by retaining direction over the acquisition of land and over large-scale expenditure, the Board, indeed, became the obvious repository for new functions. These included the Metropolitan Fire Brigade in 1865 (a response to the terrible Tooley Street fire in Southwark in 1861, the worst in terms of damage since the Great Fire of 1666), parks in 1866, and tramways in 1870, as well as major roads and bridges, drains, the administration of the 1855 Building Act, and the naming of streets. Such functions reflected the sense that existing provision, especially in fire services, was inadequate, and that the London area, instead, was the appropriate level of organisation. Fire services had been the responsibility of the Fire Engine Establishment founded in 1833, which was financed by the fire insurance offices. Major fires suggested that it was not up to the task.

Meanwhile, the 1852 Metropolitan Water Act obliged the London water companies to move their water supply sources to above the tidal reach of the Thames. The improvement in the water supply produced a large fall in mortality figures, but a sign of only patchy improvement was provided by the 1866 cholera epidemic which was moderate in the western areas, where the drainage and sewerage systems had already been improved, but still deadly in the crowded poor areas further east. By 1874, the death rate per 1,000 had fallen from a mid-eighteenth-century figure of forty-eight for London to eighteen, compared to thirty-two for Liverpool and Newcastle. The war against disease revealed both failure and success.

The process by which John Snow ascertained the means of the transmission of cholera was typical of the research-based nature of public policy that proved so important to Victorian governance. This type of policy indeed was the very opposite to the world of the Circumlocution Office, and Dickens' depiction of an unreformed system was increasingly anachronistic. At the same time, such criticism was an aspect of the process by which the world of print in London served to focus reform tendencies.

This process was more generally a characteristic of the public politics of the period. Agitation against slavery proved a good example.

Disease, which, other than in generalities, Dickens is sometimes apt to deal with less convincingly than the idea of a good death, was particularly the problem of the crowded big cities where people lived cheek-by-jowl. The Bradford Sanitary Committee visited over 300 houses in 1845 and found an average of three people sleeping per bed. In addition, there were serious problems elsewhere. An 1850 report on the Sussex town of Battle depicted scenes similar to those presented by Dickens:

> There is no provision for the removal of any offensive or noxious refuse from the houses and gardens of the poorer classes; all the decomposing and putrescent animal and vegetable matter which is brought out of the house is thrown into a pool, around which is engendered an atmosphere favourable to the production of febrile epidemics.

Yet, there was also substantial change. In part, this arose from the abandonment of earlier practices of limited and local regulation, in favour of a more self-conscious commitment to change. Indeed, the report above was not by a novelist, although Dickens dealt with such issues, but by Edward Cresy, a superintending inspector under the General Board of Health as well as an architect. The board was created by the Public Health Act of 1848, a major piece of legislation that established an administrative structure to improve sanitation and to ensure clean water. Opposed in 1847 on the basis of cost and centralisation, this Act was effectively swept onto the statute books, in part because cholera does not discriminate between social groups.

The Act was made more effective by the creation of local boards of health. They took action. Thus, the one established in Leicester in 1849 was instrumental in the creation of a sewerage system and in tackling slaughterhouses and smoke pollution. Similarly, Cresy's critical report on Derby led its Whig councillors to embark on a programme of works, including public baths and wash houses. The powers the Act gave were limited and left much work to the often-reluctant authorities. Once the cholera pandemic fizzled out, interest in the Act, indeed, fell. Nevertheless, despite its limitations and the opposition that it encountered, the legislation was a definite advance in the awareness of public health as an issue, and in organisation to try to further it.

More active local government was an important source and instrument of reform, with not only the public health movement from the 1840s, but also the laying out of public parks which were regarded as crucial to public health in offering fresh air and were regulated accordingly. In contrast, commercial pleasure parks gradually passed away. The owners of Vauxhall Gardens went bankrupt in 1840; the gardens reopened, but finally went out of business in 1859, in part, in a form of inverse gentrification, as a result of rowdiness among the changing clientele, and in part due to the advance of industry. In turn, the Recreation Grounds Act of 1859 supported the laying out of public parks as sites for improving public health and securing popular morals by bringing the recreations of the populace into contact with those of their supposed betters and also under the scrutiny of the police. In London, Primrose Hill was bought as a park in 1842 and Victoria Park opened in 1845. This major project was a contribution to the well-being of the East End. The West End was well provided with the Royal Parks, Regent's Park having recently been added to their number. In 1857, Halifax opened the People's Park, paid for by Sir Francis Crossley, a Nonconformist MP, philanthropist, and owner of the local carpet mills.

Such parks were a welcome antidote to the somewhat lifeless nature that Dickens frequently depicted in London. In *Great Expectations*, Pip finds 'a melancholy little square' with 'the most dismal trees in it, and the most dismal sparrows'.[5] A similar square is found in *Bleak House*.

The confidence that public health could be improved increasingly rested on the belief in science, and the conviction that it could be joined with government. Adam Sedgwick, Professor of Geology at Cambridge, told the 1833 meeting of the British Association for the Advancement of Science, a national organisation that spread the gospel of science-based progress:

> By science I understand the consideration of all subjects ... capable of being reduced to measurement and calculation. All things comprehended under the categories of space, time, and number properly belong to our investigation.

That year, the influential geologist William Whewell coined the term scientist. The re-conceptualisation of knowledge was thus linked to a new social category. Precision thanks to measurement by experts became important. Aside from becoming prestigious, science was also popularised, notably with public lectures, shows and museums. The cult of science was seen in the fame and fate of James Watt, who was celebrated with a monument in Westminster Abbey for which the subscription meeting in 1824 was chaired by Prime Minister Robert Jenkinson, 2nd Earl of Liverpool, while George IV gave £500, a twelfth of the sum raised. In *Bleak House*, Watt is the name given to a positive individual redolent of the promise of the present. Such naming was deliberate.

Greater prestige for science, scientists and engineers, as well as access to new data, encouraged the desire to fix information, and thus furthered classification as both goal and method. The spread of communications contributed directly to this process, as scientists and others were made more aware of discoveries and categorisations elsewhere. Issues of taxonomy helped make Charles Darwin conscious of animal variation, and thus persuaded him that individual species were not fixed. This conviction proved a significant stage on the route to his *On the Origin of Species by Means of Natural Selection* (1859), and, subsequently, to his and others' attempts to reconstruct the 'tree of life' by which evolutionary morphology had occurred. Dickens briefly discussed different theories of human classification and development in *Oliver Twist*. In *Martin Chuzzlewit*, Dickens referred to the 'Monboddo doctrine' and the 'Blumenbach theory'.[6] He is, however, more interested, as in *Dombey and Son*, but not only there, with the question of what behaviour was natural for human beings, and how far harsh nurture was passed on to the individuals who suffered from it and, indeed, as a result of their behaviour, to their children.

For others, confidence in science drew on a Whiggish culture of development. In his *Universal History* (1838), Edward Quin, a London barrister, described the 'darkness of the Middle Ages' being dispelled 'by the light of science, literature, and commerce'. Science and industrialisation indeed contributed to a sense of change that encouraged people to trace its course. This led to a decline in the interest in citing Classical sources, other than for information on the Classical world. Dickens only relatively rarely cited such sources or drew on Classical stories.

Alongside confidence, there was a powerful degree of resistance to science and utilitarianism, and not only from religious and conservative circles. Indeed, in intellectual and cultural spheres, literature competed with science in claiming to offer the truth about inherent realities, as well as guidance to the future. In *Hard Times*, the novel of his which was most on the immediate present, Dickens saw the emphasis on facts, and on paper information and arguments, as contributing to a deadening distancing from the real nature of social problems. This argument prefigured concerns in our own time that talk of transformation through modern technology has, however, neglected social context and consequences.

The relationship between knowledge and process is an issue in Dickens' work, although not to the fore. In *Bleak House*, the endless legal case of *Jarndyce* v. *Jarndyce* showed how sclerotic systems could subvert the primacy of knowledge and the good of society. This was seen with his presentation of sympathetic characters. So also with the ecclesiastical jurisdiction discussed in *David Copperfield*. In contrast, Dickens referred to the new Birmingham polytechnic favourably: 'for I *know* that on the wise regulation and success of such establishments, in such places, the future happiness and character of the people mainly depend; and that they are the most important and salutary influence at work for their improvement.'[7]

There was opposition in England to the idea of the prestige of knowledge being solely vested in scientists. Instead, there was a degree of amateur engagement in both science and the accumulation of information across a broad tranche of society in a way different from that which became the norm in the twentieth century. Like other novelists, including George Eliot and Elizabeth Gaskell, Dickens was also concerned about the need, in the face of the pressure for statistical aggregation arising from growing numbers, to reserve a place for the individual in society. In *Dombey and Son*, Solomon Gills, a sympathetic character who can distinguish fiction from fact, unlike his lively friend Captain Cuttle, an astonishing fictional fancy, wants Walter to work in the City, and not to go to sea.[8] The romantic Walter goes to sea, initially apparently to his doom, but, as so often with Dickens' good male characters, with eventual success. On the other hand, due to the interest in individuals, there could be, with Dickens, a tendency to underappreciate the requirement of reform, for new institutions, and for the standardisation of provision.

The common theme in society was that of usefulness, and this was generally interpreted in terms of social utility. Science could serve to validate the progressivism of newcomers and outsiders seeking recognition, such as the élite of industrialising Manchester, a city that was the scene of some of Dickens' greatest triumphs in public readings. Yet, as well as endorsing change, new élites and outsiders also looked to those values of the established culture that appeared conducive to them as well as adapting these values to their own interests.

The commitment of liberalism to information was related to its support for change, as well as to liberals' ideological, and frequently stated, backing for freedom of opinion, religious tolerance, freedom of the press, and the spread of free public education under state control, rather than that of the Church. At the same time, the understanding and use of information rested on conventions about appropriate knowledge and the reasonable expression of beliefs. Utilitarianism and scientific attitudes were treated as being largely compatible with spiritual renewal, and notably in the form of Evangelicalism. Catholicism was regarded as different.

In 1859, in the opening address at the meeting of the British Association for the Advancement of Science, a self-consciously reforming body that argued for the wider utility of science, Prince Albert defended statistics and science from claims of godless reductionism. The 'ownership' of expertise and information was of significance because the sense of change, in both society and understanding, made improvability seem latent and improvement possible. Objective information was employed to make arguments appear scientific, and thus to remove them, or try to remove them, from the sphere of simple contention.

Moreover, the use of information was presented as an aspect of competent and objective government, and of the professionalism and knowledge which that entailed. Different to Dickens' savagely satirical view of the Circumlocution Office in *Little Dorrit*, this approach served a politico-social purpose in enabling the use of expertise as a requirement with which to criticise traditional aristocratic amateurism as well as popular agitation. Instead, expertise provided a way to justify the opening up of government and its branches, notably the military, to talent and, more specifically, to the professional middle class.

Expertise was a necessity given the belief that government action should rest on an understanding of a science of society that would deploy knowledge and information to solve problems. This process inherently entailed the consideration of change. Moreover, although science offered apparently fixed answers, the process of scientific exposition entailed an inherent changeability stemming from new validation. Advances in measurement encouraged higher standards of accuracy and precision, and produced new results. Technological change included the naval shift to steam-powered ships which led to an arms race with France: science was not entirely peaceful in its implications. This change made most of the contents of Solomon Gills' shop redundant.

Government's dependence on science was understood in part as a matter of the scientific laws that supposedly regulated the economy. These laws could be understood so as to guide government policy, notably on commercial regulation, and to maximise the social benefits. Thus, information for production and profit was more than a matter of capitalism. A statistical department was established at the Board of Trade in 1833. Economic liberalism was understood as a necessary and progressive order that was to be utilised appropriately by an appreciation both of these laws and of the information that explained their application. For example, James Deacon Hunt, Joint Secretary of the Board of Trade, made an official tour in 1831, gathering information about silk manufacture, and, in 1832, gave evidence accordingly before a parliamentary committee on silk duties. He also gave evidence, and wrote, against the protectionist Corn Laws. Alongside governmental expertise came a local infrastructure of commercial lobbying, notably with the establishment of Chambers of Trade and Commerce which accumulated data in support of their arguments.

In contrast, Dickens presented economic liberalism as anarchic, cruel and open to fraud. Ralph Nickleby, himself a crook, is happy to be involved in the totally fraudulent 'United Metropolitan Improved Hot Muffin and Crumpet Baking and Punctual Delivery Company. Capital, five millions',[9] which is discussed at length. *Hard Times* provided Dickens with an opportunity to be highly sarcastic about such economic liberalism:

> Surely there never was such fragile china-ware as that of which
> the millers of Coketown were made. Handle them never so lightly,
> and they fell to pieces with such ease that you might suspect them

of having been flawed before. They were ruined, when they were required to send labouring children to school; they were ruined when inspectors were appointed to look into their works; they were ruined, when such inspectors considered it doubtful whether they were quite justified in chopping people up with their machinery; they were utterly undone, when it was hinted that perhaps they need not always make quite so much smoke.[10]

Alongside the flux of society, with moving people a very frequent plot device in Dickens' novel, came the fixedness offered by information. As with the population census, which began in 1801, this information sought to locate people and to record relevant data. Subjects mapped in England in the 1840s included literacy, crime, bastardy, pauperism, improvident marriages, savings-bank deposits and 'spiritual constitution'. The official Census of Religious Worship in 1851 provided spatial information on religious activity. All places of public worship were recorded, along with the frequency of services, the size of the church, and the number of attendees. The census reflected not only the Victorian conviction of the value of data, but also vocal concern about the spiritual state of the nation, a concern that encouraged church-building. John Davies, Rector of St Clement's, Worcester, reported in the census:

> The parishioners of St Clement's consist chiefly of the working class (some very poor indeed) many of whom seldom ever attend Sunday Morning Service. The Saturday Market and the late payment of wages on the evening of that day contribute probably in no small degree to produce this result. The same cause operates injuriously also with reference to the attendance of children at school and church on Sunday morning, the parents being up late on Saturday night ... Many parents, well-disposed to attend public worship absent themselves on account of their dress and the same remark is applicable to their children as relating to school and church.

Davies added of the Worcester Episcopal Floating Chapel:

> The opening of this chapel appears to have been productive, through the Divine Blessing, of beneficial effects ... But the prevalence of Sunday traffic has an injurious tendency upon the morals of this class of men [boatmen] ... Not only fishermen, but scavengers, sweeps, beggars have occasionally joined the congregation ... I have often noticed people present, who I had reason to believe would have never attended their own parish church or any other on account of their dress, etc.[11]

Dickens responded to fashionable concern in *Bleak House* when referring to

> ... ladies and gentlemen of the newest fashion, who have set up a Dandyism – in Religion, for instance. Who, in mere lackadaisical want of an emotion, have agreed upon a little dandy talk about the Vulgar wanting faith in things in general; meaning, in the things that have been tried and found wanting, as though a low fellow should unaccountably lose faith in a bad shilling, after finding it out! Who would make the Vulgar very picturesque and faithful, by putting back the hands upon the Clock of Time, and cancelling a few hundred years of history.[12]

The attack on 'Dandyism' in religion was aimed at the new High Church ritualism which Dickens detested. With reference to the 1851 census, he also observed in 1870 that to find out an individual's religion 'would be immensely difficult for the state, however statistical, to do'.[13]

People were not alone in being located for analysis. Geological mapping was an important variation in the development of thematic information. The understanding of different geological strata was the main analytical tool. William Smith's *Delineation of the Strata of England and Wales with Part of Scotland* (1815) was accompanied by a stratigraphic table, geological sections, and county geological maps. Popular understanding was transformed, but, as so often, it is less important to look not only at the creator-figure but also at a larger context that included less prominent but still influential figures, and at the role of subsequent entrepreneurs. In particular, George Bellas Greenough used Smith's map when preparing his own geological map of England and Wales for publication in 1820 by the Geological Society of London, of which he was president. Official geological mapping developed in the 1830s. It was seen as a way to provide information on the location of minerals, building materials, and rock strata appropriate for reservoirs or for artesian wells. Previous practices, such as the use of divining rods, were criticised and to a great degree discarded.

Meanwhile, devices for displaying information developed. Isolines – lines linking points of equal measurements – were developed, showing barometric pressure from 1827, precipitation from 1839, and, with contours, height. The latter replaced earlier, impressionistic systems, such as hachures and numbering peaks in terms of their relative height.

A key element of information was that of population numbers. The importance of the census encouraged work on improving and understanding demographic records. This led to the Births and Deaths Registration and Marriage Acts in 1836, and to the establishment of the General Register Office, which was responsible for this registration and, from 1841, for taking the census. Hitherto, only the parish registers were eligible for use in law courts as evidence of lines of descent. In their place, the civil system of registration was linked to Nonconformist assertiveness, as well as to parliamentary determination to support middle-class titles to property. The greater precision brought by the census was a challenge to the ability of individuals to invent identities and/or conceal family links, the key to many of Dickens' plots.

The importance of statistics to the General Register Office was shown in the increase in the number of staff in its Statistical Department, from four in 1840 to sixteen by 1866. So also with income tax, which was reintroduced by Peel in 1842, initially for a three-year trial, and was increased from 3 to 5 per cent in 1848. With his finances under pressure on the side of an expenditure he was unwilling to contain, Dickens disliked the tax,[14] not least because it had to be paid in arrears after much of the income had been spent, a practice that challenged the improvident. In Birmingham alone in the 1850s, the Clerk to the Commissioners for the Income Tax issued about 30,000 Schedule A and more than 5,000 Schedule D assessments annually. Again, there were commissioners to consider.

Statistics encouraged the evidence-based formulation and implementation of policy, and were central to the enquiries that gathered evidence and helped serve as the basis for discussion. An emphasis on the influence of the social environment encouraged a transformation in state activity, and notably so with education and public health. Concern over the latter played an important role in the collection of local mortality rates, which were seen as the basis for the application of sanitary legislation. The principal organising concept in the data collected was the nature of the materials being worked on by labourers. Edwin Chadwick's *Inquiry into the Sanitary Conditions of the Labouring Population of Great Britain* (1842), which attracted much attention, was important in the background to the Public Health Act of 1848. Dickens supported the formation of the Metropolitan Improvement Society in 1842.

Dickens' attitudes were contradictory. He enthusiastically backed Chadwick over sanitary reform, but opposed him over the Poor Law and, later, lampooned 'Chadwickism' rather nastily in *Hard Times*. This was significantly at a time when Chadwick's political stock was low and he was an easy target. In this and much else, Dickens was not a 'joined-up thinker'.

At the same time, the frame of reference in policy discussion, formulation and application was scarcely value-free, and, while use of enquiries made the process appear ideologically and politically impartial, in practice it was greatly affected by relevant presuppositions on problems, solutions and outcomes, as well as by the difficulties of establishing common standards of statistical objectivity. With ignorance typecast as a key reason for resistance to policy, indeed as the prime source of friction in the bureaucratic information state, persistence in pushing through new structures and policies, both internally and externally, was justified and encouraged.

Public health was a key concept, one that encouraged scrutiny of the population. The understanding that micro-organisms were responsible for serious diseases, such as cholera and tuberculosis, encouraged campaigns against both the diseases and the social milieux in which they were believed to thrive, for example rookeries (slums), such as that in which Bill Sikes takes refuge at the end of *Oliver Twist*. Campaigns to ensure public health created regulatory bodies and practices. In 1861–4, the *Lancet*, the leading medical periodical under its reforming editor Thomas Wakley, MP for Finsbury in London from 1835 to 1852, published a series of reports from the Analytical Sanitary Commission attacking the adulteration of food and drink. In turn, this pressure led to a Parliamentary Select Committee in 1855 and to legislation in 1860 which began modern food regulation in Britain.

Alongside demands for action by government, there was pressure for social change by bodies pledged to moral reform, such as temperance (moderation or abstinence in drinking) campaigns. As a result, with movements seeking validation for their views, the poor in particular were the subject of scrutiny, admonition and regulation both secular and religious, while government expanded its scope through advancing the claims of reform, and was expected to do so, notably by liberal commentators. Changes in public and institutional attitudes in the 1830s and 1840s, including impassioned arguments over the Corn Laws, were of particular significance. Discussion of regulation brought into dispute competing notions of governmental responsibility, namely duty of care versus *laissez-faire*, the latter held to be a matter of freedom and a cause of economic growth. The whole issue of the free market and the changes it tended to produce were never simple, despite the prevalent idea of a *laissez-faire* society.

In this politicised and value-rich environment, government moved towards regulation, and did so in partnership with new organisations of the actively committed. It was symptomatic that the most dramatic display of mid-century initiative, the Great Exhibition of 1851, did not owe its genesis to London's traditional system of government, but rather to the Society of Arts. Prince Albert and the politicians came later.

The public was to be taken along with change as part of a process of accountability that was moral as well as political. There was publication of many of the relevant documents and findings by public inquiries; and this process encouraged publication of other works in debates about conditions and remedies. In the 1830s, the Royal Commission of Inquiry into the Poor Laws led to a large-scale production of information. Official accounts of policymaking were compiled in the form of parliamentary Blue Books, in order to explain government decisions, and this process extended to the frequently appearing reports of royal commissions. In *Hard Times*, Dickens was scathing about Blue Books, which were favoured by the malevolent Tom Gradgrind MP, arguing that they could prove 'anything you like'.[15] The area covered by state inquiries and the resulting publications became a public space of information and opinion, but it was very much one directed by the state and the lobbies exerting public pressure.

At the same time, the very volume of information produced was such that publication was necessary in order to give it shape and definition. Robert Baker, a factory inspector, a post only recently created, addressed the volume of laws on working conditions by publishing *Factory Acts Made Easy* (1854), followed by *Factory Acts Made as Easy as Possible* (1867). So also with works on railways.

Dickens' fiction, both novels and short stories, was a form of accountability, but, understandably, was not comprehensive, nor always accurate. Thus, in the case of finance, Dickens depicted fraud, most prominently with Merdle and Carker, and also with an insurance fraud of the 1830s the point of reference in *Martin Chuzzlewit*. In practice, most financiers were not swindlers, while many were eager to invest in shares, including Dickens who, with much more information and freedom, proved more successful in investment than Jane Austen. Dickens' depiction of the situation has been seen as producing both melodrama and scapegoats,[16] which is more generally true of his stance. Fraud, however, was part of Dickens' secretive backstory. His maternal grandfather, Charles Barrow, was found guilty of embezzlement from the Navy Pay Office in 1810 and absconded, first to the Continent and later to the Isle of Man.

As a key instance of a widespread attempt to counter risk and thus provide progress,[17] the development of the life assurance industry, which fascinated Dickens, was an aspect of demand, wealth and the ability of the industry to respond. Building on the earlier development of maritime and fire insurance, there was, with life insurance, which represented a certain democratisation of the idea, an expansion of product types, driven by the need to match the expectations of different social groups, varied levels of wealth, and the needs of employers. With Britain at the leading edge of commerce, there was a move to composite companies, providing a broad range of policies. Moreover, there was increased technical efficiency as actuarial knowledge developed on the life side was spread to other areas of insurance. Professionalisation came in the mid-nineteenth century. The Institute of Actuaries was founded in 1847 to elevate 'the attainment and status and promoting the general efficiency of all who are engaged in the occupation'.

New life assurers specialising in insuring the professional classes, including Standard Life (1825), and the Prudential (1848), were launched. By 1850, there were about 180 life assurers and about £150 million in life covers in the United Kingdom. Godfrey Nickleby considers insuring his life before committing suicide; while, in *Great Expectations*, Herbert Pocket wants to 'buy up some good Life Assurance shares, and cut into the Direction'.[18]

As with banking and railway companies, there were challenges. A rapid turnover of companies did not always lead to good policyholder outcomes. Mismanagement, bankruptcies and the fraud revealed by a Parliamentary Select Committee under

Gladstone's chairmanship in 1841 encouraged tighter regulation. Dickens referred to the fraud in *Martin Chuzzlewit* with the Anglo-Bengalee Disinterested Loan and Life Assurance Company. This is described as a bird of prey, the term used for the body scavenger working in the River Thames in *Our Mutual Friend*.[19] The bird of prey returns in *Martin Chuzzlewit*, with Elijah Pogram, the ludicrously patriotic American politician compared to a raven.[20] Although the comparison with slavery was not drawn, the plight of those in the hands of the company, and, by extension, of other such companies, was brought out:

> 'B is a little tradesman, clerk, parson, artist, author, any common thing you like ... besides charging B the regular interest, we get B's premium, and B's friends' premiums, and we charge B for the bond, and, whether we accept him or not, we charge B for "inquiries" ... and we charge B a trifle for the secretary; and in short, my good fellow, we stick it into B, up hill and down dale, and make a devilish, comfortable little property out of him. Ha, ha, ha! I drive B, in point of fact,' said Tigg, pointing to the cabriolet, 'and a thorough-bred horse he is.'[21]

The most active insurance centre was London, but the industry was national and key companies with lasting importance were established outside London. Thus, Royal Insurance was founded in Liverpool in 1845, while what was renamed the Britannic Assurance Company in 1905 was founded in Birmingham in 1866 and named the British Workman's Mutual Assurance Company.

Regulatory procedures improved. The failure in 1869 of the under-capitalised Albert Life Assurance Company led the following year to the Life Assurance Companies Act, which required new companies to deposit money with the Accountant General as security, imposed the standardisation of revenue accounts and balance sheets, and directed that the insurance funds attributable to life business should be kept separate from other business and should be independently audited every five years. The principles of investment as laid down in the Act were clear. In order to provide a regular income, and to be certain of meeting liabilities, there was an emphasis on dated securities with a guaranteed capital repayment, rather than undated ones or ones the value of which could vary. Thus, the stress was on debentures, and not on ordinary shares.

Dickens, however, was sceptical about all financial instruments. In *Our Mutual Friend*, he referred to a gentleman of property:

> As is well known to the wise in their generation, traffic in Shares is the one thing to have to do with in this world. Have no antecedents, no established character, no cultivation, no ideas, no manners; have Shares. Have Shares enough to be on Boards of Direction in capital letters, oscillate on mysterious business between London and Paris, and be great. Where does he come from? Shares. Where is he going to? Shares. What are his tastes? Shares. Has he any principles? Shares. What squeezes him into Parliament? Shares. Perhaps he never of himself achieved success in anything, never originated anything, never produced anything! Sufficient answer to all; Shares. O mighty Shares! To set those blaring images so high, and to cause us smaller vermin, as under the influence of henbane or opium, to cry out night and day, 'Relieve us of our money, scatter it for us, buy us and sell us, ruin us, only, we beseech you, take rank among the powers of the earth, and fatten on us!'[22]

In the event, the man is a fraud.

Alongside life assurers providing cover for the middle and wealthier classes, plus an increasingly strong element of long-term contractual savings, came life assurance companies at the lower end of the market. Their role was driven largely by the absence of a welfare state beyond the workhouse, and by the desire of the working class to be able to provide for funeral expenses, or for a small income following retirement or long-term sickness; an absence that is in the foreground of Dickens' plots. Many of these companies began as Burial Societies or Friendly Societies. Their common feature was that their policies were sold directly on a door-to-door basis and that premiums were at very low levels (often only a few pence) and were collected physically by an agent, usually weekly. These contracts involved very high expenses because of the low premiums and the high collection costs. However, in the shadow of fears of the workhouse and the 'pauper's funeral', fears that Dickens amplified, huge volumes were sold to the working class. The combination of low premiums and regular personal collections ensured that policyholders were better able to meet their contractual obligations. In addition, in what was very much a shame culture, the penalty of default was too shameful to contemplate. This class of life assurance eventually became known as Industrial Assurance. Early examples of successful offices of this type were Royal Liver in Liverpool, Prudential and Pearl in London, and what became Britannic in Birmingham. Some of these companies, including Royal Liver, were mutual friendly societies, as opposed to being shareholder-owned.

With insurance and other matters, Dickens, however, was more inclined to note the deficiencies of a situation. This was understandable as the long term frequently only appears in perspective, but the short term is very much felt in the present. In 1865, Dickens commented on the response to a cattle plague which led to the slaughter of infected cows:

… we are groaning under the brigandage of the butcher, which is being carried to that height that I think I foresee resistance on the part of the middle-class, and some combination in perspective for abolishing the middle-man, whensoever he turns up (which is everywhere) between producer and consumer. The cattle plague is the butcher's stalking-horse, and it is unquestionably worse than it was; but seeing that the great majority of creatures lost or destroyed have been cows, and likewise that the rise in butchers' meat bears no reasonable proportion to the market price of the beasts, one comes to the conclusion that the public is done. The [Royal] Commission has ended very weakly and ineffectually, as such things in England rather frequently do; and everybody writes to *The Times*, and nobody does anything else.[23]

Insurance helped provide some security for the public. Nevertheless, indicators such as height, physical well-being, and real earnings drive home Dickens' depiction of shifts and expedients, real and psychological. As he shows, this was the case not only for the poor, but, indeed, for much of society, notably also the lower middle-class, especially clerks, the dependents of the wealthy, and women seeking marriage with security. While living standards were rising in aggregate, the situation remained harsh and uncertain for many.

6

PUBLIC ORDER AND PRESSURE FOR CHANGE

I quite agree with you in your admiration of the forbearance and long-suffering of the poor – everyone who knows them must. Their outbreaks, whenever they recur, can surprise few, I think, but Governments and Parliaments, who are always disposed to virtuous wonder.

Dickens to James Clephan, 1844[1]

Dickens' London is a city with little real order and where the figures of authority generally are dubious at best. Policing London was certainly an unprecedented issue due to the size of the city. Moreover, the example of Paris succumbing to disorder in the French Revolutions of 1789, 1830, 1848 and 1870 was scarcely encouraging. There was strong opposition in England to improved policing, which was seen as a threat to liberty. Yet, there was a long-standing belief that London's policing, including by the Bow Street Runners established in 1749, was inadequate and ineffective, and this argument was pushed hard by Sir Robert Peel, the Tory Home Secretary from 1822 to 1827 and 1828 to 1830. The 1828 House of Commons Committee of Investigation discovered corruption among the Runners, and Dickens, who was to imply the same in 1862, presented the old-fashioned police as inefficient or unimpressive in *Great Expectations*. The police respond to the assault on Pip's sister:

> The Constables, and the Bow-Street men from London – for, this happened in the days of the extinct red-waistcoated police – were about the house for a week or two, and did pretty much what I have heard and read of like authorities doing in other such cases. They took up several obviously wrong people, and they ran their heads very hard against wrong ideas, and persisted in trying to fit the circumstances to the ideas, instead of trying to extract ideas from the circumstances. Also, they stood about the door of the Jolly Bargemen, with knowing and reserved looks that filled the while neighbourhood with admiration; and they had a mysterious manner of taking their drink, that was almost as good as taking the culprit. But not quite, for they never did it.[2]

In *Oliver Twist*, the Bow Street Runners, Blathers and Duff, are easily misled.[3] Mr Fang, the harsh magistrate in the novel, was based on Allan Stewart Laing, a bad-tempered magistrate in Hatton Garden, whom Dickens met in 1837 and who was to be dismissed in 1838 for his harshness. In his treatment of the law, as of other matters, Dickens was not impressed by show and keen to get below the surface in order to reveal the person beneath: 'Would you care a ha'penny for the Lord Chancellor if you know'd him in private and without his wig – certainly not.'[4]

Believing that society could survive in turbulent times only if secular authority was resolutely defended, Peel, a Staffordshire gentleman from a paternal background in textile manufacturing, conflated threats he and others perceived from crime, radicalism and immorality, and had a hostile view of London as a centre for all three that required rigorous control. Passed in 1829, in part also to deal with corruption in existing police provision, Peel's Metropolitan Police Act created a uniformed and paid police force. This professional service was designed to maintain the law and to keep order against radicals, but also to check what was seen as working-class immorality. Despite being unpopular among those used to libertarian views about English freedoms, the police were a means to defend the existing system, as well as an alternative to the army which otherwise was the major force at the disposal of the government.

Reflecting the importance of the task, the new Metropolitan force was controlled by the Home Office, rather than the local authorities, and was initially made responsible for Marylebone, Finsbury, Tower Hamlets, Westminster, Southwark and Lambeth, an area within 7 miles of Charing Cross. In 1839, with crime rates in London having fallen markedly, this radius was extended, under the Second Metropolitan Police Act, to 15 miles, a distance that took in the suburbs. The 4,300-strong force represented an overriding of the existing pattern of local control and also a cost that could not be controlled by the local authorities. Instead, the cost was a police precept (rate), which critics saw as taxation without representation. Indeed, the Metropolitan Police were not particularly popular, either with the major vestries or with ratepayers. The critics had hoped that the Whigs would overthrow the Tory measure, but, instead, they strengthened it in 1839, in part as a force against radicals. The Whigs had been scared by Chartism in 1837, and wanted to keep the reassurance of a professional force. As much of London opinion supported the Whigs, the new force became established.

Dickens, however, was more sceptical, arguing in *Oliver Twist*, which is largely set in London, that a police officer 'is generally the last person to arrive' in the pursuit of thieves, and also complaining about the state of the cells in the police stations.[5] The rich were not exposed to such cells. During the public launch in London of a fraudulent company in *Nicholas Nickleby*, the police in attendance are able to do nothing with those near the stage who are making a noise

... but entertaining nevertheless a praiseworthy desire to do something to quell the disturbance, immediately began to drag forth, by the coat tails and collars, all the quiet people near the door; at the same time dealing out various smart and tingling blows with their truncheons, after the manner of that ingenious actor, Mr Punch: whose brilliant example, both in the fashion of his weapons and their use, this branch of the executive occasionally follows.[6]

In 1841, Dickens observed, 'Any man who goes to a Police Office without absolute necessity, must be raving mad.'[7] Chevy Slyme thinks it shaming to be a police officer.[8] However, *Our Mutual Friend* was more positive. John and Bella go to a police station in London, of which John is not fearful. It is a 'kind of criminal Pickford's. The lower passions and vices were regularly ticked off in the books, warehoused in the cells, carted away as per accompanying invoice, and left little mark upon it.'

The 1835 Municipal Corporations Act gave the reformed corporations responsibility for policing in their boroughs, replacing in many cases police or watch commissions established under local Acts. This meant that the borough forces, unlike the Metropolitan Police, were under the authority of elected bodies, the 'ratepayer democracy'. These boroughs were given powers that were denied to most of London, although the City was, as a municipal borough and the most important, permitted to keep its own police force separate from the Metropolitan Force, as remains the case today.

Under the County Police Act of 1839, Parliament enabled counties to raise uniformed police forces, although they were not compelled to do so. The number of constables was not to exceed one per 1,000 of the population, which scarcely offered assurance in years of living standards under pressure and public agitation, notably 1842 when the police were heavily employed against Chartism, both in London and in the provinces. Purpose-built police stations were opened, such as that in Doncaster in Yorkshire in 1846. The police force of County Durham, established in 1839, consisted of sixty-five officers under Major James Wemyss, a Waterloo veteran. This force was used to police the miners' strike of 1844. 'Specials' – volunteer police officers known as special constables – were also deployed, as in London during the Chartist petition rally in 1848. That year, the police were also extensively employed in the provinces against Chartism.

The County Police Act was discretionary. It left the decision on forming a force to each individual county. Governments feared the county gentry, many of whom sat in Parliament, and were not going to treat the counties as they did London or even the boroughs. Some counties, not least in the West Country, for example Devon, put off establishing a county force as long as they could. Whereas the usual modern view is that the Metropolitan Police was a major improvement, most of society preferred having no significant professional force at all if this was practical. The cost was a factor, as was the issue of control.

The County and Borough Police Act of 1856 made the formation of paid police forces obligatory on local authorities. There were linked changes in the law. The new police largely replaced individuals as prosecutors in cases of criminal justice in England and Wales.

Alongside policing, the legal code was transformed. Contemplating his gains from theft, Fagin offered praise to capital punishment: 'Dead men never repent; dead men never bring awkward stories to light. Ah, it's a fine thing for the trade! Five of 'em strung up in a row; and none left to play booty, or turn white-livered.'[9] However, from the 1830s, hanging, which to Dickens was 'ever worse than useless',[10] was confined to murderers and traitors, while the transportation of convicts to Australian dumping grounds had ceased by his death. Instead, prisons were built and reformatory regimes developed. From 1868, hanging was no longer carried out in public.

Dickens was concerned about miscarriages of justice, past and present. At the same time, he saw crime as widespread, Wemmick telling Pip: 'You may get cheated, robbed, and murdered, in London. But there are plenty of people anywhere, who'll do that for you … if there's anything to be got by it.'[11] A convict reveals that he would sell all the friends he ever had for £1.[12] Yet, Dickens also noted that miscarriages could include the conduct of the defence in legal cases. On 23 and 26 June 1840, the *Morning Chronicle* published letters from him in which he condemned Charles Phillips, the defence lawyer in the case of the murderer François Courvoisier, a valet convicted for murdering his employer, Lord William Russell, uncle of Lord John Russell. To Dickens, Phillips' attacks, in the Old Bailey, on the prosecution witnesses were wrong, and might discourage future witnesses coming forward. Dickens also criticised Phillips' frequent citation of God and his warning to the jurors that they risked their salvation if they convicted the defendant, who would thereby be hanged. Courvoisier confessed after the sentence was passed. He was hanged, outside Newgate, on 6 July, with Dickens and a shocked Thackeray among the large crowd.

Nevertheless, while the police, magistracy and judiciary served in the necessary supervision of society, Dickens was justifiably harsh about the extent of unfairness that was involved:

> ... the same enlightened laws which leave the debtor who can raise no money to starve in jail, without the food, clothing, lodging, or warmth, which are provided for felons convicted of the most atrocious crimes that can disgrace humanity. There are many pleasant fictions of the law in constant operation, but there is not one so pleasant or practically humorous as that which supposes every man to be of equal value in its impartial eye, and the benefits of all laws to be equally attainable by all men, without the smallest reference to the furniture of their pockets.[13]

The poor were especially affected by policing, but not only them. Thus, characteristically capturing his social mood, that of all of society as open to the moralist's gaze, Dickens wrote of an episode in Preston in 1842:

> The policeman who supposed the Duke of Brunswick [exiled nephew of George IV] to be one of the swell mob [well-presented pickpockets], ought instantly to be made an inspector. The

suspicion reflects the highest credit (I seriously think) on his penetration and judgment.[14]

Practices judged unacceptable, such as public drunkenness and prostitution, were subject to regulation and action. Policing sought to bring order and decorum to the streets. Under the 1824 Vagrancy Act and later laws, the police were able to arrest street entertainers, part of the attempt to regulate the streets. Moreover, in 1854, pubs were forced to close at midnight on Sunday and, except for Sunday lunch and evening, not to reopen until 4 a.m. on Monday. The 1869 Wine and Beerhouse Act brought more regulation. There was a tension between beer-drinking – largely seen as healthy, not least because of serious problems with the water supply – and the consumption of spirits, which, on a long-standing pattern, was regarded as deplorable.

The courts, moreover, dealt with unacceptable beliefs that led to action that could be monitored, for example claiming to be a witch: related crimes resulted in court cases, including eight in Birmingham and the Black Country in the 1860s.

Dickens was a master of irony, although he preferred his irony obvious rather than subtle. An ironical testimony to regulation was paid by Bill Sykes in *Oliver Twist* when complaining about the shortage of boys for housebreaking. His usual helper was

... that young boy of Ned, the chimbley-sweeper's [*sic*]! He kept him small on purpose, and let him out by the job. But the father gets lagged; and then the Juvenile Delinquent Society comes, and takes the boy away from a trade where he was earning money, teaches him to read and write: and in time makes a apprentice of him. And so they go on.[15]

A different form of public order was provided by religious Evangelicalism, which was by no means confined to the middle class. This Evangelicalism further encouraged a sense of national distinctiveness and mission, or was at least presented in that light.

Evangelicalism was especially strong in attacks on drunkenness and in the promotion of temperance.

There were also the cross-currents, sometimes hypocritical, captured by Dickens:

> Muggleton is an ancient and loyal borough, mingling a zealous advocacy of Christian principles with a devoted attachment to commercial rights; in demonstration whereof, the mayor, corporation, and other inhabitants, have presented at divers times, no fewer than one thousand four hundred and twenty petitions against the continuance of negro slavery abroad, and an equal number against any interference with the factory system at home; sixty-eight in favour of the sale of livings in the Church, and eighty-six for abolishing Sunday trading in the street. (*Pickwick Papers* 7)

Politics, as Dickens shows, was part of the world of élite condescension, civic concern, group activity, individual enthusiasm and hucksterish entrepreneurialism. The last is particularly apparent in Dickens' depiction of elections, as with the fictitious constituency of Eatanswill, and the corruptly competing Blues and Buffs in *The Pickwick Papers*. This account was probably based on Dickens' coverage of an election in Northamptonshire North, more specifically Kettering, in 1835, although Sudbury, Ipswich, and Bury St Edmunds have also been mentioned. In *The Moonstone* (1868), Wilkie Collins wrote:

> The guests present being all English, it is needless to say that, as soon as the wholesale check exercised by the presence of the ladies was removed, the conversation turned on politics as a necessary result ... this all-absorbing national topic.

In practice, although excluded from the vote in national elections, women were also very interested in politics. There was an attempt to provide and secure a stable civic order, based on the rule of law, through which liberties could be safeguarded, prosperity enjoyed, and progress maintained. This prospect

'London from Greenwich Park', Joseph Stadler after Joseph Farington. (Yale Center for British Art)

The Duke of Wellington equestrian statue in front of the Royal Exchange. (Library of Congress)

Green Park Arch – or Constitution Arch, or the Wellington Arch – as it appeared in Dickens' day. (Wellcome Collection)

Cleopatra's Needle on the Thames Embankment. (Library of Congress)

Drury Lane photographed by Alfred H. Bool in 1876. (Cleveland Museum of Art)

Above, both pages: Robert Havell's panorama of London, 1831. (Yale Center for British Art)

'The Royal Mail's departure from the General Post Office', Richard Gilson Reeve after James Pollard. (Yale Center for British Art)

'A Bird's Eye View of Smithfield Market, Taken from the Bear & Ragged Staff', John Bluck after Thomas Rowlandson. (Metropolitan Museum of Art)

Above and below: The construction of the 'Great Leviathan', Brunel's *Great Eastern*. (University of Bath Digital Archives)

Kate Nickleby. (Wellcome Collection)

'The Bull's-eye', Gustave Doré.

Auguste Blanchard's 'The Derby Day' after Frith. (Yale Center for British Art)

An illustration by Hablot Browne for *Nicholas Nickleby*: 'Mr Mantalini poisons himself for the seventh time'. (Wellcome Collection)

An illustration by Hablot Browne for *Bleak House*: 'Attorney [Vholes] and client [Carstone], fortitude and patience'. (Wellcome Collection)

'The Parish Beadle' by Abraham Raimbach after David Wilkie. (Yale Center for British Art)

'A London hair-dresser's shop: a barber shaves a man; a young woman who is having her hair cut recognizes another customer; and a man who rents the upper part reads the Sunday newspaper', Hablot Browne, 1892. (Wellcome Collection)

Little Nell held by her grandfather in an illustration by F. O. C. Darley for *The Old Curiosity Shop*. (Library of Congress)

Charles Dickens in 1867.

A late nineteenth-century
photograph of the (closed)
Marshalsea prison, where
Dickens' father was imprisoned
for a time. The Marshalsea
would feature prominently in
Little Dorritt.

Left: One of George Cruikshank's illustrations for a work by Dickens, in this case for his short 'The Next-door Neighbour'. (Wellcome Collection)

Below: A noisy London street scene by Cruikshank. (Wellcome Collection)

'A drunken man sits at home with his family who must pawn their clothes to pay for his habit', George Cruikshank, 1847. (Wellcome Collection)

'A drunken scene in a gin shop with children being given alcohol', George Cruikshank, 1848. (Wellcome Collection)

'Outdoor Relief', an illustration by Hablot Browne from James Grant's *Sketches in London (1840)*. (Wellcome Collection)

'The Workhouse, Poland Street, Soho: the interior' aquatint by T. Sunderland after Thomas Rowlandson (1809). (Yale Center for British Art)

'Black Lion Wharf, James McNeill Whistler, 1859. (Metropolitan Museum of Art)

'The Pool', James McNeill Whistler, 1859. (Metropolitan Museum of Art)

'The Lime-Burner (W. Jones, Thames Street)', James McNeill Whistler, 1859.
(Metropolitan Museum of Art)

required what was seen as responsible and rational conduct, and the control of emotionalism. The extension of civil rights to those outside the Established Church, most obviously with the repeal of the Test and Corporation Acts in 1828 (thus benefiting Protestant Nonconformists) and the passing of an Act for Catholic Emancipation in 1829, was presented as another aspect of national reason and superiority; and such moves were contrasted with the situation on the Continent, more particularly in Catholic countries.

Politics and culture were both affected by democratisation. The newly literate did not have a passive response to either, but proved active voters and consumers, supporting, or being encouraged to support, new products and novel arguments. A host of political and social trends was linked to the rise of a more literate populace, and these trends implied demands for information as well as leading to the related expression of opinion. The major rise in literacy stemmed from government policy in the shape of mass education. The situation was made more dynamic by the pace and extent of technological change, including inexpensive books. With reason, Dickens saw himself as responding in

> ... the tone I tried to take about the eternal duties of the Arts to the People. I took the liberty of putting the Court and that kind of thing out of the question, and recognising nothing but the Arts and Peace. The more we see of Life and its brevity, and the World and its vanities, the more we know that no exercise of our abilities in any art, but the addressing of it to the great ocean of humanity in which we are drops, and to bye-ponds (very stagnant) here and there, ever can or ever will lay the foundation of an endurable retrospect.[16]

In favour of reform, Dickens was concerned with the root cause of conditions. He was careful to discriminate in his analysis of the causes of problems, and therefore concerning possible remedies. As a key indicator, Dickens was not a supporter of the temperance movement, distinguishing crucially between the value of individual abstinence as a remedy for drunkenness and the problem posed by prohibition:

> I can no more concur in the philosophy of reducing all mankind to one total abstainment level, than I can yield to that monstrous doctrine which sets down as the *consequences* of Drunkenness, fifty thousand miseries which are, as all reflective persons know, and daily see, the wretched *causes* of it ... I cannot get it into my mind that his [total abstinence] is just or wise.[17]

He fell out with Cruickshank, who became a prohibitionist and whose powerful series of narrative illustrations, 'The Drunkard's Curse', was specifically aimed at the evil of gin. Indeed, Dickens saw drunkenness as beginning 'in sorrow, or poverty, or ignorance'[18] rather than vice, which led him to press the need for a radical approach to the problem rather than one aimed at tackling individual sin. Dickens was also concerned to defend public entertainments, notably music halls from the claim that they contained 'loose women'.[19] In practice, the music halls were a place in which prostitutes operated but it was wrong to treat single women as prostitutes.

Dickens' lack of belief that hereditary vice was at play in criminality led him to offer comments to the latter effect to those presented as fools. An instance was the response of Charlotte to Oliver Twist standing up for himself: 'I only hope this'll teach master not to have any more of these dreadful creeturs, that are born to be murderers and robbers from their very cradle.'[20]

Reflecting social concerns and intellectual ideas, reform activism drew on both the locality and the state, but the process, as Dickens was very aware, was not one of automatic improvement, nor always sufficient. Thus, working-class communities found their neighbourhoods rebuilt or reorganised without reference to them. New Oxford Street was driven through the St Giles' rookery, an overcrowded slum of courts and yards, in 1847. Dickens was appalled by the degradation of the rookery. Agar Town, a shanty town of poor-quality housing with no sewerage or lighting, rapidly built in the 1840s, was demolished to make way for warehouses for St Pancras railway station in the late 1860s. These clearances were seen as ways to civilise society as well as improving traffic flow. Cleared from a slum, the poor moved on to other poverty-stricken neighbourhoods. It is understandable that Dickens did not always emphasise the extent to which activism also both helped to counter the worst ravages of social distress and to introduce a broader pattern of improvement. Activism, moreover, combined local initiatives and central supervision administered by inspectors, the latter part of a major shift in the character of government. The clearing of the rookeries helped reduce mortality and disease as a rebuilt London was a healthier one. So also with the steady suppression of ancient fairs, St Bartholomew's the most famous, held in Smithfield being finally suppressed in the 1860s. Fairs came to be seen as occasions of crime, riot and immorality.

Although conservative in some respects, Dickens was highly sceptical of existing arrangements, and this attitude characterised his treatment both of current-day England and of the more strongly etched 'leprosy of unreality' in pre-Revolutionary France.[21] Dickens responded in 1849 to the pardon for William Barber, a London solicitor sent to the penal station at Norfolk Island in 1844 for forging a will:

> It is a tremendous illustration of the inefficiency of Lords and Gentlemen as Home Secretaries – of the manner to which they may receive Memorials from innocent men in the agony of supposed guilt, and endurance of frightful punishment – put them away in drawers, and never so much as read them – and of the indispensable necessity there is, for a public and solemn Court of Appeal in all criminal cases.[22]

In the event, none was established until 1907. More generally, Dickens presented social improvement as the necessary good, and not as retributive control. He used Pecksniff's self-interested talk of his duty to society to attack the ethos and practice of the latter:

> Oh late-remembered, much-forgotten, mouthing, braggart duty, always owed and seldom paid in any other coin than punishment and wrath, when will mankind begin to know thee! When will men acknowledge thee in thy neglected cradle, and thy stunted youth, and not begin their recognition in thy sinful manhood and thy desolate old age! Oh ermined Judge whose duty to society is, now, to doom the ragged criminal to punishment and death, hadst thou never, Man, a duty to discharge in barring up the hundred open gates that wooed him to a fellon's dock, and throwing but ajar the portals to a decent life!

And so on.[23]

Yet, Dickens could also be highly sceptical about government, as in replying to a philanthropic pamphlet in 1866:

> I have not sufficient faith in any Parliament that could be got together in England, or in any Public Department that could be established, or in any Administration that could be formed, to trust to such bodies the sole undertaking of all great works for the public benefit and use. I do not in the least believe through such agencies Jobbery would cease out of the land. Quite the contrary. Nor can I assume that such authorities would achieve none but profitable works. Quite the contrary again ... I should very strongly object to any Governments having the power to force me to accept a piece of paper in lieu of a sovereign, so I cannot conscientiously recommend the public to vote for that Legal Tender of which you think so highly. And concerning that 'mere stroke of the pen' which is to make a country prosperous and virtuous, I ... utterly unable to receive the belief.[24]

Yet, soon after, with reference to 'the neglected children of London ... an interesting subject to me ever since I began to write', Dickens suggested:

... a better House of Commons, and (consequently) a better form
of Government altogether – I have used the wrong word, for I
mean a reality and not a form – alone can deal with the gigantic
and unchristian horror.[25]

At the same time, the repeated theme in the novels is that public
intervention can only achieve so much unless joined by a vigorous
public morality shot through by a charitable purposefulness.
Thus, Brownlow, a positive figure, at the conclusion of *Oliver
Twist*, rejects the villain's description of Oliver as a bastard: 'The
term you use is a reproach to those who long since passed beyond
the feeble censure of the world. It reflects disgrace on no one
living, except you who use it.'[26] This was very much Dickens'
morality.

Complacency, censure and greed are the vices most in
Dickens' gaze. They ensure a failure to engage with the terrible
circumstances that turn so many to the faults more commonly
discussed in terms of vice. Hereditary factors are also a major
problem, and, in Dickens' plots, with the rich rather than the
poor: 'What lawsuits grow out of the graves of rich men, every
day: sowing perjury, hatred and lies among near kindred.'[27] As he
shows, these family issues focus greed and aspiration, and thereby
give rise to conspiracy and malice. All can be affected.

In *Martin Chuzzlewit*, Dickens made it clear how rapidly
people could fall in fortune and, with that, self-respect. This
happens to the protagonist, in but five weeks, during which he
has to support himself by pawning his clothes, which would have
been a terrible experience for many of his readers. In this episode,
Dickens penned a powerful attack on conventional morality,
which is presented as ignorant and hypocritical:

Oh, moralists, who treat of happiness and self-respect, innate in
every sphere of life, and shedding light on every grain of dust in
God's highway, so smooth below your carriage-wheels, so rough
beneath the tread of naked feet, bethink yourselves in looking on
the swift descent of men who *have* lived in their own esteem, that

there are scores of thousands breathing now, and breathing thick with painful toil, who in that high respect have never lived at all, nor had a chance of life! Go ye, who rest so placidly upon the sacred Bard who had been young, and when he strung his harp was old, and had never seen the righteous forsaken, or his seed begging their bread; go, Teachers of content and honest pride, into the mind, the mill, the forge, the squalid depths of deepest ignorance, and uttermost abyss of man's neglect, and say can any hopeful plant spring up in air so foul that it extinguishes the soul's bright torch as fast as it is kindled! And, oh! ye Pharisees of the nineteen hundredth year of Christian knowledge, who soundingly appeal to human nature, see first that it be human. Take heed it has not been transformed, during your slumber and the sleep of generations, into the nature of the Beasts.[28]

Dickens was also sceptical about the intellectual approach, giving the honest Charles Cheeryble the remark:

You fall into the very common mistake of charging upon Nature matters with which she has not the smallest connexion, and for which she is in no way responsible. Men talk of Nature as an abstract thing, and lose sight of what is natural while they do so.[29]

The inconsistency and fluctuation of Dickens' views on many political and social issues reflected in part his humane engagement with complex issues.

7

CULTURE

Tradesmen and clerks, with fashionable novel-reading families, and circulating-library-subscribing daughters, set up small assemblies in humble imitation of Almack's.

Dickens, 'London Recreations',
Evening Chronicle, 17 March 1835

1851, the year of the Great Exhibition, also saw the opening of the Canterbury Theatre at Lambeth by Charles Morton (1819–1904), the 'father of the music hall'. He was one of the entrepreneurs so important in the cultural marketplace, a marketplace in which Dickens was to be prominent, and as both writer and, increasingly, performer. Publishers who treated culture as a commodity, the value of which was set by the market, were key instances of this entrepreneurship. Dickens, who was concerned about obtaining value for his own work as a producer, was not kind in his depiction of entrepreneurs, as with the unattractive calculating victualler with 'a complete edition of Cocker's arithmetic in each eye' who managed the edgy singing house in his short story 'Poor Mercantile Jack'. Some politicians were not all that dissimilar in their entrepreneurial methods, for example addressing both public meetings and the wider nation through the press, as with Palmerston.

In politics, as in culture, there was a fluid market, in which style and novelty were important in enhancing value and attracting recognition and support. At the same time, old hobbies and sports continued, and notably rural ones, especially hunting and shooting. Thus, the Pickwickians go rook shooting in Kent before observing a rural cricket match.[1] The customer was the key element, as when Vincent Crummles' theatrical company, one of the most attractive groups in Dickens' writing, seeks patronage from the public:

... everybody wanted a different thing. Some wanted tragedies, and others comedies; some objected to dancing; some wanted scarcely anything else. Some thought the comic singer decidedly low, and others hoped he would have more to do than he usually had. Some people wouldn't promise to go, because other people wouldn't promise to go; and other people wouldn't go at all, because other people went. At length, and little by little, omitting something in this place, and adding something in that, Miss Snevellicci pledged herself to a bill of fare which was comprehensive enough, if it had no other merit (it included among other trifles, four pieces, divers songs, a few combats, and several dances).[2]

In both culture and politics, the market was changing, largely owing to the movement of the bulk of the population into positions of access, and therefore purchasing power, which had hitherto been limited. In particular, the bulk of the male working class, especially the relatively well-paid skilled artisans, gained not only the vote but also more time and money for leisure. Much of this time and money was spent on sport; and football especially emerged as a very popular spectator sport. This was a national game and one that benefited from the Victorian zeal for organisation alongside entrepreneurship, indeed for enterprising organisation. The Football Association, formed in 1863, sought to codify the rules of the game. Other sports, such as horse racing, also attracted a large working-class following, as did pigeon racing. Sporting activities, like other branches of leisure, became increasingly organised, competitive and commercialised, and with a much more distinct division than hitherto between participant and observer. Successful new sports included rugby.

There was a boom in middle-class sports, such as golf and lawn tennis. As a result, sporting institutions and facilities were created across England. Northumberland Cricket Club had a ground in Newcastle by the 1850s. More generally, the expansion of organised middle-class cultural activity owed much to the growth of the middle class in the cities, and also to its pursuit of culture not only for pleasure but also as a way of defining its purpose and leadership. The site of new and imposing buildings, such as the Free Trade Hall (1853–6) and the Town Hall in Manchester (1867–77), cities established major art collections and musical institutions, for example the Hallé Orchestra in Manchester in 1857. Such patronage helped support popular art movements, for example that of the Pre-Raphaelite painters, who, alongside criticism, enjoyed considerable popularity from the early 1850s.

Although much of the expansion of cultural expression was the product of commercial, urban, middle-class wealth, its purpose was more broad-ranging. Labouring men and women queued for hours to file past Ford Madox Brown's painting *Work* when it was finally finished in 1863, and many hung up cheap reproductions of paintings and bought sheet music, an important industry of the period. Again, Dickens' public readings can be set in this context.

Painting, like fiction, reflected the eclecticism and energy of English culture. There was a major role for public favour, as in *Little Dorrit*, with the well-deserved failure of Henry Gowan, a very distant connection of the politically crucial Barnacle family, who had become a painter:

So it had come to pass successively, first, that several distinguished ladies had been frightfully shocked; then, that portfolios of his performances had been handed about o'nights, and declared with ecstasy to be perfect Claudes, perfect Cuyps, perfect phaenomena; then, that Lord Decimus had bought his picture, and had asked the President and Council [of the Royal Academy] to dinner ... and, in short, that people of condition had absolutely taken pains to bring him into fashion. But somehow it had all failed. The prejudiced public had stood out against it obstinately. They had determined not to admire Lord Decimus's picture.[3]

The legacy of the past was seen with the strong interest in earlier schools of Continental painting, and their display as in the Stafford Gallery, which was finally installed by Lord Francis Egerton in the new Bridgewater House in 1851.[4] At the same time, there was an engagement with the present and, accordingly, the patronage of modern painters, such as J. M. W. Turner (1775–1851). Although both Dickens and Turner were Londoners who spent time in coastal Kent, they did not really interact. Some of Dickens' writing, notably about fog, contains comments on light that echo Turner's use of it.

A key establishment figure was Edwin Landseer (1802–73), the favourite painter of both Victoria and her subjects. Knighted in 1850, he was able to offer both a sentimentality and an exemplary image of bravery that appealed to contemporary tastes. In 1851, Landseer exhibited *The Monarch of the Glen*, a dramatic depiction of a stag; in 1853 *Night* and *Morning*, pictures of a duel between stags; and in 1864 *Man proposes, God disposes*, featuring polar bears amid the relics of Sir John Franklin's disastrous Arctic expedition. The last, an episode in the long-unsuccessful attempt to find a North-West Passage from the Atlantic to the Pacific, was presented in terms of an exemplary selfless, yet disciplined, heroism. The failure of the expedition was the basis of *The Frozen Deep* (1856), a play by Wilkie Collins in which Dickens acted, and which inspired him in the plotting of *A Tale of Two Cities*, more particularly with the love triangle and the related self-sacrifice. In 1857, Victoria and Albert were in the audience for a performance of the play.

Engravings of Landseer's paintings were printed in large numbers. Not noted as an explorer of the urban scene, he nevertheless left his mark on London when he sculpted the lions at the foot of Nelson's Column (1867). This was part of the process by which Trafalgar Square was scripted as the symbolic centre of empire. Alongside obvious contrasts, notably that Landseer offered animals where Dickens, who had relatively little to say about animals, instead provided children, there are instructive similarities between Landseer's style and that of Dickens, who laid on his words with oils, and not watercolours.

Dickens was a keen observer of paintings, as in his comments in 1842 on his close friend Daniel Maclise's depiction of the play within the play in *Hamlet*. Dickens captured its theatricality as well as the use of supporting echoes:

> ... what a notion is that, which hoods this murderer's head, as who should say to the real King – 'You know what face is under that!' What an extraordinary fellow he must be, who so manages the lights in this picture, that on the scene behind, is an enormous shadow of this group – as if the real murder were being done by phantoms! And what a carrying-out of the prevailing idea, it is, to paint the very proscenium of the little stage with stories of Sin and Blood – the first temptation – Cain and Abel – and such like subjects – crying Murder! from the very walls.[5]

Very differently, the term Pre-Raphaelite had been adopted in 1848 by a group – or, as, they called themselves, Brotherhood – of young English painters, the most prominent of whom were William Holman Hunt, John Everett Millais and Dante Gabriel Rossetti. They attempted to react against what they saw as the empty formalism of the then fashionable 'subject' painting and, instead, offered a stress on the moral purpose of art. The great popularity of Hunt's paintings of Biblical scenes, such as *The Hireling Shepherd* (1851) and *The Light of the World* (1851–3), underlined the strong Christian commitment of society. However, there was a negative reaction in 1850 to the first showing of

Christ in the House of His Parents, for daring to present the Holy Family as ordinary. Dickens commented that 'their very toes have walked out of St Giles', a notorious slum with many Irish immigrants.

Social-problem paintings included George Frederic Watts' *Found Drowned* (1849–50), a reference to the lists of women, mostly prostitutes, found dead in the Thames. This was very much a concern of Dickens. He also criticised paintings that failed to match up to reality, most dramatically in *The Chimes* when Will Fern, just come from jail for vagrancy, tells the truth at Lady Bowley's birthday banquet:

> You may see the cottage from the sunk fence over yonder. I've seen the ladies draw it in their books a hundred times. It looks well in a picter, I've heerd [sic] say; but there an't weather in picters, and maybe 'tis fitter for that, than for a place to live in. Well! I lived there. How hard – how bitter hard, I lived there ... 'tis harder than you think, gentlefolks, to grow up decent, commonly decent, in such a place.

This is a criticism of the bucolic style, for example of John Constable and Clarkson Stanfield, the illustrator of the scene. Dickens' illustrators were important, and notably so in a society with limited literacy.

There were parallels in the discussion about paintings with the moral presentation of contemporary social themes by novelists. The writers of the age sought a wide readership, not only for personal profit but also because they thought it important to write for the unprecedented mass readership being created by increased education. Such a goal was not seen as incompatible with literary excellence, and these attitudes reflected the distance between the literary world of the nineteenth century and that of two centuries earlier which had displayed a self-conscious elitism and had operated in the context of widespread illiteracy.

William Wordsworth's successor as Poet Laureate in 1850 was Alfred Tennyson (1809–92), a favourite of Victoria whose

The Mermaid and *A Dream of Fair Women* were praised by Dickens in July 1842 for their striking imagery. Helping to reconcile poetry and the Establishment, Tennyson was no bluff rhymester, but, like many prominent contemporaries, a neurotic and withdrawn figure who understood sadness. A protagonist of morality and empire, Tennyson was a moralist as well as a master of poetry as understood in the period. Sentimentalism was to the fore. The self-sacrifice endorsed in poems like his *Enoch Arden* (1864) was very popular. It was self-sacrifice not of the Byronic outcast but of the servant of a social morality. Despite the importance of the prolific and talented Robert Browning (1812–89), Tennyson dominated the poetic world even more than Dickens did that of fiction. Dickens was not a poet, despite the blank verse in *Martin Chuzzlewit*; but *Household Words* fulfilled his plan for having 'a little good poetry'.[6]

The current theatrical repertoire includes very few works from Dickens' lifetime. Indeed, there is generally a gap between Sheridan in the 1770s and Pinero/Wilde in the 1890s; Pinero in the 1890s mattered more than Shaw, although Shaw has clearly outlasted him. Contemporary successes included comedies of T. W. Robertson, notably *Society* (1865), *Ours* (1866), *Caste* (1867), *Play* (1868), *School* (1869), and *M.P.* (1870). Described as 'cup-and-saucer drama', these have been seen as offering a detailed account of domestic life that laid the basis for the later revival of serious drama by Shaw. Theatre managers preferred long runs of uncontentious single plays which could best be secured by prominent stars, and spectacular productions with an emphasis on scenery and music. This system scarcely encouraged adventurous drama, but it brought profits, encouraging investment in new theatres, which were particularly prominent in central London. Theatre was an aspect of a commodity culture that linked advertising and spectacle.[7]

The staging of melodrama was popular. It joined theatre with fiction in the drama of public readings, such as those held, with great success, by Dickens. He, in contrast, in his 'Two Views of a Cheap Theatre', published in *The Uncommercial Traveller* (1860), criticised preachers for being unable to reach out to as large a social range as the theatre. Indeed, Dickens linked this to the failure to speak of the New Testament as 'the most beautiful and affecting history conceivable by man'. The issue was approached in a different light in *Little Dorrit* at Merdle's dinner when

> Bishop conversed with the great Physician on that relaxation of the throat with which young curates were too frequently afflicted, and on the means of lessening the great prevalence of that disorder in the church. Physician, as a general rule, was of opinion that the best way to avoid it was to know how to read, before you made a profession of reading. Bishop said dubiously, did he really think so? And Physician said, decidedly, yes he did.[8]

Theatre and the Bible, notably the New Testament, were linked in Dickens' fiction, as in *Oliver Twist* where Oliver retells his history, the novelist reflecting:

> Oh!, if when we oppress and grind our fellow-creatures, we bestowed but one thought on the dark evidences of human error, which, like dense and heavy clouds, are rising, slowly it is true, but not less surely, to Heaven, to pour their after-vengeance on our heads; if we heard but one instant, in imagination, the deep testimony of dead men's voices, which no power can stifle, and no pride shut out; where would be the injury and injustice: the suffering, misery, cruelty, and wrong: that each day's life brings with it![9]

Dickens was far from alone in his social concerns; although, as was characteristic of much work of the period, Thackeray's panoramic *Vanity Fair* (1847–8) offered a realistic account of individual drives, rather than a prescription for social action. Elizabeth Gaskell (1810–65) wrote about industrial strife, working-class living standards, and the role of entrepreneurs in *Mary Barton: A Tale of Manchester Life* (1848). She was more positive about entrepreneurs in *North and South* (1855). George

Eliot, the pseudonym of Mary Anne Evans (1819–80), depicted a seducing squire in *Adam Bede* (1859), social ostracism in *The Mill on the Floss* (1860), the cruel selfishness of the two sons of the squire in *Silas Marner* (1861), corrupt electioneering in *Felix Holt* (1866), a hypocritical banker in *Middlemarch* (1871–2), and the decadent mores of society in *Daniel Deronda* (1878). Social rank is presented as divisive in *Middlemarch*. These novelists saw the need, in the face of the pressure for statistical aggregation arising in large part from urban numbers, to reserve a place for the individual in society. In their loose and compendious form, they were able to seek to do this and much else.

The alternative wisdom of philosophers was gently mocked in Dickens' Christmas book *The Battle of Life* (1846):

> Dr Jeddler, in spite of his system of philosophy – which he was continually contradicting and denying in practice, but more famous philosophers have done that – could not help having as much interest in the return of his old ward and pupil, as if it had been a serious event.[10]

At the same time, it is too easy to imply that 'condition of England' topics dominated fiction. Instead, there was a range of topics,[11] including heroic nationalism, as in Bulwer Lytton's *Harold, the last of the Saxon Kings* (1848) and his epic poem *King Arthur* (1849). Much of the contemporary interest in the historic (or imagined) past began with Walter Scott, who was also the first man to make a fortune from writing novels.

Heroic nationalism was facetiously echoed in *Our Mutual Friend* when 'Mr Lightwood murmured "Vigorous Saxon spirit – Mrs Boffin's ancestors – bowmen – Agincourt and Cressy"',[12] referring to dramatic English victories over the French in the Hundred Years War in 1415 and 1346 respectively. Charles Kingsley, a well-connected clergyman who was an unqualified Regius Professor of Modern History at Cambridge from 1860 to 1869, wrote a number of historical novels glorifying heroes from the English past. These included *Westward Ho!* (1855), an account of the Elizabethan struggle with Philip II of Spain, in which the Inquisition and the Jesuits appear as a cruel inspiration of Spanish action, and *Hereward the Wake* (1866) about resistance to the Norman conquest. Bulwer Lytton's highly successful *The Last Days of Pompeii* (1834) was another aspect of the fascination with the past. The huge sales of Thomas Babington's Macaulay's *The History of England from the Accession of James the Second* (1848) indicated strong public interest. History was on offer in several ways. In *Our Mutual Friend*, the Boffins have Wegg read to them Edward Gibbon's *Decline and Fall of the Roman Empire* (1776–88).

History painters ranged across time for their subjects, as with Benjamin Robert Haydon (1786–1846), whose subjects included the Black Prince, a hero of the Hundred Years War with France, the Duke of Wellington, *The Burning of Rome by Nero*, and *Alfred and the First Trial by Jury*, the last two images of bad and good monarchy. Haydon's financial problems, which included imprisonment for debt, contributed to his suicide. Dickens thought him a very bad painter. The demand for an exemplary visual national history was seen in Maclise's *Wellington and Blücher at Waterloo* (1861) and *The Death of Nelson* (1864), painted for the new Palace of Westminster, as well as with his *Alfred the Great in the Camp of the Danes* (1852).

Life in a more exalted sphere than that usually tackled by Dickens, and with a very different didactic tone, was the forte of the popular and wealthy novelist Anne Marsh (1791–1874). Dickens was moved by her *Emilia Wyndham* (1846), a sentimental tale of romance, love, manners and duty among the well-connected, but was unwilling to accept a piece by her for *All the Year Round* on the grounds that it lacked 'some special individuality'.[13] Margaret Oliphant's *Miss Marjoribanks* (1866) was an example of the corpus of social observation that focused on the comic. As a reminder of the range of fiction, she also came to write stories in which ghosts play a key role.

As part of the range of writing, there was also the contrast between homosocial and heterosexual themes and plots. The military, exploration, universities and clubs were key settings for the former, as was much, but not all, historical adventure fiction; and the household for the heterosexual themes and plots. With the exception of Pickwick, Dickens dealt with the latter. Homosexuality left few traces in his fiction.

Dickens' fiction, both prolific and appearing over several decades, was at one with the standard corpus of many writers. As such, there was a tension for Dickens between responding to change, both individual (writer) and collective (readers and writers), but also the pressures of familiarity in style (writer) and audience response (readers). As Dickens found it easiest to write from his experience, and that was strongest in terms of his narrative of his youth, which in part remained a felt injustice, so there was a 'backward'-looking character to some of his prose. This injustice was extrapolated onto many of his characters.

The context of writing in the shape of publication, however, was very much altering. The appearance of large numbers of relatively inexpensive books reflected the impact of technology in allowing a far greater ease in moving timber thanks to railways and steamships; the development of papermaking using esparto grass and wood-pulp in place of linen and cotton rags; speedy, steam-powered production processes; and lower printing and binding costs. These changes, which Dickens does not consider in his novels, provided opportunities for entrepreneurial publishers, a group whom Dickens avoids in his novels, unlike in his life. Visiting Salisbury, Mr Pinch surveyed the bookshops:

> in the window were the spick-and-span new works from London, with the title-pages, and sometimes even the first page of the first chapter, laid wide open: tempting unwary men to begin to read the book, and then, in the impossibility of turning over, to rush blindly in, and buy it![14]

In their tone as well as plots, novels themselves were affected by the changing nature of information and connections caused by the postal services, telegraphy, and the railway. Each of these influenced the perceptions and assumptions of readers, as well as the authorial imagination and plot repertoire. In addition, the very form of these systems affected their content and impact. Thus, an immediate realism, as well as timed precision, was significant in the postal services, telegraphy and railways, and indeed in novels, with the 'fact' seen as a key player in each.

Devices, moreover, helped enhance reality. In particular, the camera provided an apparent fixity for vision and memory,[15] although spiritualists were to have success in manipulating photographs in the 1860s. With his interest in ghosts and, even more, the ghostly, his commitment to the imagination, and his dislike of utilitarianism, Dickens, who does not give his characters cameras, is very careful not to commit himself automatically to a fact-based analysis. Nevertheless, Dickens' concern with social equity, as with poor relief and the workhouse in *Oliver Twist*, means that he deploys facts to challenge complacency.

Religion was a major aspect of the culture and society of the period. The opening of the Great Exhibition in 1851 included a religious element in the form of a prominent benediction from John Bird Sumner, the Archbishop of Canterbury, and there were displays, by the Religious Tract Society and the British and Foreign Bible Society, of religious works in many languages. The presentation of copies of the Bible in 165 languages impressed Evangelicals. The translation of God's works in order to build a new Jerusalem in accordance with divine providence was a seductive view that appeared to align human inventiveness with moral purpose, as did overseas proselytising missions. Alongside the underlying idea of a benevolent God who had equipped humans with the means to serve his purposes, there was also the powerful conviction that moral purpose was necessary in all endeavours to assuage divine wrath, as well as with the ending of the slave trade and, later, slavery.

In his influential *Bridgewater Treatise* (1833), William Whewell found evidence of divine design in the laws of nature, notably in the way they had combined to support human life. This theme was also important to Charles Babbage, the key figure in the attempt to develop mechanical computation, which was a vital process for both business practice and theoretical developments. With his emphasis on final causes, and his argument that science had a moral purpose, not least in shaping inchoate data into order and meaning, Whewell contributed strongly to the presentation of information in a context of meaning or, rather, of a specific meaning. The possibility of alternative explanations was challenged when Whewell denied that there were inhabitants of other planets. This denial joined the state of scientific knowledge to a concern that the situation should be within the prospect offered by Scripture and Christian redemption rather than challenging them as the theory of evolution was to do.

There was also a major effort to interpret the discoveries of geology and the very process of geological research, a subject that enjoyed much public attention, so that they did not invalidate the historical framework of theology. To a degree, this effort matched the attempt in Britain to ensure that the counter-revolutionary tendencies of the period were still capable of being aligned with the idea of a belief in progress. William Buckland, who became Professor of Mineralogy at Oxford in 1813, published his proof of the Biblical Flood, *Reliquiae Diluvianae, or Observations on the Organic Remains Attesting the Action of A Universal Deluge* (1823), following it, in 1836, with his own *Bridgewater Treatise*, which sought to use geology and other scientific tools to prove the power of God as shown in the Creation. In *Man as Known to us Theologically and Geologically* (1834), Edward Nares, Regius Professor of Modern History at Oxford from 1813 to 1841, and a clergyman, attempted to reconcile theology and geology. This was a task different from his need in 1832 to explain why he had given no lectures for a decade, or, indeed, visited Oxford: Nares blamed the students' lack of interest. Dickens, who had no personal knowledge of the universities, did not use them as a setting.

The development of the idea of uniformitarianism proved a fundamental challenge to Biblical ideas such as the Flood. In the *Principles of Geology* (1830–3), Charles Lyell, Professor of Geology at King's College, London from 1831, argued that current processes had acted over time. In turn, this view was challenged in the 1840s by catastrophism, in the shape of glaciation, which had a long time span. Geology contributed to other aspects of science and culture of the period. Discussion of the age of the Earth and of the extinction of animal and plant species encouraged a sense of change, and the latter encouraged thought about evolution. Geological debate also influenced the contemporary aesthetic of poetry and art by revealing the majesty and antiquity of the earth, exploring slow but profound processes, and imagining great catastrophes and vast subterranean depths. Information was thus mapped onto the psyche, a process seen with engravings of paintings that captured these ideas. The impact of geological thought was apparent at the start of *Bleak House*, with a striking reference to a megalosaurus in London.

At the same time, there was a considerable degree of ecclesiastical hostility to aspects of science. John Cumming, a Scottish cleric prominent in London who used prophecy to claim in a series of sermons and writings that the 'last vial' of the Apocalypse was soon to be poured out, argued that sciences should only be studied in so far as they clustered round the Cross, a potent image and one that presented the Crucifixion as a continuing theme. There was concern in clerical circles that an emphasis on science extending to human actions and morality – the latter presented as determined by natural laws – led to materialism and possibly atheism, a process that was unacceptable to most. Separately, Biblical criticism in *Essays and Reviews* (1860) caused a sensation in the 1860s with heresy trials for some contributors.

More generally, the Gothic Revival expressed a religious taste and one that aspired to different values from those offered by the Neoclassical. Both were a reminder of the still strong hold of the élite on national culture. Thus, in the Neoclassical Temple of Worthies at the stately home of Woburn of John, 6th Duke of Bedford (1766–1839), there were such figures of Classical Roman probity as the Elder and Younger Brutus, all serving as remembrances of heroic virtue. A pediment by John Flaxman depicted Liberty and a frieze by Richard Westmacott the march of heroic virtue. Liberty was asserted and carefully grafted onto Whig family trees. This was not the culture on offer in Dickens' novels, although he glimpsed it in some of his social links, notably with the Watsons of Rockingham Castle.

The case for the Neo-Gothic was pushed hard by Augustus Pugin, an architect who saw Gothic as the quintessentially Christian style. His arguments and designs hit home at the right moment as, after a long period in which relatively few new churches had been built, there was a massive wave of church-building. This owed much to the expansion of the cities and to a determination to resist 'godlessness' there. Dickens sarcastically referred to a fairground booth as 'an ecclesiastical niche of early Gothic architecture'.[16] There was also much secular building in the Gothic style, notably from the 1850s, including the Houses of Parliament by Sir Charles Barry. More generally, pride was readily apparent in new cityscapes. 'Visit to Birkenhead', a piece published in *The Living Age* on 5 July 1845, referred to Merseyside becoming 'the grandest monument which the nineteenth century has erected to the genius of Commerce and Peace'. Offering a different and critical view, Dickens' account of the vain and mediocre Pecksniff in *Martin Chuzzlewit* provided a necessarily brutal portrayal of architectural plagiarism.

Opposition to scientific approaches was scarcely surprising since the biological understanding of human collectivities and destiny suggested by Darwinism clashed with clerical precepts; and England remained a religious society in which the Bible played a prominent role. In contrast, evolutionary accounts left scant room for divine intervention. In response, some advocates of scientific approaches, such as Robert Chambers, the author of *Vestiges of the Natural History of Creation* (1844), a work containing emerging ideas about evolution, complained about clerical obscurantism and resistance.

Religion alone, however, was not responsible for opposition to evolutionary ideas. There was also social snobbery, as with the ridiculous Eugene Wrayburn complaining in *Our Mutual Friend* about being referred to bees for a lesson of life:

> As a biped ... as a two-footed creature; – I object on principle, as a two-footed creature, to being constantly referred to insects and four-footed creatures. I object to being required to model my proceedings according to the proceedings of the bee, or the dog, or the spider, or the camel.[17]

Meanwhile, research into the context and content of the Bible was designed to help explain faith in a rational fashion, not least by pruning seemingly bizarre elements of Scripture. Biblical scholarship challenged the liberal inspiration. David Friedrich Strauss contradicted the historicity of supernatural elements in the Gospels in his *Das Leben Jesu* (1835–6), which was translated by George Eliot as *The Life of Jesus, Critically Examined by Dr David Strauss* (1846), and led to the loss of her faith. Such scholarship affected Anglicanism as well as English Presbyterianism and Congregationalism. Protestantism was reconceptualised, as the traditional authority of the Bible was challenged, while private judgement in religious matters was increasingly stressed by Protestants. These shifts also reflected the inroads into conventional religious beliefs made by scientific developments, as well as by the impact of a more optimistic view of human nature.

These factors could be seen with the contemporary Broad Church movement, which sought to draw on the spirit of the age, and, in more political terms, with the reaffirmation of a sense of national superiority through a combination of the notion of the leader of civilisation with the precepts of a competitiveness that was to be focused by the concept of Social Darwinism. The implications of change for the understanding of religion was apparent with the impact of anaesthetics which helped contain pain and transformed the understanding of this pain so that it was not simply in the hands of God.[18]

The compassionate and individualistic Dickens was strongly committed to God and the Bible, rather than the Church, a common distinction that was consistent with anticlericalism:

There would be happier lives and happier Deaths, perhaps, if we read our Saviour's preaching a little more, and let each other alone. If men invest the Deity with their own passions, so much the worse for them. He remains the same; and if there be any truth in anything about us, and it be not all one vast deceit, he is full of mercy and compassion, and looks to what his creatures do, and not to what they think.

Nine days later, Dickens commented on the need for Christian aid and instruction to be open to all.[19] In 1865, he wrote to his son Alfred, then *en route* for Australia:

You know that I never interfere with the religious opinions of my children, preferring they should reflect for themselves, as they grow old enough to do so: but in parting from you, as in parting from Sydney and Frank I tell you that if you humbly try to guide yourself by the beautiful new testament, you can never go wrong: also that I hope you will never omit under any circumstances to say a prayer by yourself night and morning.[20]

Dickens' writings dealt frequently with what were also central issues of religious discussion, notably death. In doing so, he captured individual and collective experience, for Victorians were accustomed to the deathbed. Dickens conveyed reassurance, and did so with reference to Christianity largely in the broader sense of consolation. Women took on an importance in this context that they lacked in the Church itself.[21]

Dickens was bothered about how the Church treated women, and he showed this notably in the planning of Burdett Coutts's 'Home for Homeless Women'. The choice of the chaplain concerned him:

... a knowledge of human nature as it shews itself in these tarnished and battered images of God – and a patient consideration for it – and a determined putting of the question to one's self, not only whether this or that piece of instruction or correction be in itself good and true, but how it can be best adapted to the state in which we find these people, and the necessity we are under of dealing gently with them, lest they should run headlong back on their own destruction – are the great, merciful, Christian thoughts for such an enterprise, and form the only spirit in which it can be successfully undertaken.[22]

With religion as with other aspects of society, Dickens distinguished between true values and meaning, as when Rose Maylie correctly tells Nancy in *Oliver Twist* that it is 'never too late for penitence and atonement',[23] and, on the other hand, outward form. Thus, in 1847, Dickens replied to a cleric:

As I really do not know what orthodoxy may be, or what it may be supposed to include – a point not exactly settled, I believe, as yet, in the learned or unlearned world – I am not in a condition to say whether I deserve my lax reputation in that wise. But my creed is the creed of Jesus Christ, I believe, and my deepest admiration and respect attend upon his life and teaching, I know.[24]

This attitude also reflected Dickens' consistent response to pressure for temperance,[25] which, to him, was an aspect of the way in which 'Philanthropists are always denouncing somebody' and 'are so given to seizing their fellow-creatures by the scruff of the neck, and ... bumping them into the paths of peace'. In *Edwin Drood*, Luke Honeythunder of the Philanthropists talks about men being brothers but has no sense of humour and takes space from the driver of the carriage, while, as a pedestrian, he forces people off the road. Honeythunder wishes to impose universal concord by force.[26] Dickens was troubled by 'the wickedness and foolishness of our social arrangements',[27] but also worried about those who preached improvement.

In contrast to contemporary norms, Dickens was pretty negative about religion. His parents were Anglicans, but he seems to have been cynical about the Church, and sometimes negative. In denominational terms, Dickens was hostile to the Oxford Movement, referring to 'that preposterous abuse, Puseyism' and attacking it in a piece in the *Examiner* on 3 June 1843, one that glanced at its favour for 'little boys'.[28] Dickens was also sarcastic about clerical opposition to public readings by novelists.[29] Like Victoria, Dickens, whom George Orwell saw as 'part of the English puritan tradition',[30] was in favour of a Broad Church approach, one hostile to the Oxford Movement and Evangelicals alike. Indeed, when the Convocation of the Province of Canterbury, presided over by the Archbishop of Canterbury, was held in 1866, mostly discussing ritualism, Dickens wondered whether his health was affected by his resulting irritation: 'a preposterous Clerical Body ... the weakened hopefulness of mankind which such a dash of the Middle Ages in the color and pattern of 1866 engenders'.[31]

Three years later, Dickens was dismayed by what to him was the mechanical nature of the service in Canterbury Cathedral. Moreover, many of the individual London churches described by Dickens are life-draining mausoleums, dusty and cold.[32] The oppressiveness not only of Sabbitarianism but also of religious observance is captured in *Little Dorrit* when Arthur Clennam returns to London:

> In every thoroughfare, up almost every alley, and down almost every turning, some doleful bell was throbbing, jerking, tolling, as if the Plague were in the city and the dead-carts were going round. Everything was bolted and barred that could by possibility furnish relief to an over-worked people. No pictures, no unfamiliar animals, no rare plants or flowers, no natural or artificial wonders of the ancient world – all *taboo* with that enlightened strictness, that the ugly South Sea gods in the British Museum might have supposed themselves at home again ... such a happy time, so propitious to the interests of religion and morality.[33]

There is also clear cynicism in *David Copperfield*: 'We had an adjourned cause in the Consistory that day – about excommunicating a baker who had been objecting in a vestry to a paving-rate ... we got him excommunicated for six weeks, and sentenced in no end of costs.' This is followed by a broad attack on ecclesiastical jurisdiction on the basis of Spenlow's praise of it.[34]

The disagreeable Dean in *Edwin Drood* intones: 'Our affections, however laudable, in this transitory world, should never master us; we should guide them, guide them.' This is clearly not Dickens' view. In *Oliver Twist*, the presiding clergyman only bothers with four minutes of the pauper funeral, while Dickens writes that 'there are a great many ladies and gentlemen, claiming to be out-and-out Christians, between whom, and Mr Sikes's dog, there exists very strong and singular points of resemblance'. The dog's hatred of 'other dogs as ain't of his breed' and growling when he hears a fiddle playing have just been mentioned.[35] Yet, there are good Anglican clerics in the novels alongside the selfish ones. Septimus Crisparkle does not 'preach more than I can', and repays a confidence 'not with a sermon' but by seeking aid from Heaven, as well as giving practical help.[36]

Dickens was more critical of Catholicism than of the Church of England. There was a sense of challenge from Pope Pius IX's decision to restore the Catholic hierarchy in England. In response, the Ecclesiastical Titles Act of 1851 prohibited Catholics from assuming episcopal titles. Dickens himself was no friend to Catholicism. Indeed, in 1847, he observed: 'My sympathy is strongly with the Swiss Radicals. They know what Catholicity is; They see, in some of their own valleys, the poverty, ignorance, misery, and bigotry, it always brings in its train wherever it is triumphant.'[37] Two years later, Dickens responded to a proposal for opening an embassy in Rome: 'As I am not favourable to Censorships generally, or to Papal Censorships in particular, I hope your pamphlet will always remain the curiosity it has become.' In response to the proposal from John Armstrong, an Anglo-Catholic cleric who supported female penitentiaries, Dickens reflected that the pamphlet was probably

... written by somebody who has conceived Puseyite ideas, and who has got one foot and the best part of one leg into the Romish Church. The suggested place is but a kind of Nunnery. If it be meant to be anything else, it is a mere vision, which, reduced to practice, would come to that. I think such places very promising offshoots from the root of all mischief, and believe this sprig would blow, in time, like the rest.[38]

In *Barnaby Rudge*, the Catholic Haredale flees

... to a religious establishment, known through Europe for the rigour and severity of its discipline, and for the merciless penitence it exacted from those who sought its shelter as a refuge from the world, he took the vows which thenceforth shut him out from nature and its kind, and after a few remorseful years was buried in its gloomy cloisters.[39]

At the same time, Dickens' villains, for example the truly sinister Carker in *Dombey and Son*, scorn Christianity in word or deed.[40] Another villain, Jonas Chuzzlewit, turns down the opportunity to say a prayer before dying.

A very different view into the soul was offered by physiognomy, the analysis of character from the shape of the head. This appeared to be made more scientific by photography, offering apparently objective evidence for differences between peoples, just as intelligence was clarified and supposedly assessed by developments in science including cranial measurement and psychology. Photography and physiognomy contributed to the arguments of eugenicists about inherited characteristics and the need to foster what would be presented as meritorious choices in marriage partners and in encouraging couples to have children – or not. Far from being dependent on governments, photography also provided individuals with additional means to acquire and retain their own information about the outside world. Despite the cumbersome and expensive nature of early equipment, very large numbers of photographs were taken.

Dickens was fascinated by the full range of culture, and depicted it in his novels, as with the singing at the Three Cripples pub in *Oliver Twist*,[41] and Vincent Crummles' lively theatrical company in *Nicholas Nickleby* which included the pony:

> His mother was on the stage ... She ate apple-pie at a circus for upwards of fourteen years ... fired pistols, and went to bed in a nightcap; and, in short, took the low comedy entirely. His father was a dancer ... He was rather a low sort of pony ... he had been originally jobbed out by the day, and he never quite got over his old habits. He was clever in melodrama too, but too broad – too broad. When the mother died, he took the port-wine business ... Drinking port-wine with the clown ... but he was greedy, and one night bit off the bowl of the glass, and shocked himself, so his vulgarity was the death of him at last.[42]

Dickens' interest in popular culture and pastimes, as well as his readiness to quarry them for his writing, were seen in the connection he made in a letter to John Forster in September 1842 during his visit to Broadstairs:

> At the Isle of Thanet races yesterday I saw – oh! who shall say what an immense amount of character in the way of inconceivable villainy and blackguardism! I even got some new wrinkles in the way of showmen, conjurors, pea-and-thimblers, and trampers generally. I think of opening my new book on the coast of Cornwall, in some terribly dreary iron-bound spot.[43]

Far from Wiltshire being dull, as he had anticipated, Mark Tapley in *Martin Chuzzlewit* found the Dragon Inn there a centre of activity, with 'skittles, cricket, quoits, nine-pins, comic songs, choruses, company round the chimney corner every winter's evening'. The snobbish Pecksniff, in contrast, typically finds 'the very sight of skittles ... far from being congenial to a delicate mind', and an amusement of the 'very vulgar'.[44]

At the same time, popular culture could be wearing for Dickens, who wrote in 1847:

> Vagrant music is getting to that height here, and is so impossible to be escaped from, that I fear Broadstairs and I must part company in time to come. Unless it pours of rain, I cannot write half-an-hour without the most excruciating organs, fiddles, bells, or glee-singers.[45]

In *Our Mutual Friend*, Dickens was sardonic about

> ... a sort of little Fair in the village. Some despairing gingerbread that had been vainly trying to dispose of itself all over the country, and had cast a quantity of dust upon its head in its mortification, again appealed to the public from an infirm booth. So did a heap of nuts, long, long exiled from Barcelona, and yet speaking English so indifferently as to call fourteen of themselves a pint. A Peep-show which had originally started with the Battle of Waterloo, and had since made it every other battle of later date by altering the Duke of Wellington's nose, tempted the student of illustrated history. A Fat Lady, perhaps in part sustained upon postponed pork, her professional associate being a Learned Pig, displayed her life-size picture in a low dress as she appeared when presented at Court, several yards round. All this was a vicious spectacle, as any poor idea of amusement on the part of the rougher hewers of wood and drawers of water in this land of England ever is and shall be.

Yet, Dickens replied to criticism of popular culture, for example from teetotallers, writing:

> In my opinion the Street Punch is one of those extravagant reliefs from the realities of life which would lose its hold upon the people if it were made moral and instructive. I regard it as quite harmless in its influence, and as an outrageous joke which no one

in existence would think of regarding as an incentive to any course of action, or a model for any kind of conduct. It is possible, I think, that one secret source of the pleasure very generally derived from this performance, as from the more boisterous parts of a Christian Pantomime, is the satisfaction the spectator feels in the circumstances that likenesses of men and women can be so knocked about, without any pain or suffering.

Dickens then added a comment that ironically challenged the entire idea of fiction as social commentary:

In countries where Punch is still a censor of the follies of the day, his influence is not beneficial. In the most popular Theatre in Naples, that is still his character every day and night; and Naples is perhaps the wickedest city upon earth.[46]

As he was well aware, culture had numerous contexts and many meanings. His writings did not seek to cover all of these contexts and meanings, but he contributed greatly in advancing the repertoire and fame of the novel, one of the major English contributions to culture.

8

THE 1810s

Dickens recalled seeing George IV when he was the Prince Regent pass through Chatham in a royal carriage. This would have been a spectacle for a child, but George faced a difficult situation. Loyalism had been a reaction to the French Revolution and Napoleon, but it confronted a growing challenge in the mid-1810s. Waterloo in 1815 brought a victorious close to the Napoleonic Wars. However, economic strains and social discontent, already serious, were exacerbated from 1815 by post-war depression and demobilisation. The unprecedented mobilisation for the wars was necessarily followed by unprecedented demobilisation. Population growth also led to under-employment and unemployment, and thus low wages and poverty, both for those in work and for those without any. Unemployment, moreover, owed something to new technology (and thus inspired Luddites to destroy new industrial machines in 1811–12), the unbalanced nature of industrial change, and the economic problems it caused. Poor harvests and agitation for political reform, combined with unemployment to produce a volatile post-war atmosphere. In addition, there was a string of bad winters, which hit economic activity. These winters were to influence Dickens when writing *A Christmas Carol*, and therefore strongly influence our image of Christmas to this day. The explosion of the Krakatoa volcano in the Far East led to a worsening of the global climate for several years. The year 1816 came to be known as the year with no summer.

The papers of Henry, Viscount Sidmouth, the Home Secretary, indicate the range of concern about popular radicalism. They include, for March 1815, the resolution of gentlemen members of the vestry of St Marylebone, London:

> Letters having been received from the magistrates at the Police Office in Marlborough Street recommending immediate steps be taken for the prevention of tumultuous meetings. And information which can be relied upon having been given to this meeting that it is the intention of a mob to destroy the houses of the members of both Houses of Parliament in this parish. Resolved that it is expedient that the Secretary of State should be applied to by a deputation from this meeting for a strong military force to act under the direction of the magistrates in this district.

The same month, George, 13th Earl of Rothes wrote in to say that the presence of the yeomanry in Kingston, Surrey, had helped lessen the impact of an attempt 'by some of the most inferior class to raise a mob by carrying about an effigy of a farmer who had dismissed some of his labourers'. Sidmouth referred to 'fresh and lamentable indications of the turbulent spirit which prevails amongst the lower orders of the people of Nottingham'.[1] Indeed, disorder continued. In Carlisle, the handloom weavers rioted in 1819.

Dominated by the landed interest, in 1815 Parliament passed the Corn Laws. These prohibited the import of grain unless the price of British grain reached 80 shillings a quarter. Thus, the price of the essential component of the expenditure of the bulk of the population was deliberately kept high, setting food producers against the consumers. The result was food riots among hungry agricultural labourers, with attacks on farmers and on corn mills, and demands for wage increases. The price of wheat per bushel was seen as a key indicator in *David Copperfield*, being linked by Spenlow to the rate of litigation.[2] The level of 80 shillings per quarter was well below some of the peaks achieved during the war period when imports from the Continent were not possible. Even the Corn Laws did not prevent a sharp deflation in agricultural prices and agricultural depression in the 1820s, including low wages and underemployment, contributing to the 'Captain Swing' riots in wheat-producing southern England in 1830.

Meanwhile, income tax, intended as an emergency wartime measure, was repealed in 1816. Prefiguring Dickens, William Cobbett (1762–1835), a leading radical political writer, denounced 'The Thing' – the Anglican, aristocratic establishment that dominated society, politics, religion and learning by means of patronage. This system, which was focused on stability and providing sound money and adequate food supplies, was run by the highly talented Robert, 2nd Earl of Liverpool, Tory Prime Minister from 1812 until a major stroke in February 1827.[3] In contrast, the Prince Regent, his stamina weakened by laziness, self-indulgence and poor health, was not a man effectively to resist the trend toward a lesser political role for the monarch, however much he might spasmodically insist on his own views of his importance.

Luddism was in part about strengthening the wage-bargaining position of trade unions, but governmental attitudes in the 1810s were hostile to these aims and not conducive to the development of popular activism outside the context of self-consciously loyalist activity. The Combination Acts of 1799 and 1800 had made trade unionism illegal. They were not repealed until 1824. Discontent and violence led to repressive legislation in the late 1810s, most prominently the Six Acts of 1819. Cobbett fled to America in 1817, when Habeas Corpus was suspended, and the Blasphemous and Seditious Libels Act and Publications Act, both of 1819, were intended to limit press criticism. However, by the standards of modern totalitarian regimes as well as of Early Modern equivalents, there was no police state, and that despite the problems and instability the country went through.

Nevertheless, a panic charge by the yeomanry ordered by the over-excitable Manchester magistrates on an enormous crowd gathered to support demands for parliamentary reform by speakers such as Henry 'Orator' Hunt led, in the Peterloo Massacre of 1819, to eleven deaths and many injuries. It elicited widespread revulsion: the radical poet Percy Bysshe Shelley referred, in *The Mask of Anarchy*, to

> Trampling to a mire of blood
> The Adoring multitude

Presented the Tories as repressive:

> I met murder on the way
> He had a mask like Castlereagh.

And called for a popular rising:

> Ye are many – they are few.

The *Times* deplored 'the dreadful fact that nearly a hundred of the King's unarmed subjects have been sabred by a body of cavalry in the streets of a town of which most of them were inhabitants, and in the presence of those magistrates whose sworn duty it is to protect and preserve the life of the meanest Englishman'.

In practice, the radicals were divided and most, including Hunt, rejected the use of force after Peterloo, which, like the more serious massacre at Amritsar in India in 1919, received so much attention because it was untypical.[4]

In the person of the young – but not therefore foolish – Pip, Dickens referred ironically to these years after Waterloo in *Great Expectations*:

We Britons had at that time particularly settled that it was treasonable to doubt our having and our being the best of everything: otherwise, while I was scared by the immensity of London, I think I might have had some faint doubts whether it was not rather ugly, crooked, narrow, and dirty.[5]

9

THE 1820s

The situation of the greater part of the operative manufacturers, in this county, in Nottinghamshire, and in Leicestershire, is said to be truly deplorable. There are supposed to be thirty thousand stocking-frames; and the wages of the weavers have declined to such a point, as to leave the poor creatures scarcely the means of bare existence. ... one of the consequences ... their dress, their looks, their movements, and the sound of their voices, correspond with their debasement with regard to their food. Potatoes appear to be the best of their diet. Some live upon boiled cabbage and salt ... And this is ENGLAND!

William Cobbett, Derby, 1829

'Albion [England] is still in the chains of slavery.' So declared Arthur Thistlewood at the end of his trial for treason. He had led a small group of London revolutionaries who had plotted to murder the entire Cabinet at dinner and to establish a radical government. They were arrested in Cato Street in 1820. A rising in Huddersfield, Yorkshire, also in 1820, was unsuccessful. There were also attacks on local privileges, attacks which reflected the volatile social relations of the period. Local opposition to the tolls on the bridge over the Tees at Stockton led to a riot that September in which the gates were pulled down and thrown into the river. The tolls were abolished in 1821. That March, Addington warned Wellington: 'The accounts from Manchester, Leeds, Glasgow etc are unsatisfactory. A simultaneous explosion appears to be meditated.'

There were threats to George IV's life, including one stating: 'I claim on behalf of thousands of my suffering fellow countrymen to cut off the head of the King.' As a result, that September, George was warned not to return to his cottage in Windsor Forest, as he wished to do. The popularity of his estranged wife, Caroline of Brunswick, was a reflection of the low regard in which the king was held, as well as being a way to attack him.

Yet, although 1820 was the most threatening year of Liverpool's peacetime ministry, popular discontent did not set the agenda for national politics. Liverpool's government contained the situation, firmly resisting both agitation and reform, but offering a more liberal Toryism in the 1820s. Able to offer neither leadership nor charisma, George IV was proof that government was no longer dependent on the calibre of the monarch. Tensions eased during the prosperous years of the early 1820s, and in response to a more moderate government policy. The *Birmingham Chronicle* of 12 February 1824 suggested that prosperity was leading to a general 'apathy' about Parliament.

However, in the late 1820s, an industrial slump and high bread prices helped cause a revival in popular unrest. Indeed, concern that the capital contained tinder for revolutionary outbreaks was the main factor in the decision by Wellington and Peel to create a fully professional Metropolitan Police force in 1828, and, moreover, one that was directly under Home Office control. A caricature of 1829, possibly by Robert Seymour, showed ragged and thin workers clinging to a broken shaft labelled

'Manufactures and Commerce'. They are pulled down by two larger employers, and, in turn, as the caption explains:

> Manufactures and Commerce support the Workmen
> they the Merchants and Masters who are the
> chief taxpayers and thereby support
> The great tax eater Church-and-State.

Arson and animal-maiming were common in many rural areas. The invention of friction matches in 1826 by the Stockton chemist John Walker, and their subsequent manufacture as 'strike anywhere Lucifers', made arson easier. In *Great Expectations*, the initial action takes place before it was possible to get 'a light by easy friction'.[1]

Public opinion, meanwhile, was treated as socially specific, as in *On the Rise, Progress and Present State of Public Opinion* (1828) by William Mackinnon, who was to be elected as a Tory MP in 1830:

> Public opinion may be said to be, that sentiment on any given subject which is entertained by the best informed, most intelligent, and most moral persons in the community, which is gradually spread and adopted by nearly all persons of any education or proper feeling in a civilized state. It may be also said, that this feeling exists in a community, and becomes powerful in proportion as information, moral principle, intelligence, and facility of communication are to be found. As most of these requisites are to be found in the middle class of society as well as the upper, it follows that the power of public opinion depends in a great measure on the proportion that the upper and middle class of society bear to the lower, or on the quantity of intelligence and wealth that exists in the community.

In the late 1820s, religious issues focused and contributed to a sense of change. In Ireland, where Catholics had had the vote since 1793, there was growing pressure for emancipation in the shape of representation in Parliament and holding office. Against this background, there was change. Liverpool's stroke in 1827 helped release tensions within the political world. The crisis of his succession was eventually resolved by making George Canning head of the Tory government, against the initial wishes of George IV, but Canning's death in August 1827 reopened the political situation. Keen not to turn to Wellington, whom he distrusted politically, George helped to put in a government under Frederick, Lord Goderich, a former Chancellor of the Exchequer, but the agreeable Goderich was weak and could not control his colleagues. Disillusioned with Goderich, whose willingness to blubber was unimpressive, George accepted his resignation in January 1828, and finally turned to Wellington.

The Duke wanted change. In 1828, the Test and Corporation Acts that maintained the Anglican ascendancy over Dissenters were repealed. The following year, Catholics gained full representation with the passage of the Roman Catholic Relief Act. This was highly contentious. Not just ultra-Tories regarded equality for Catholics as a fundamental challenge to the Protestant constitution. Indeed, the extent of petitioning, local meetings and newspaper agitation was firmly set against the change. An editorial in the *Exeter Weekly Times* of 8 November 1828 noted:

The Gunpowder Plot.

The return of the Fifth of November calls forth all over the country, for Protestant execration on Catholic bigotry; and the anniversary of a national deliverance is seized on, as a pretext for exciting by-gone prejudices for sowing dissentions, and inflaming ancient animosities. Catholic intolerance is descanted on by Protestant bigots, and ready invectives supply the place of historical truth. To how few, even among the liberals, have the real features of this conspiracy been lain open; and among the vulgar, who knows the gunpowder treason by any other name than the Popish Plot?

In practice, the term Papist was less frequently employed for Catholics than in the past. Catholic emancipation split the Tories, with the ultra-Tories seeing it as a betrayal, prefiguring the division over the repeal of the Corn Laws in the 1840s. Wellington, a pragmatist, had to press the obdurate George IV very hard to obtain his consent to the legislation. George, having threatened to abdicate, bowed to necessity, as his father had done with American independence.

Meanwhile, part of the London of Dickens' life was being built, including many of the most dramatic cityscapes, such as the new London Bridge (1824–31) as well as bridges at Vauxhall (1816), Waterloo (1817) and Southwark (1819). These bridges were crucial to the opening up of south London, a process encouraged by the draining of marshland, for example in Waterloo. Meanwhile, in the West End, George supported John Nash's 'Royal Way', which was designed to link the new Regent's Park to his palace at Carlton House Terrace near Pall Mall. With the attractive sweep of Regent Street, and the imposing Nash terraces alongside Regent's Park, this is one of London's few successful large-scale schemes of town planning. More gloomily, and an expression of a very different sort of power, Millbank Penitentiary, the 'great blank Prison' in *David Copperfield*, was opened in 1816.[2]

The last stages of George's life deserve the attention of a novelist. Very sickly and heavily drugged with laudanum, he still ate heavily and showed a variety of interests. Alongside concern about horse racing, including eagerness for news of the results and for details about horses he wished to buy, came signs of religious devotion. George read the Bible frequently, took solace in receiving the sacrament, and declared his repentance of his youth, saying that he hoped the mercy he had shown others would be offered him. In practice, he had presided over the legal system discussed in *Great Expectations*. His decline took several months, during which he displayed considerable courage and calm. In his last moments, George looked at Sir Watkin Waller, who was holding his hand, and said, 'My boy, this is death!' He then fell back dead on his chair: the rupture of a blood vessel in his stomach had killed him. The *Times* commented: 'Never was there a human being less respected than this late king ... What eye weeps for him?'[3]

Dickens, meanwhile, was experiencing great change, change that reflected not so much general economic circumstances as the particular problems of his father John, a clerk in the Navy Pay Office, whose different jobs had led to Charles living in Portsmouth, London and Chatham in the 1810s. In 1822, the family returned to London, with his father working at Somerset House. Unable to cope, John went to the Marshalsea, the debtors' prison, as happened to many middle-class men. To help with the family economy, the ten-year-old Charles went to work for Warren's blacking business, sticking labels on pots; rather as David Copperfield, also aged ten, was to work at Murdstone and Grinby's warehouse. Warren's factory was at Hungerford Stairs, part of London's Thameside economy, at once dynamic and sordid.[4]

This was a total humiliation for Charles, whereas many others in such circumstances responded in a more phlegmatic way or did not have the opportunity to express hurt. Dickens kept the episode a secret for most of his life, and referred to it as 'the secret agony of my soul'. The episode, which left him with conflicted attitudes towards his parents, was followed in the fashion of one of his novels by a legacy that took all the Dickens family out of penury and enabled Charles to have some education. In 1827, he became a junior clerk in a solicitor's office, moving on, in 1829, to become a reporter in one of the offices of Doctors' Commons. From these roles, he acquired a lifelong loathing for the pomposity and even malignity of the law. In the decade as a whole, Dickens matured. However, the adversity of part of the decade affected, even tarnished, the rest of his life. That was the case with family dynamics as well as circumstances.

An illustration of humiliation of a different type was provided in *The Wolf and the Lamb* (1819–20), a painting by William Mulready (1786–1863) that was purchased by George IV. Much admired by contemporaries, it showed a boy being bullied by another.

10

THE 1830s

The early 1830s saw, alongside the continuing pressures of daily existence that Dickens was to capture so well, a widening of political and social divisions. In 1830, 'Swing' riots affected large parts of southern and eastern England. Machine-breaking, arson and other attacks often followed letters signed by 'Swing' threatening trouble if labour-saving – and thus job-destroying – machines were not removed. The identity of 'Captain Swing', a pseudonym appropriated by the protestors, is unclear. He was as if a figure out of fiction. The riots probably spread spontaneously, rather than reflecting central control. Wage and tithe riots also contributed to the atmosphere of crisis in 1830, but, in much of rural England, although rick-burning continued, with an upsurge in 1843, it was the last episode of large-scale riot until the 1870s. However, the Plug Riots of 1842 which affected factories, mills and mines, notably in the North, kept rioting as an issue to the fore, as did the Rebecca Riots in Wales in 1839–43.

Dickens referred back to the 'Captain Swing' riots in *Martin Chuzzlewit* when upbraiding social neglect: 'Oh Magistrate, so rare a country gentleman and brave a squire, had you no duty to society, before the ricks were blazing and the mob were mad; or did it spring up, armed and booted from the earth, a corps of yeomanry, full-grown!'[1] So also with Lincolnshire, in *Bleak House*, where Sir Leicester Dedlock fears 'a body of some odd thousand conspirators, swarthy and grim, who were in the habit of turning out by torchlight, two or three nights in the week, for unlawful purposes'.[2]

In 1830, there was also much political and popular pressure for reform of the electoral franchise to make it more representative of the wealth and weight of the community. The Tories were not only hit by this pressure. They also lost power because they were split badly over two other issues: Catholic emancipation (1829), which had alienated many on the religious and constitutional right of their supporters; and free (or at least freer) trade, on which the Canningites or Huskissonites, notably Goderich and Palmerston, had fallen out with Wellington. This latter group became part of Grey's new ministry in 1830. Looking back to earlier support for reform, the Whig ministry of Charles, 2nd Earl Grey, which took power after the elections of 1830 (although not immediately), believed such reform necessary as part of a confidence in a future they could determine. The Tories were opposed to such reform. Introduced into the Commons in March 1831 by Lord John Russell (the son of a peer and therefore in the Commons, not the Lords), the Reform Bill was defeated at the committee stage in April after passing the second reading by only one vote.

Dickens possibly began his parliamentary reporting in this period, at least as suggested by him in a letter of 7 March 1831. His uncle's *Mirror of Parliament* was launched in January 1828, and acted as a competition to *Hansard's Debates*. In *David Copperfield*, Dickens describes how the narrator, David, trains himself to be a parliamentary reporter.

Grey then sought a dissolution of Parliament, preparatory to a new election designed by the Whigs to lead to a more reform-minded Commons. William IV's agreement to this dissolution, and thus to the second general election in quick succession, was very popular among supporters of reform, and was to be favourably recalled. Indeed, in the debate on Victoria's accession in 1837, Grey claimed: 'If ever there was a Sovereign entitled to the character, his Majesty may truly be styled "a Patriot King".' In 1831, William, instead, could have sought to appoint another Prime Minister, as he did in 1834.

The second Reform Bill passed the Commons in September 1831, after the general election had returned Grey with a very large majority, but it was thrown out by the Tory-dominated Lords. While the prospects of a compromise Bill were probed in discussions, there was much popular agitation, including bitter riots in Bristol, Derby and Nottingham.

A third Reform Bill, which reflected modifications arising from the recent discussions, was introduced in the Commons on 12 December 1831, passing its second reading with a large majority on 18 December. The attitude of the Lords, however, remained crucial and it was unclear that the modifications would ensure sufficient support. William was asked to appoint enough peers to secure the success of the Bill. Although respectful of the position of the Lords, and worried both about the content and tendency of the Reform Bill, and by Grey's inability to distance his policy from that of the radical Whigs, William felt he had to support the government. Reluctantly he agreed, on 15 January 1832, to create enough peers to support passage of the Bill in the Lords, if such a course was necessary, and also to press the peers to pass the measure.

The press world in which Dickens was increasingly engaged took a role. On 5 March, the *True Sun* was launched, with Dickens reporting on Parliament for it, but he soon found the paper in difficulties and decided to leave.[3]

Having passed its third reading in the Commons by 355 votes to 239 on 22 March 1832, the Bill went to the Lords four days later. Its second reading there was secured on 14 April, but by a majority of only nine, on a division of 184 to 175. This majority was judged insufficient by Grey. After being amended in committee, the Bill went back to the Lords for its third reading, only to meet with defeat on an amendment on 7 May by a majority of 161 to 116. Grey then asked William for fifty new peers, and when William, who had been thinking of about twenty-one, refused on 9 May, he resigned. William accepted the resignation of the ministry, and turned to the Tories, first asking Robert Peel, their leader in the Commons, who refused, and then Wellington, to form a government.

Handicapped by Tory divisions, Wellington failed, obliging William, who did not wish to see another general election, and the disruption and uncertainty that would cause, to turn to Grey, and to accept the need to create peers as the Whigs wished. He recalled Grey, as Wellington advised, on 15 May and agreed to create new peers if necessary three days later. Rather than doing so, however, William was responsible for a circular letter to Tory peers that led many to decide to abstain, as Wellington promised to do. Under this pressure, the Lords yielded, passing the third reading on 4 June. With the royal assent, the Reform Act became law on 7 June 1832.

At the moment of crisis, William had been led to back Grey by the widespread support for reform, by the view that the choice was between reform and widespread disorder, but also, in the confusion created by Tory divisions, by Grey's opposition to further changes, and by the sense that the legislation would not be followed by a total transformation of politics. William and Grey both wished to avoid revolutions like those of 1789 and 1830 in France. William was regarded as wanting to be a 'constitutional' monarch, which, indeed, he sought to be. His stance was a precedent for later Parliament Acts in 1911 and 1949. William's alleged support for the Bill had been used extensively, and to considerable effect, by supporters of reform in the 1831 election. Many pubs were named after William, including one in Exeter near where I live that only closed in 2019; unlike the case with George IV. William was to help bequeath a secure monarchy to his young and inexperienced niece Victoria in 1837.

A former naval officer, William may be glanced at by Dickens in his account of the contested election for a vestry beadle in which a former naval officer leads the reform party. The navy, and all matters maritime, tends to get a much better press from Dickens than the army. Lacking the purchase of commissions, the navy's officer corps was more meritocratic than the army's and quite a few naval officers sat as Whig MPs in the 1830s and 1840s.

The first major change to the franchise and political geography of England and Wales since the short-lived Interregnum constitutions of the 1650s, the First Reform Act (1832), misleadingly described by its authors as final, established more consistency in the right to vote and brought the franchise to the middle class. The act also reorganised the distribution of seats in order to reward growing towns, such as Birmingham, Blackburn, Bolton, Bradford, Leeds, Manchester, Oldham, Sheffield and Sunderland, and counties, at the expense of 'rotten boroughs', seats with a small population that were open to corruption. The latter were very much part of the *ancien régime* structure and character of English politics that Dickens derided, both in terms of electioneering and with reference to the products, such as Cousin Feenix and his reminiscences in *Dombey and Son*. The information-driven preference of reform was shown in the use for redistribution of the specially commissioned 'Drummond Scale', which ranked parliamentary boroughs on criteria including the number of houses they contained and the amount of assessed taxes paid. This information was collated from four different sources, including the census.

As a result of the Act, the size of the electorate was increased by 50 per cent, albeit from a low base so that it remained small. Most men and all women still could not vote, voting qualifications still differed between boroughs and the counties, electoral registration remained an issue, and the size of the electorate continued to vary greatly from the vote. The Act maintained the distinction between borough and county franchises, a distinction that continued until 1884. The county franchise, though extended in 1832, remained a freeholder and large tenant one, and was more conservative in character than the new borough franchise. The registration of voters stimulated party organisation in the shape of getting as many of one's own supporters as possible on the register while challenging the registration of those of one's opponents. Opportunities for fraud were present. Meanwhile, economic independence remained a fundamental principle of the right to vote.

Nevertheless, the Act helped underline the extent of popular representation through, and participation in, the electoral system; and thus it sustained the broad popular acceptance of the political system. London in particular gained a larger electorate. There were also five new constituencies: Tower Hamlets, Finsbury, Marylebone, Southwark, and Lambeth. This ensured that London was better represented than it had been prior to 1832, although it still had too few MPs for both its population and its electorate.

The general election of December 1832 was the first under the reformed system. Reform enthusiasm was still high. It was also the third general election in just over three years, and, as a result, the resources of Old Corruption had been exhausted. The election produced the biggest Whig majority of the century and convinced many Tories that they would not see office again for many years, if ever. Wellington described it as completing 'a revolution by due process of law'.

The 1832 Reform Act was not alone. Instead, it began a process of continuous reform, notably under the Whig government. The Emancipation Act of 1833 was the most significant step, both to contemporaries and in hindsight. The slave trade itself had become illegal in 1807. Attention then turned to slavery. Abolitionist tactics reprised those earlier directed against the slave trade, with press agitation, public meetings, pressure on Parliament, and a prominent role for women. Thus, a large meeting in Exeter on 3 April 1833 supported Abolitionist petitions, pressing for nothing short of 'the immediate and entire extinction of slavery'; the proceedings were reported at length in the *Western Times* of 6 April. A week later, the paper noted that the Anti-Slavery Committee in London had told the Devon Society that pressure on the government had to be maintained in order to indicate public concern, and that there had been between 1,500 and 1,600 people present at an anti-slavery public meeting in Exeter, including a 'great number of elegantly dressed ladies who could not procure seats'. The 1831 census figure for the city was 28,242.

Concern about the plight of Christian slaves, especially those who were fully converted by Methodist missionaries, who often established schools for slaves, made the issue more potent, as did increased scepticism that the end of the slave trade would lead to the end of slavery. Instead of confidence that the situation would gradually improve, pressure grew for immediate emancipation. Moreover, reports of the slave rising in Jamaica in 1831–2, and of the brutality of its suppression, helped make slavery appear undesirable and redundant, as the colonists clearly could not keep order. Influenced by Evangelicals, many Whig candidates included an anti-slavery platform in their electoral addresses and Whig victories in the general elections of the early 1830s were crucial. The Reform Act of 1832 contributed directly to this legislation as many seats with small electorates traditionally occupied by members of the West Indies interest group were abolished and replaced by constituencies that favoured abolition. These seats tended to be large or medium-sized industrial or shipping towns, especially those with many Nonconformists. Slaves were emancipated from 1 August 1834, Emancipation Day, although, until 1838, they had to work for their former masters as apprenticed labourers.

Very clear in his opposition to slavery, Dickens has Edward 'Monks' Leeford, the prime mover of the villainous plot in *Oliver Twist*, as the owner of an estate in the West Indies.[4] Such ownership was now a negative indicator, and to a degree not yet seen in Jane Austen's *Mansfield Park*.

There were also important legislative changes within England. In particular, the Municipal Corporations Act of 1835 reformed and standardised the municipal corporations of England and Wales. Elected borough councils, based on a franchise of rated occupiers, were given control over the local police, markets and street lighting. This legislation made town governments responsible to the middle class and was a crucial precondition for a wave of reforming urban activism. At the same time, much of this was slow in coming. Although the reformed corporations were often Liberal at first, many pretty quickly swung back to Tory dominance, for example Exeter which opposed sanitary legislation in the 1840s. Local ratepayers tended not to like the high rates which municipal activism required.

Other Acts of the period indicated the spreading role of reform agitation, the greater scope of legislation and, also, the extent of accommodation with existing interests. In 1833, there was a Factory Act and a Bank Charter Act, and Parliament voted the first grant to support education for the poor in the shape of annual grants for new school buildings to two voluntary bodies: the Church of England's National Society, and the British and Foreign School Society, which was formally non-denominational although most of the support was Nonconformist. The Bank Charter Act gave the Bank of England new powers, renewed its charter for twenty-one years, and established its notes for sums of £5 or more as legal tender throughout England and Wales. This was a measure of national standardisation, but also added the accountability that was a steadily greater theme of public office, for the bank was required to publish its accounts on a quarterly basis. The introduction of the civil registration of births, marriages and deaths in 1837 lessened the role of the Established Church.

Reform aroused mixed feelings. Grey was to complain in 1837 that the 1832 Reform Act had made 'the democracy of the towns paramount to all the other interests of the state', which was not what he had intended, for the Whigs had little time for radicalism. Indeed, the old landowning political élite had seen its dominance of the electoral process challenged with the Reform Act, and, thereafter, a steadily decreasing percentage of MPs came from it, although the political system largely remained under the control of the socially prominent. Certainly, there was no social revolution.

Others were dissatisfied with the limited extent of reform. The radicals had long seen the Whigs as exponents of oligarchy, and with reason. Indeed, 'Orator' Hunt, whose address had triggered the violence at Peterloo in 1819, and who supported universal manhood suffrage (the right to vote), opposed the 1832 Reform Act because he feared it would link the middle and upper classes against the rest.

Meanwhile, high politics continued to reflect the interaction of monarch, ministers and parties. William IV was happy when William, 2nd Viscount Melbourne, the Home Secretary, succeeded Grey as Prime Minister in July 1834. Although his effort to get Melbourne to form a coalition with the Tories was unsuccessful, William both liked and backed Melbourne, not least because he felt he could trust him to oppose radicalism: Melbourne had been Home Secretary in 1830–2. Indeed, William had clashed with Grey in 1832 over what he felt was the latter's willingness to discourage opposition to radicalism on the Continent.

Once Melbourne (who, later, did not share Victoria's liking for *Oliver Twist*) was in office, however, he differed with William over the Church of England. Melbourne wished to make Lord John Russell, later Prime Minister and an acquaintance of Dickens, Leader of the House of Commons. However, on one of the last occasions on which a monarch resisted an individual Cabinet appointment, William would not accept this. He saw Russell's support for the Irish Church Temporalities Bill as a threat to the rights of the Irish Church that was a breach of his coronation oath. This was an echo of George III and George IV's strong concerns over Catholic emancipation.

Using the excuse that the government was divided on the issue, which was indeed the case, William dismissed it on 14 November 1834. The dismissal reflected his conviction that he had the right to choose the government and that, while that government needed to command parliamentary support, it also needed to be his government and to back him. George III had followed such a course successfully in 1783–4. George IV, however, had not pushed through such a step, and it struck many contemporaries as a disturbing development.

The Tories, under Sir Robert Peel, then formed a government. In the event, the Tories lost the January 1835 election, although they did gain an additional ninety-eight seats. By then, Dickens was working as a reporter for the *Morning Chronicle*. Supported by the editor, John Black, he enjoyed this and earned a reasonable salary. Based in Chelmsford during the election campaign, Dickens reported on the elections in Essex and Suffolk, visiting Colchester among other places. Of Braintree, he wrote: 'I wish to God you could have seen me tooling in and out of the banners, drums, conservative emblems, horsemen, and go-carts with which every little Green was filled as the processions were waiting for the Tory candidates.'[5]

The election results did not stop Peel trying to continue in office, but defeats in the Commons led him to resign on 8 April 1835, having been in office for one hundred days. Now dependent on the support of Irish MPs, Melbourne returned to office on 11 April after the Whigs had rejected William's pressure for a coalition with the Tories. Queen Adelaide took Peel's failure to create a Commons' majority, and in the subsequent election, as signs of incipient revolution, but this response greatly exaggerated the extent of instability in 1834–5. Even in 1831–2, the disturbances, although violent, were relatively modest, considering the issues at stake and the apparent difficulty of ensuring a satisfactory constitutional outcome. Politics was certainly more peaceful than on the Continent.

William adapted well to Melbourne's return to office. He had to see Russell become Home Secretary and Leader of the House of Commons, Dickens reporting his nomination meeting for re-election for South Devon in which Russell in the event was defeated amid much Tory rejoicing, as well as a later speech by Russell at Bristol. However, Melbourne was careful not to alienate the elderly King, while William, in turn, accepted the new state of constitutional monarchy; although there were quarrels and disagreements reflecting the difficulties of 'bedding down' a new practice of politics. Fortunately for William, Melbourne's ministry rested on Tory support and was adaptable to Tory views. Melbourne was largely concerned to consolidate Grey's legacy, rather than to press on with radical reforms which Dickens would probably have preferred; while Peel, who was no ultra-Tory, was more comfortable with Melbourne than with many Tories. William could share this view. Nevertheless, he had to accept that Crown and Lords could not prevail together against the Commons. William's (eventual) willingness to be pliable was a crucial element of the Crown's position, and continued George IV's more grudging stance in the late 1820s.

At a different political level, dissatisfaction with the political situation led in the late 1830s to a working-class protest movement, known as Chartism, which called for universal adult male suffrage, a secret ballot and annual elections. The Six Points of the People's Charter (1838) also included equal constituencies, the abolition of property qualifications for MPs, and their payment. The last two were designed to ensure that the social élite lost their control of the representative system. The *Northern Star or Leeds General Advertiser*, launched in 1837, which was the leading Chartist newspaper, benefited commercially from its move to London in 1843, although the Chartists' pastoral form, for example the Chartist Land Company which partly reflected Irish enthusiasm for the idea of peasant farming, represented a rejection of London's urban life, and the sense that London's urban existence was in some way 'unnatural'. In London, where there were Chartists, the poor saw Chartism largely as a movement against taxes that hit them hard, a point exemplified in the caricature *The Man Wot Pays the Taxes*, in which the hapless protagonist with broken shoes exclaims: 'In what better condition am I now that the Reform Bill has past. I have been obliged to rob my family to pay taxes and now they tell me I'm Frenchised [for Franchised], that is I suppose lean, meagre, and to live upon frogs.'

Chartism as a 'movement' embraced temperance, land reforms, and educational themes, as well as political issues. Although

Chartists disagreed over tactics as well as goals, there was general support for the argument that peaceful agitation should be used. Many Chartists argued that force could be employed to resist what they saw as illegal action by the authorities, but, in practice, there was great reluctance to endorse violent policies. The Chartist Convention held in Birmingham in 1839 presumed that Parliament would reject the Chartist National Petition, and called on the people to refrain from the consumption of excisable goods, and thus hit tax revenues, to put pressure on the government and the middle classes, and pressed for the people to exercise a right to arm. This was seen as a preparation for a general strike or 'sacred month' for the Charter, which was in fact not implemented due to disagreements over appropriate action and a lack of preparedness.

Dickens himself responded to Chartism with great unease, as seen with his concern about the crowd in both *Barnaby Rudge* and, less histrionically, *A Tale of Two Cities*. The historical settings of these novels did not lessen their relevance and immediacy to readers. Based on the Gordon Riots in London in 1780, *Barnaby Rudge* was very much intended by Dickens to have contemporary relevance. It reflected his distaste for the mob and his concern about what it could lead to. Separately, Chartism also added to the reaction against the Whigs, who did badly in by-elections in the late 1830s.

Meanwhile, competing agendas for reform came to the fore. Moral politics were important. Concern over the state of the population led to a widespread determination to 'reform', that is to change, popular pastimes. Leisure was to be made useful: drink was to be replaced by sport. The teetotal movement was well developed by 1833, and temperance excursions were developed by the Secretary to the South Midland Temperance Association, Thomas Cook, as the basis for an industry of leisure trips and for a company that lasted until 2019.

When William IV died in 1837, he was succeeded by Victoria, the daughter of George III's fourth son, Edward, Duke of Kent, who had died in 1820. She had been in effect adopted by William and Adelaide as the daughter they could not have. William greatly disliked Victoria's meddlesome mother, Maria Louisa Victoria, whom he publicly insulted at a banquet in 1836. A crucial part of this rift was that Maria had snubbed Adelaide by failing to attend her birthday celebrations (which preceded those of William by eight days), arriving only in time for those of the king. William also quarrelled with Maria over Victoria's establishment – he wanted one for her that was separate from her mother's – and over a husband for Victoria.

William was determined to survive until Victoria, whom he liked, came of age on 24 May 1837, so that the Duchess of Kent should not be regent, a position she had been appointed to in 1830 in the event of William dying while Victoria was still a minor. Despite falling seriously ill on 20 May, William succeeded in his objective, finally dying a month later, early on 20 June.

The impact of parliamentary politics on the population was amply displayed by Dickens in his contextualisation of the 1834 Poor Law in *Oliver Twist*. The novel also enabled him to poke fun at the entire nature of control and regulation. The totally hypocritical and very callous Beadle Bumble, coming himself from kissing his intended, finds Noah Claypole and Charlotte romancing. Dickens uses this to mock the socially conservative:

> 'Kissing!' cried Mr Bumble, holding up his hands. 'The sin and wickedness of the lower orders in this porochial [*sic*] district is frightful! If parliament don't take their abominable courses under consideration, this country's ruined, and the character of the peasantry gone for ever!'[6]

Noah and Charlotte end up going to London where they fall into Fagin's clutches, Noah displaying a great eagerness to do so. The consequences are grim, but, in the description of this episode, there is none of the savagery of *King Lear* with its reference to a 'rascal beadle' whipping a whore after whom he is lusting.[7]

In his correspondence, Dickens provided a blunter account of the nature of electoral politics, one in which he vilified the Tories, than that which he offered his newspaper readers. From Kettering, where he was reporting the North Northamptonshire by-election in December 1835 for the *Morning Chronicle*:

> ...we had a slight flare here ... just stopping short of murder and a riot ... As the Tories are the principal party here, *I* am in no very good odour in the town ... Such a ruthless set of bloody-minded villains, I never set eyes on, in my life. In their convivial moments ... they were perfect savages. If a foreigner were brought here on his first visit to an English town, to form his estimate of the national character, I am quite satisfied he would return forthwith to France, and never set foot in England again. The remark will apply in a greater or less degree to all Agricultural places during the pendency of an Election ... Would you believe that a large body of horsemen, mounted and armed, who galloped on a defenceless crowd yesterday, striking about them in all directions, and protecting a man who cocked a loaded pistol, were led by Clergymen and Magistrates.[8]

To Dickens' fury, the Tories won. That this situation persisted after the 1832 Reform Act helped explain Dickens' criticism of Merdle's electoral interests in *Little Dorrit*:

> The three places in question were three little rotten holes in this Island, containing three little ignorant, drunken guzzling, dirty, out-of-the-way constituencies, that had reeled into Mr Merdle's pockets.

In Merdle's eyes, 'they are perfectly aware of their duty to Society'.[9] Dickens makes Gregsbury, the awful MP in *Nicholas Nickleby*, a Tory:

> 'With regard to such questions as are not political,' continued Mr Gregsbury, warming; 'and which one can't be expected to care a curse about, beyond the natural care of not allowing inferior people to be as well off as ourselves – else where are our

privileges? – I should wish my secretary to get together a few little flourishing speeches, of a patriotic cast.'[10]

The radical tone Dickens adopted in *Nicholas Nickleby* was directed at society as a whole:

A thief in fustian is a vulgar character, scarcely to be thought of by persons of refinement; but dress him in green velvet, with a high-crowned hat, and change the scene of his operations, from a thickly peopled city to a mountain road, and you shall find in him the very soul of poetry and adventure.[11]

Looked at differently, the Kettering episode showed how badly Dickens identified or reflected prevailing popular sentiment in his political reporting. For Dickens, nevertheless, alongside the evils of society, the world was opening up for him, as he later recorded for David Copperfield, who has the author's initials transposed:

I had been writing, in the newspaper and elsewhere, so prosperously, that when my new success was achieved, I considered myself reasonably entitled to escape from the dreary debates. One joyful night, therefore, I noted down the music of the parliamentary bagpipes for the last time, and I have never heard it since; though I still recognise the old drone in the newspapers, without any substantial variations.[12]

Married in 1836, Dickens had a growing family with a child each born in 1837, 1838 and 1839. By William IV's death, Dickens was a tenant at 48 Doughty Street (now a museum), near Gray's Inn, a twelve-room household with a staff of four. The following March, the first episode of *Nicholas Nickleby* was published. It was a major success. At the end of 1839, Dickens moved to 1 Devonshire Terrace, which was opposite to the York Gate entrance of Regent's Park. This was a larger house, and the annual rent, at £160, was twice that of Doughty Street. The house was a splendid setting, indeed stage, for Dickens' life, writing (with a large study) and hospitality.

Although maintaining the edgy feeling of an outsider, one whose position was due to continual effort, and felt inherently precarious, Dickens had fully arrived. Nevertheless, the tension between Dickens' attitude and his position remained important. It helped explain his angry concern over copyright and American pirate editions, but also his more general stance.

11

THE 1840s

Briefly Prime Minister in 1834–5, Sir Robert Peel, the Tory leader, gained power more conclusively in 1841, and was then Prime Minister until 1846. He was a new sort of Tory leader: an industrialist and not an aristocrat, although a landowner. Peel won a comfortable majority in the general election of 1841. This was thanks to the support of the counties and the numerous small boroughs that it is all too easy to forget, and not to the industrial towns. In the 1841 election, two of the City of London seats were also gained by the Tories. Dickens declined to stand against them in Reading. The 'Derby Dilly', Whigs under Edward, Lord Stanley, who left the party in 1834 over radicalism and the reorganisation of the Church of Ireland, who became Tories by 1837, were important to the undoubted success of Peel's party between 1837 and 1845 and did much to liberalise old Toryism.

Peel cut import and export duties, thus helping trade, and introduced the first peacetime income tax to make up the shortfall in government revenues. Peel came to advocate the cutting and eventual ending of the Corn Laws, because he saw their continuation as likely to increase popular radicalism, as well as hitting the free trade that the exporting industries required. Peel was not a free-trader from the start. In the 1841 general election, he and his followers supported the Corn Laws and the sliding scale of duties against the Whig proposal of a 5-shilling fixed duty. It was probably the scare of 1842, a real horror year for the economy and for employment, that persuaded him of the merits of cheaper bread – hence the 1842 and 1845 revisions of the sliding scale. That, however, meant that Disraeli and others could accuse him of betraying his party's commitments of 1841.

In 1843, in the first editorial of the *Economist*, which was launched by James Wilson, a former Financial Secretary to the Treasury and a virulent free-marketeer (and an opponent of most parliamentary measures for social reform), in order to attack the Corn Laws, Wilson drew attention to a general malaise:

> It is one of the most melancholy reflections of the present-day, that while wealth and capital have been rapidly increasing, while science and art have been working the most surprising miracles in and of the human family, and while morality, intelligence, and civilisation have been rapidly extending on all heads; – that at this time, the great material interests of the higher and middle classes, and the physical condition of the labouring and industrial classes, are more and more marked by characters of uncertainty and insecurity.

That year, in *Past and Present*, Thomas Carlyle stressed the disadvantages of unemployment. He was to be depicted in Ford Madox Brown's painting *Work* (1863), a painting presenting a scene in London, alongside F. D. Maurice, the Christian Socialist head of the Working Men's College at which Brown taught.

In 1842, when Dickens had thanked God that 'Peel continues hideously unpopular',[1] the Prime Minister reduced the Corn duties, and in 1845, when Dickens planned the *Daily News* in part to attack the Corn Laws, Peel decided that they had to go; not that there was any link. The advent of the potato blight in Ireland in 1845, and the subsequent savage famine, provided the occasion for Peel's acceleration of policy, but, unable to convince the Cabinet, he stood aside in December 1845, only to return to office when the Whig leader, Lord John Russell, could not form a ministry. Peel then pushed through the repeal of the Corn Laws on 15 May 1846, but it was carried only thanks to the support of Whig MPs, and with a majority of Tories, concerned about agricultural interests, voting against repeal, many with great bitterness.

Having lost control of his party, Peel resigned on 29 June 1846. This Tory baronet was presented as the figure who had given the people cheap bread, and had shown that the political system could satisfy public demands. When, his political life cut short by a riding accident, he died in 1850, Peel was commemorated in statues, engravings, street names, and celebration mugs and plates. The commemorations of Peel were heavily orchestrated by Liberal and Peelite free-traders to embarrass Derby's Conservatives. Peel certainly tried to present (and romanticise) himself as the giver of 'the people's bread', although in fact grain prices did not fall significantly until the 1870s when American imports began to arrive in bulk. [2]

However, with the rural interest hit hard, the Tory party was now divided. Micawber complains that 'the sale of corn upon commission ... does *not* pay'.[3] The repeal of the Corn Laws badly divided the Tories, as Catholic emancipation had done beforehand. In 1846, a minority Whig ministry under Russell came to power.

Dickens supported Whig parliamentary candidates with 'liberal and enlightened principles',[4] such as more public educational provision. In *Martin Chuzzlewit*, Dickens made fun of those, the Tories, 'returned upon the Gentlemanly Interest', of whom the representative voter really knows nothing.[5] For *Edwin Drood*, Dickens revised the phrase, referring to the complacent Mr Sapsea as 'voting at elections in the strictly respectable interest'.[6] In *Dombey and Son*, Dickens used Cousin Feenix, a former MP, to criticise the Tories as a group living in the shadows of William Pitt the Younger, Prime Minister from 1783 to 1801 and 1804 to 1806:

when a man had leave to let off any little private pop-gun, it was always considered a great point for him to say that he had the happiness of believing that his sentiments were not without an echo in the breast of Mr. Pitt ... upon which, a devilish large number of fellows immediately cheered, and put him in spirits. Though the fact is that these fellows, being under orders to cheer most excessively whenever Mr Pitt's name was mentioned, became so proficient that it always woke 'em.[7]

Dickens, who followed the political news, could be scathing. On 2 February 1849, he read the Queen's Speech on opening Parliament the previous day – the declaration of government policy, and the subsequent debate. Having referred to 'most frightful humbug', Dickens added:

Oh that I had the wings of a dove, and could flee (with a select circle) to some pleasant climate, where there are no Royal Speeches, and no professed Politicians! Heavens and Earth, to read the circumcised Dog D'Israeli apropos of War and Cobden![8]

This was a blunt response to Benjamin Disraeli, an opponent of Peel and able speaker who had become a prominent Tory in the Commons. Of Jewish background, although a convert to Christianity, Disraeli was a focus for anti-Semitic prejudice. Disraeli had attacked reformers as dangerous radicals threatening the constitution and the Church, and, in particular, Richard Cobden, onetime head of the Anti-Corn Law League, who was influencing the government to cut military expenditure. Dickens subsequently referred to Disraeli as 'conscience-less'.[9]

Not only the landed élite was divided. In addition, although Peelite conservatism appealed to an important segment of the middle class, the Anti-Corn Law League was a symbol of middle-class aggression. The repeal of the Corn Laws was followed by that of the Navigation Acts (1849), and by Cobden's Treaty with France (1860), which cut duties on trade, as did Gladstone's free-trade budget of the same year. Free trade became a central theme of national policy. Dickens' views on its value were reflected in his comment about 'that rickety national blessing, the British farmer'.[10] His observation of 1865 is also notable: 'I have strongly urged the case of the Music Halls against the prosecutions of the Theatrical Managers and have advocated Free Trade in entertainments as in all other speculations.'[11]

Meanwhile, Victoria's marriage, the fuss over which did not impress Dickens,[12] who had no emotional commitment to monarchy, was much happier than those of the élite depicted by Dickens. The lucky princeling, Albert of Saxe-Coburg-Gotha (1819–61), his case pushed hard by his uncle, the influential Leopold, King of the Belgians, was a happy case of dynastic choice becoming love-match, and the couple were married in 1840. He was an ardent husband whose life with Victoria was surprisingly passionate for those who think that Victorian values means sexual repression.

Rapidly educating himself in the details of the political system, Albert emphasised the need for the Crown to adopt political neutrality, and helped lessen Victoria's highly partisan preference for the Melbourne Whig ministry, which was necessary as Tory popularity revived. He was against public partisanship by the Crown, which had become dangerous after the defeats of 1829–41. However, Albert was not against covert politics by the Palace. In fact, he encouraged it, in support of Peel as Prime Minister and then over the Corn Laws, against the Conservatives from 1846 until his death, and against Henry, 3rd Viscount Palmerston as Foreign Secretary (1846–51) as too anti-German. Indeed, Victoria and Albert helped Russell to sack Palmerston in 1851. Some politicians saw Albert's covert interference as unconstitutional. Crucially, Albert did his dynastic duty by fathering many children, and thus avoiding the danger of the unpopular Ernest, Duke of Cumberland, George III's fifth son and Victoria's uncle, being next in line for the throne: Ernest inherited that of Hanover in 1837 as there was no female succession there.

Albert was also active in a host of spheres across public life. His prestige, drive and tact helped make him a sound committee man, and, through his position as the chairman of committees, he helped drive forward the cause of national improvement. Thus, after Parliament burned down, Albert was appointed as Chairman of the Royal Commission that was formed to choose frescoes to decorate the inside of the new Parliament buildings. He supported using the rebuilding as an opportunity to promote British arts.

More dramatically, Albert played a major role, not least as President of the Society for Arts from 1843, in promoting the Great Exhibition. In 1846, he told a deputation that 'to wed mechanical skill with high art is a task worthy of the Society of Arts and directly in the path of its duty'. In contrast, George IV had sponsored high art, most flamboyantly with the highly decorated Royal Pavilion in Brighton, but not mechanical skill. Albert's visit to Birmingham in 1843 had developed the affirmation of a link between monarchy, industry and modernity. Due to radical agitation, Albert was advised not to visit the city, but he did so, touring five major factories and being favourably received. The accounts of his visit were very different from that by Dickens of Little Nell's arrival there.

Although he struck Dickens, who gleefully cited xenophobic popular hostility to the match, as 'a good example of the best sort of perfectly commonplace man, with a considerable desire to make money',[13] Albert was a self-conscious moderniser, willing to work hard to acquire the detailed knowledge necessary to understand how best to implement change successfully. He was a practical paternalist, keenly committed to improvement, and concerned to lessen social discontents. At a meeting of the Society for Improving the Condition of the Working Classes in 1848, Albert argued that progress would not come from revolution and that the wealthy had a duty to help. He was committed to the improvement of public health and policing.

Albert indicated the range of support for reform. As government became more activist and regulatory, so the goal of the political groupings that controlled it increasingly became that of seizing the opportunity to push through policy; as much as office-holding for personal profit and prestige which was

Dickens' theme in *Little Dorrit*. The nature of power within society was now discussed to a greater extent than a century earlier. Moreover, consciously mimicking the anti-slavery movement in the mobilisation of public opinion, the large-scale popular petitions against the Corn Laws in the 1830s and 1840s reflected widespread interest in, and commitment to, key issues in public economy, and understandably so given their significance. The period was once known as 'The Hungry Forties' and indeed 1842, the worst year of the century, was horrific. However, it was followed by the Railway Boom of 1843-7. Moreover, the gold discoveries in California and Australia in 1849 were a major influence on economic growth and prosperity thereafter, particularly for a gold standard economy like Britain.

Dickens' work and audience can in large part be located with reference to the middle-class criticism of existing practices and their pressure for reform, as well as to the extent to which 'morality' and reform agitation were not only middle-class causes but also involved self-improving artisans whose support was increasingly an issue. Earning consistent criticism from Tory critics, notably the *Morning Post*, Dickens' powerful support for reform was readily apparent in his writings. These included a vigorous article in the *Morning Chronicle* of 25 July 1842 backing the Mines and Collieries Bill which excluded from the pits all women and girls as well as boys under ten (originally thirteen). The bill had passed in the Commons with support from Peel; but the Lords was more hostile, with mine owners, notably the very wealthy Charles, 3rd Marquess of Londonderry, opposing reform. In the event, although there were amendments, the bill was largely passed. Dickens very strongly attacked complacency and hypocrisy and brought up the theme of exploration and proselytization in which Britain was then very active and of which it was very proud:

That for many years these mines and all belonging to them, as they have been out of sight in the dark earth, have been utterly out of legislative mind; that for so many years all considerations of humanity, policy, social virtue, and common decency, have been left rotting at the pit's mouth, with other disregarded dunghill matter from which lordly colliers could extract no money; that for very many years, a state of things has existed in these places, in the heart and core of a Christian country, which, if it had been discovered by mariners or missionaries in the Sandwich Islands (Hawaii), would have made the fortune of two quarto volumes, filled the whole bench of bishops with emotion, and nerved to new and mighty projects the Society for the Propagation of the Gospel in Foreign Parts, is well known to every one.[14]

In turn, the Chartists' *Northern Star* strongly praised Dickens' *The Chimes* (1844). In its original version, *The Chimes* included criticism of Disraeli's feudalist 'Young England' Social Toryism movement that was more pointed than what finally made it into print. The pointed criticism included a ridiculous attack, attributed to the feudalist movement, on the present as 'degenerate times', in comparison with 'the good old times, the grand old times, the great old times!' This was a theme repeated without meaning, and one that Dickens despised.

Meanwhile, Parliament resisted Chartist mass petitions in 1839, 1842 and 1848. These petitions certainly captured many of the inequalities of society. That of 1842 noted: 'The borough of Guildford with a population of 3,902 returns to Parliament as many members as Tower Hamlets with a population of 300,000.' The latter was a testimony to the enormous expansion of the East End, which was within Dickens' perambulatory gaze. However, despite considerable distress among sections of the working class, England did not share in the political breakdown of 1848, the year of revolutions on the Continent, although the French Revolution of that year was applauded by radicals, including Dickens.

London in 1848 was also not the setting for any confrontation comparable to the Gordon Riots of 1780 described at length by Dickens in *Barnaby Rudge* (1841) and leading him to the conclusion that the riots should have taught a lesson of 'reproof or moderation'. Dickens tackled a very different riot in *Nicholas Nickleby* when the Squeers' regime in Dotheboys Hall is overthrown.[15] There had indeed been public school riots in the eighteenth and early nineteenth centuries, notably at Westminster in 1791, Charterhouse in 1792, Rugby in 1797, and Winchester in 1818. Some of these disturbances matched that in Dotheboys Hall.

Benefiting from modern technology in the shape of trains and the telegraph, the scale of government preparations was impressive. The Chartist mass meeting on 10 April 1848 saw the deployment of over 8,000 troops and army pensioners, as well as the 4,000 members of the Metropolitan Police and the enrolling of about 85,000 special constables, including Gladstone, although not Dickens. Charles Grenville noted that 'every gentleman in London is become a constable', although there were also working-class specials. Wellington was put in charge of the capital. Thirty cannon were prepared at the Tower. The government was resolved to stop a mass procession taking the petition to Parliament, and, to do so, decided to stop the Chartists crossing the Thames. The confrontation in London was stage-managed by Russell's government with deliberate overkill when the real worry was Ireland, especially Dublin where a rising was brewing.

In the event, despite claims of half a million Chartists assembling on Kennington Common in Lambeth, the number was probably only 20,000. The violence that action against the Chartists could entail was noted by the Chartist poet John Leno:

> I saw a meeting announced to be held on the old tilting ground, Clerkenwell Green. ... an army of constables and detectives swept the Green ... I was standing on the pavement discussing the Irish question when a disguised policeman gave the order to move on ... I still kept my ground when he commenced to belabour me with a truncheon ... The blood fairly poured down my face.

In turn, the Chartists were blamed by critics for the disorder of that year. In June, in face of renewed Chartist action,

5,000 troops were deployed, but again there was no fighting. There was a revolt in Ireland, but it was premature and disorganised, and failed.

Dickens had some sympathy for the Chartists – 'working men who are Chartists' – but also thought they lacked 'vitality' and was critical of 'the amateur members of that body', the leaders. He was particularly hostile to George Reynolds, a radical Chartist and a rival of Dickens as a popular writer and successful journalist.[16] Earlier, Dickens had opposed the idea of mentioning in his magazine Robert Owen's Socialist weekly, *The New Moral World*, which itself had praised Dickens' depictions of social evils in *Sketches of Boz*. Dickens was worried that the goal of the weekly was notoriety.[17]

It is unclear whether Chartism failed because of the iron fist of the state, because the government meeting some of its demands left it looking passé, because of its failure to achieve its objectives due to growing prosperity, or because of its own internal divisions – or a combination of these factors. Chartism was badly divided in terms of leadership, regional character and interests. It was a composite of various regionally based movements, rather than a cohesive and integrated single movement. The Irish element was a strong factor in both London and Lancashire. Mass support for Chartism was apparent only in times of recession. In London, the poor saw Chartism largely as a movement against taxes that hit them hard. Similarly, rural protest movements against heavy rent and tithe burdens did not change the situation in the countryside.

In the longer term, whereas Whiggism, certainly in the eyes of its supporters, was progressivism without autocracy or democracy, this prospectus ceased to be a realistic option as democratic and populist politics became more important. Linked to this came tensions in progressivism. In place of a focus on constitutional, political and imperial themes came notions of social welfare. What that would mean in practice was less clear.

In his proposals for social amelioration, Dickens presented himself as responding to the changing exigencies of the period.

The 1840s saw him more prominent and successful, and writing in different forms. *The Old Curiosity Shop* (1840–1), a major success, and *Barnaby Rudge* (1841), which had lower and falling sales, began the decade with the pressure of weekly instalments. That both demanded consistent publication and provided less space for development in each issue, and therefore demands for revision. Dickens then turned to monthlies. He had found *Barnaby Rudge* very difficult to start. From *Pickwick Papers* on, although there were precursors from other hands, Dickens was the great protagonist in this period of serial novels.[18]

In his shorter fiction, his Christmas books were great successes, notably *The Cricket on the Heath* (1845). They contributed to the Victorian 'invention' of Christmas, including trees, cards, carols and stories. Dickens' Christmas pieces were later subsumed into his magazines, with *Household Words* launched on 30 March 1850.

Dickens' politics were seen in a variety of ways, for example in a response to a magazine contribution on Wat Tyler, the key figure in the unsuccessful 1381 Peasants' Revolt, killing a tax collector after an insult to his daughter:

> I object on principle to making Wat such a thorough-paced villain, because a rebel on such grounds has a certain claim to one's sympathy, and I feel that if I had lived in his time, I should have been very likely to have knocked out the collector's brains myself, – or at all events to have looked upon the man who did so, as a demi-God. Fathers may naturally object to having gross indecencies practised upon their daughters even by government servants; and bystanders can scarcely shew their manhood better than be resenting such things when they are done before their eyes. Therefore, if Wat Tayler and his followers when their passions were once let loose, had burnt down the City and got drunk with blood, I should still entertain some respect for their memory.[19]

Dickens followed on by saying that the sight of 'such miseries and horrors among these little creatures' helped radicalise people, and made him, also seeing the children of the nobility, 'sick'.[20] In *A Tale of Two Cities* (1859), revolution in France in 1789, for the details of which Dickens drew on Carlyle's history, is presented as the destructive and cruel product of a destructive and cruel social system, with neither having much to offer in comparison to the necessary moral character of any society. The theme is intended as universally valid and, therefore, as pertinent for Dickens' readers.

12

THE 1850s

So many hundred hands in this Mill; so many hundred horse Steam Power. It is known, to the force of a single pound weight, what the engine will do.[1]

In *Hard Times* (1854), a much tauter and more urgent novel than his earlier ones, Dickens contrasted the subordination of human experience to the obsession with mathematical facts of the industrial new world. Indeed, the statistics of industrialisation were part of the utilitarian, measurement-based, outcome-oriented mentality that economic change enabled. The impact of industrialisation on the very physique was seen with the deplorable Mr Bounderby who had 'a metallic laugh'.[2]

Dickens himself benefited greatly from mechanisation, both in travel and in the publication of his works. Indeed, on both heads, mechanisation provided him with the prospect of profit. It also helped explain the conviction expressed by the *Western Luminary* in its issue of 2 January 1855: 'Progress is the great animating principle of being. The world, time, our country have advanced and are advancing.' Optimism in the expansion and application of knowledge was widespread. The narrator in Edward Bulwer Lytton's (1803–73) ghost story 'The House and the Brain' (1859) explained his theory that 'what is called supernatural is only a something in the laws of Nature of which we have been hitherto ignorant'. This approach reflected faith in reason, but also the strong interest in the supernatural that was readily apparent. Lytton was a friend of Dickens.

A sense of the congruence of Christianity, reform and science played a major role in the optimism of the present. In his *History of England from the Fall of Wolsey to the Defeat of the Spanish Armada* (1858–70), James Anthony Froude presented the English Reformation as providential, while, in his hugely successful *History of England* (1848–62), Thomas Babington Macaulay offered a Whig view of 1688–1702, comparing what he presented as the backward Stuart England of 1688 to the more progressive present that the Whigs had created as a result of the overthrow of James II in 1688–9. Dickens added a sardonic note in *Hard Times*, with strangers in Coketown praising Bounderby:

> They made him out to be the Royal arms, the Union-Jack, Magna Carta, John Bull, Habeas Corpus, the Bill of Rights, An Englishman's house is his castle, Church and State, and God save the Queen, all put together.[3]

Optimism took physical effect in the Great Exhibition of 1851, which was planned to speak for Britain past, present and future. Opened at the specially built Crystal Palace in London's Hyde Park, it was intended as a demonstration of British achievement, and was a proclamation of the nation's mission, duty and interest to put itself at the head of the diffusion of civilisation, and thus to take forward history. The exhibition was seen as an opportunity to link manufacturing and the arts, in order to promote a humane practicality and inspired, progressive society, in which Britain would be foremost, and from which the British people and economy could benefit.

The exhibition proclaimed the supposed triumph of free trade which was linked to manufacturing supremacy. To some extent, indeed, the exhibition was a political stunt of the free-traders, a very successful Whig/Peelite enterprise to push free trade and embarrass the Conservatives, as the Tories can now be called. Although a partisan occasion, the exhibition also symbolised the coming of a less fractured and more prosperous society after the often divisive and difficult experiences of the 1830s and 1840s, notably the contentious repeal of the Corn Laws and the pressure from the Chartist movement for political reform.[4]

The Great Exhibition reflected an attempt to embrace and to channel the country's dynamic industry, the New Britain; an attempt in part arising from the 1843 visit to Birmingham of Prince Albert, a key promoter of the exhibition. With its massive block of coal by the entrance, the exhibition was a tribute to British manufacturing skill, prowess and confidence in the future, one abundantly displayed in its central space, the first wonder of the modern world, Joseph Paxton's iron and glass conservatory, which was 1,850 feet long, 460 feet wide and 108 feet high. It included 294,000 panes of glass and contained almost 1 million square feet of space. This was a public palace of Britain's prowess and future. The British public celebrated their future with their presence: with 6.2 million visitors in the 140 days of the exhibition. It had been agreed that it should be entirely self-financing, with no public money involved: this goal more than succeeded, thanks to a lovely summer in 1851, and the role of the railway, and of Thomas Cook, the entrepreneur of tourism, in bringing large numbers of visitors to London.

Also that year, Dickens purchased the forty-five-year lease on Tavistock House for £1,542. A further £577 15s 6d, an enormous sum, was then spent on alterations, including a well-furnished library and a cold shower. He owned it until 1860, when he both sold the lease and destroyed the letters he had received. Dickens settled, instead, in Gad's Hill Place, which he had bought in March 1856 for £1,790, and then adapted, initially spending part of each year there. The decision to write

Great Expectations was to be encouraged by the return to Kent: the novel was partly set there.

In his unprecedentedly successful *Bleak House* (1852–3), a bleak masterpiece, Dickens not only indicted the coldness of law and Church but also society, in the haughty personages of Sir Leicester Dedlock – 'his family is as old as the hills, and infinitely more respectable' – and his wife who is concealing a guilty secret. Such accounts served to identify and criticise an entire class. Sir Leicester's attitude to the interminable Chancery suit of *Jarndyce* v. *Jarndyce* is used to characterise conservatism as snobbish folly. He has

> ... no objection ... It is a slow, expensive, British, constitutional kind of thing. ... he regards the Court of Chancery, even if it should involve an occasional delay of justice and a trifling amount of confusion, as a something, devised in conjunction with a variety of other somethings, by the perfection of human wisdom, for the eternal settlements (humanly speaking) of everything. And he is upon the whole of a fixed opinion, that to give the sanction of his countenance to any complaints respecting it, would be to encourage some person in the lower classes to rise up somewhere – like Wat Tyler.[5]

Wat Tyler is introduced again, as are the earlier Dedlocks having backed Charles I, who is described by their housekeeper as excellent and a blessed martyr. The authoritarian Sir Leicester also seeks to close up a green pathway, and uses both force and the law to that end.[6] Social criticism indeed became more common in England in the 1850s. Under the heading 'The Lord Lieutenant and the North Devon Railway', *Trewman's Exeter Flying Post* of 3 January 1856 reported at length a clash between what it implied were the mores of aristocratic society and, on the other hand, the notion of public responsibility:

> Express trains will not do the bidding of Lords Lieutenant. Railways are not managed as are coaches; – the times of arrival

and departure, as advertised, are kept as regularly as possible; and a railway superintendent would as soon think of keeping a train back to accommodate a peer of the realm as he would of sending off a train too soon to baulk a director. Lord Fortescue, however, seems to think that in his case exceptions ought to be made to the rule which governs all railway companies. It was his misfortune to be in the down express from Bristol last Saturday afternoon week, which did not happen to reach Taunton until after the time it was due at Exeter. The North Devon train is advertised to leave the station at 3.30, – half an hour after the arrival of the express. The superintendent having ascertained by telegraph that the express was much behind its time, started the North Devon train at 3.45.

Hugh, 2nd Earl Fortescue, a prominent Whig, complained about the failure to delay the latter, despite the large number of passengers on it, leading the paper to ask, 'Does Lord Fortescue mean to say that these should have been detained an hour and a half to suit his Lordship's convenience?' Opened in 1903, Badminton station was more amenable to the wishes of the Duke of Beaufort.

Yet, alongside aspects of social criticism, this was still very much a nation in which debate was over how it was to be guided as a whole by moral conduct. Paternalistic and Evangelical concern about Christian welfare lay behind much pressure for reform, rather than egalitarianism. These values were noted in the *Western Times* of 25 January 1851:

We have only space to refer to the satisfactory report of the meeting held at Guildhall, to establish public libraries. We should prefer seeing a more direct effort to promote the education of the destitute youth and children of the city, but we receive the conclusions of the meeting as an admission of the public duty to provide a means of education for that class of society whose means do not enable it to educate its offspring.

The 11 July 1855 issue of *Chudleigh's Weekly Express* praised the situation under which 'the children of our poorer brethren here receive a sound religious and moral education'.

Tory division over Corn Law repeal had led to Peel's resignation in 1846 and to the formation of a minority Whig ministry under Lord John Russell, which Dickens referred to as 'my friends (or supposed to be)'.[7] In 1865, he was to write to Russell of 'a public admiration of you and confidence in you which were as strong and steady as any man's in England long before I owed you any'.[8] However, neither the 1847 nor the 1852 general elections left a firm Whig majority; indeed the Conservatives marginally improved their position in 1852, in part thanks to a decline in the number of Peelites. Russell depended on the strength of Conservative divisions and, accordingly, on the support of the Peelites. This set the pattern for the 1850s, as the Peelites remained able to hold the balance until 1859. Meanwhile, the abandonment of protectionism by the Conservative leaders in 1852 helped defuse the issue. It was not only the Conservatives who were divided. Prior to 1859, what became the Liberal Party was an uneasy group of Whigs, Liberals and radicals. As with much else in British society in this period, politics was in a state of flux. This remained the case throughout Dickens' life.

Rather than engaging with this complexity, Dickens preferred to focus on a continuity, in the sense of politics by a self-styled élite giving out posts while uncertain what to do 'for Noodle!' Meanwhile, in his account, democracy is at bay:

> A People there are, no doubt – a certain large number of supernumeraries, who are to be occasionally addressed, and relied upon for shouts and choruses, as on the theatrical stage; but Boodle and Buffy, their followers and families, their heirs, executors, administrators, and assigns, are the born first-actors, managers, and leaders, and no others can appear upon the scene for ever and ever.[9]

There is also the dimension of change. With regard to electioneering in *Bleak House*, Sir Leicester Dedlock, an MP himself, is angry 'that in many places the people have shown a bad spirit, and that this opposition to the Government has been of a most determined and most implacable description'. The two seats Dedlock, clearly a Conservative, habitually dominates are lost to Rouncewell the ironmaster, leading him to claim that 'the floodgates of society are burst open'.[10] This was typical of the alarmist Conservative comments of the period.

A far less positive aspect of national effectiveness than the Great Exhibition of 1851, although in a very different context, was provided by the mismanagement of the Crimean War with Russia (1854–6). The terrible conditions of the troops, especially a lack of adequate food, clean water, medical attention, shelter and clothing, helped lead to very heavy losses from disease, more so than from Russian action, and the administrative deficiencies were heavily criticised in Parliament. In this, the development of newspaper reporting, which benefited from reports sent home by telegraph and from photography, was important to identification with the soldiers and to this criticism.

Dickens was involved with the Administrative Reform Association, speaking to them in criticism of the conduct of the war, on 27 June 1855. In *Little Dorrit*, he drew on popular anger over it. In his preface to the book once it appeared as a whole, Dickens noted:

If I might offer any apology for so exaggerated a fiction as the Barnacles and the Circumlocution Office, I would seek it in the common experience of an Englishman, without presuming to mention the unimportant fact of my having done that violence to good manners, in the days of a Russian war, and of a Court of Enquiry at Chelsea.

In a letter of 19 March 1855, Dickens counterpointed 'our valiant soldiers' and 'we have got involved in meshes of aristocratic red tape to our unspeakable confusion, loss, and sorrow', adding,

'I am sick and sour to think of such things at this age of the world...'[11]

With the Circumlocution Office, Dickens offered an equivalent of the description of the law in *Bleak House* in the case of *Jarndyce* v. *Jarndyce*. In both cases, as with the Poor Law in *Oliver Twist*, the target is the devastation to innocent individuals brought by the complacency of those running institutions. Moreover, anticipating interest in German methods in the 1890s and 1900s, Dickens suggested that other states, in the shape of 'a certain barbaric power [which] ... had no idea of stowing away a great national object in a Circumlocution Office', were more effective precisely because they did not work through the obfuscation of such an institution.[12] Dickens became disillusioned about the possibility of improvement, arguing, in October 1855:

> As to the suffrage, I have lost hope even in the Ballot. We appear to me to have proved the failure of Representative Institutions, without an educated and advanced people to support them ... I do reluctantly believe that the English people are, habitually, consenting parties to the miserable imbecility into which we have fallen, *and never* will help themselves out of it.[13]

This was in line with the eighteenth-century view of radicals that universal (male) suffrage was impossible until the 'lower orders' were educated out of their 'miserable imbecility'.

Dickens' anger was very much seen in *Little Dorrit*. Led by George, 4th Earl of Aberdeen, a former Peelite, the government from 1852 to 1855 was a coalition of political groups born out of the failure of both Liberals and Conservatives to sustain a parliamentary majority in 1852. In *Little Dorrit*, the ridiculous Lord Lancaster Stiltstalking regrets that the coalition had failed to muzzle the newspapers.[14] This government proved unequal to the political strains caused by the serious British mismanagement of the Crimean War. As seen with *Little Dorrit*, this failure helped to boost middle-class values of efficiency in politics at the expense of the aristocracy.

This tendency was linked to the movement of Whiggism to Liberalism in the 1850s and 1860s and to the tension within Liberalism between Whiggism and radicalism. In acquiring middle-class support, the Whigs to a degree became a party fitted for the reformist and increasingly assertive middle class, notably to the increasing numbers of middle-class Nonconformists who were critical of Church as well as State, for instance passing a Clean Air Act for London in 1852. Although there could be criticism of centralising government, and notably so in London, reform was central to Liberal appeal. Reform also ensured that there was a real difference to Conservative assumptions and interests.

This process, however, took a while. Reform, indeed, did not greatly advance under Palmerston, who was Prime Minister from 1855 to 1858 and 1859 to 1865. In December 1853, he had resigned as Home Secretary in protest against Russell's proposals for a reform bill. Palmerston returned to office only on the understanding that the proposals were off the table. Palmerston's liberalism was of the condescending type, and he was a noteworthy opponent of any extension of the franchise.

Leading the Liberals to victories in the elections of 1857, 1859 and 1865, Palmerston focused on foreign and imperial policy, but not domestic policy. The replacement of the East India Company with more direct British control of India after the Indian Mutiny of 1857–8 was a major change. Palmerston was criticised by Dickens in *Little Dorrit* as Lord Decimus, the Chief Barnacle. Merdle's dinner in that novel was designed as a 'Patriotic Conference', which was a reference to Palmerston's declamatory style in foreign policy. It also captured a nexus of political identity. So also in *Our Mutual Friend* in which Podsnap offers a simplistic account of international relations:

> Podsnap always talks Britain, and talks as if he were a sort of Private Watchman employed, in the British interests, against the rest of the world. 'We know what Russia means, sir,' says Podsnap; 'we know what France wants; we see what America is up to; but we know what England is. That's enough for us.' (*Our Mutual Friend* 67)

In contrast, William Ewart Gladstone, the Liberal Chancellor of the Exchequer from 1859, became an increasingly vigorous focus of radical hopes and a proponent of parliamentary reform. To Dickens, he was a more attractive Liberal than Palmerston.

Dickens' radicalism, indeed, was clear cut. It was seen in particular over the discussion of a strike in Lancastrian cotton mills against cutting wages. Dickens wrote of 'this unhappy class of society who find it so difficult to get a peaceful hearing'. Dickens was ready to refute the critics of strikers: 'Nor can I possibly adopt the representation that these men are wrong because, by throwing themselves out of work, they throw other people, possibly without their consent.' In response to Harriet Martineau's attack on Dickens as 'the humanity-monger', who should confine himself to fiction, he referred to her 'vomit of conceit'.[15] Dickens also mocked the criticism directed against the press when he referred to 'the statesman at the head of the Circumlocution Office, when that noble or right honourable individual sat a little uneasily in his saddle, by reason of some vagabond making a tilt at him in a newspaper'.[16] In April 1855, he wrote to Austen Henry Layard, a Liberal MP agitating against the lack of merit in public appointments, a damaging indictment of British politics that is worth quoting at length because it also reflected anxiety about what he saw as public disillusionment:

There is nothing in the present time at once so galling and so alarming to me as the alienation of the people from their own public affairs ... They have had so little to do with the Game through all these years of Parliamentary Reform, that they have sullenly laid down their cards and taken to looking on. The players who are left at the table do not see beyond it – conceive that the gain and loss and all the interest of the play are in their hands – and will never be wiser until they and the table and the lights and the money are all overturned together ... it is extremely like the general mind of France before the breaking out of the first Revolution, and is in danger of being turned by any one of a thousand accidents – a bad harvest – the last straw too much of aristocratic insolence or incapacity – a defeat abroad – a mere chance at home – into such a Devil of a conflagration as has never been beheld since. Meanwhile, all our English Tufthunting, Toad Eating, and other manifestations of accursed Gentility ... are expressing themselves every day. So, every day the disgusted millions with this unnatural gloom and calm upon them, are confirmed and hardened in the very worst of moods. Finally, round all this is an atmosphere of poverty, hunger, and ignorant desperation, of the mere existence of which, perhaps not one man in a thousand of those not actually enveloped in it, through the whole extent of this country, has the least idea. It seems to me an absolute impossibility to direct the spirit of the people at this pass, until it shows itself. If they would begin to bestir themselves in the vigorous national manner – if they would appear in Political Unons – array themselves peacefully, but in vast numbers, against a system that they knew to be rotten altogether, make themselves heard like the Sea, all round this Island – I for one should be in such a movement, heart and soul, and should think it a duty of the plainest kind to go along with it (and try to guide it), by all possible means ... until the people can be got up from the lethargy which is an awful symptom of the advanced state of their disease, I know of nothing that can be done beyond keeping their wrongs continually before them.[17]

In April 1859, Dickens launched *All The Year Round*, a weekly magazine, as a sequel to *Household Words*, with the dramatic *A Tale of Two Cities* appearing from the first issue. This magazine format was to affect his novels, leading to *Great Expectations* becoming a weekly serial in the magazine in 1860–1, rather than the planned monthly. Dickens then made changes to the novel before the three-volume edition appeared in 1861. The commitment that journalism brought to his writing was at one with Dickens' concerns, his engagement with the present, and his location in London. That novel looked back to the early nineteenth century but was affected by Dickens' commitment to improving present-day circumstances.

At the same time, the sombre approach taken by Dickens in particular from *Bleak House* (1852-3) became more insistent. Parents ruining their children offered a bitter and disturbing theme, one seen to refer to the nation and the family alike. In *A Tale of Two Cities* (1859), Tellson's Bank, an old-fashioned one, had partners happy with its

> ... incommodiousness ... Any one of these partners would have disinherited his son on the question of rebuilding Tellson's. In this respect the House was much on a par with the Country; which did very often disinherit its sons for suggesting improvements in laws and customs that had long been highly objectionable, but were only the more respectable.[18]

Dickens' increasingly dark and negative view of his times – 'an enormous black cloud of poverty in every town which is spreading and deepening every hour'[19] – can be taken too much at face value. The 1850s were seen at the time as a blessed period of stability and recovery after the travails of the period 1815–48. Britain was more stable than the Continent, and there was nothing anticipating the civil war in America. Ireland, in the post-Famine period, was unusually quiet. Despite the Crimean War, Britain's naval supremacy helped to achieve a *Pax Britannica* outside the continental landmasses which naval power could not reach so easily.

Moreover, legislative achievements were not negligible as, except on the franchise, Palmerston was pretty open-minded to reforms and was much guided by his Evangelical son-in-law, Antony, 7th Earl of Shaftesbury. Conservative policy, under both Edward, 14th Earl of Derby, Prime Minister in 1852, 1858–9 and 1866–8, and Disraeli, was not radically different in its policies. These were relatively easy years for the country.

13

THE 1860s

... the Station had swallowed up the playing-field. It was gone. The two beautiful hawthorn-trees, the hedge, the turf, and all those buttercups and daisies had given place to the stoniest of jolting roads ... The coach that had carried me away, was melodiously called Timpson's Blue-Eyed Maid, and belonged to Timpson, at the coach-office up-street; the locomotive engine that had brought me back, was called severely No. 97 and belonged to SER [South Eastern Railway], and was spitting ashes and hot-water over the blighted ground.

'Dulborough Town' (1860) sees Dickens capture the transformation of sights, smells and much else, with the train as a cause of lost innocence as well as a source of new experience including a degree of urbanisation. The situations of both Dickens and, even more, many of his readers and listeners revealed a continuing mix of improvement and dire circumstances, notably the problems of ill health. For example, the River Tyne was dredged from 1863 by the typical combination of a reforming body (the Tyne Improvement Commissioners), an able engineer (J. F. Ure), and new technology (the world's most powerful bucket dredgers). Yet, in 1866, 43 per cent of Newcastle's population was still living in dwellings of only one or two rooms. Moreover, as a reminder of the extent of dire circumstances, gastro-intestinal disorders linked to inadequate water and sewerage systems were responsible for very high infant mortality rates in crowded parts of Newcastle, Bradford and elsewhere. This was a background to the life of Dickens' audiences. He received good audiences for his public readings in Newcastle.

Middle-class interests and views increasingly set the legislative agenda, although aristocratic influences on policymaking remained strong. In July 1865, Palmerston, leading the Liberal Party, won an increased majority over the Conservatives in the general election. Dickens had turned down the offer of standing for the Liberals for Lambeth, a London seat, feeling: 'that I am more useful, more congenially occupied, and more free, out of Parliament than I could possibly be in it'.[1] That was an accurate response to his personality and circumstances. His preference for moral admonition as the means to social improvement did not suit him for electioneering or parliamentary politics. In *Our Mutual Friend* (1864–5), Dickens remarked with regard to government, 'God Save the Queen and Confound their politics.'

In *Our Mutual Friend*, Dickens had recently been very sceptical about the way that a parliamentary seat was allegedly bought, Veneering being expected by 'Britannia' to pay £5,000. This was more pertinent for earlier periods, although, even then, the control by patronage was often circumscribed by signs of local independence. Dickens' description of Veneering's ridiculous electioneering visit to the constituency of Pocket-Breaches makes it clear that the candidate has nothing significant to say.[2] The reference to turning out 'those terrible people for us' shows that Veneering and his conceited group are Tories. Yet, the second dinner at the Veneerings' house that is discussed indicates a nexus of politics and money in which inherited status is of limited significance:

A new race of intimate friends has sprung up at Veneering's since he went into Parliament for the public good, to whom Mrs Veneering is very attentive. These friends, like astronomical distances, are only to be spoken of in the very largest figures. Boots says that one of them is a Contractor who (it has been calculated) gives employment, direct and indirectly, to five hundred thousand men ... Buffer says that another of them hadn't a sixpence eighteen months ago, and, through the brilliancy of his genius in getting those shares issued at eighty-five, and buying them all up with no money and selling them at par for cash, has now three hundred and seventy-five thousand pounds ... Lady Tippins is eminently facetious on these Fathers of the Scrip-Church: ... inquiring whether ... they will make her fortune if she makes love to them? (*Our Mutual Friend* 50)

Dying in October 1865, Palmerston was succeeded as Liberal leader and Prime Minister by Lord John Russell, now 1st Earl Russell, who had earlier been Prime Minister from 1846 to 1852. However, with his party divided over the issue of parliamentary reform, he held office again only to 1866, as he was defeated over it, much to the disappointment of Dickens.[3]

Gladstone succeeded Russell as Liberal leader in 1868 when Victoria, to the surprise of Russell, invited Gladstone to become Prime Minister of a returning Liberal government. In 1865–6, Gladstone had been Liberal leader in the Commons, as Russell sat in the Lords. Dickens meanwhile continued a radical Liberal, albeit not to the satisfaction of all other radicals. In 1865, he was cross about his daughter Mary who was electioneering for a Conservative: 'Think of my feelings as a Radical Parent! The wrong-headed Member and his wife are the friends with whom she hunts, and she helps to receive (and *deceive*) the voters, which is very awful.'[4] More generally, Dickens thought the system of political life 'horribly rotten'.[5] He was a strong supporter of the popular pressure for manhood suffrage and the secret ballot:

As to the Reform question, it should have been, and could have been, perfectly known to any honest man in England that the more intelligent part of the great masses were deeply dissatisfied with the state of the representation, but were in a very moderate and patient condition, awaiting the better intellectual cultivation of numbers of their fellows. The old insolent resource of assailing them and statements that they were politically indifferent, has borne the inevitable fruit ... I have such a very small opinion of what the great-genteel have done for us, that I am very philosophical indeed concerning what the great vulgar may do.[6]

The Second Reform Act, passed in 1867 by a minority Tory government, pushed to the left by Liberal votes on which it was dependent, nearly doubled the existing electorate and, by offering household suffrage, gave the right to vote to about 60 per cent of adult males in boroughs. The Tories were less hopeful of the effects of redistributing parliamentary seats and of developing working-class support than some of Disraeli's rhetoric suggested. The Prime Minister, Derby, referred to a 'Leap in the Dark'. The partial exception to that was in Lancashire where popular Protestantism, which largely meant opposition to the Irish, was swinging opinion towards the Conservatives. Otherwise, the main resource of the Conservatives was to leave the county franchise almost unchanged, so that until the next Reform Act, that of 1884, there was a very lopsided electorate, one that was vastly more radical and 'democratic' in the boroughs than in the counties.

The clear Liberal victory in the following general election, that of December 1868, led to the first government of Gladstone. Driven by a sense of providential agency, Gladstone was a formidable and multifaceted individual of great determination and integrity, a Classical scholar and theological controversialist who had originally planned to be ordained, a hewer of trees and, like Dickens (whose writing he found in 1842 to be 'negative'[7]), a rescuer of prostitutes. A Tory Treasury minister in the 1830s, Gladstone became the leading Liberal politician of the age, committed to reform at home and a moral stance abroad, both aims joined in a conviction that religion was a key element and purpose of government and politics. These were not the assumptions, policies or politics of Palmerston.

Gladstone's political skills bridged the worlds of Parliament and of public meetings, for, under his leadership, Liberalism became a movement enjoying mass support. Able to present himself as popular, because he came from a commercial background, and not an aristocratic one, Gladstone appealed from Parliament to the public and sought to gain mass support for his politics of action and reform. Indeed, many of Chartism's ideas, including democratic accountability, influenced popular Liberalism from the 1850s. There was a growth in interest in the working class building up its own institutions, such as a multitude of friendly societies, and clubs, and in schemes for improving the physical and moral condition of working people through education and temperance.

Measures for change were swiftly introduced by Gladstone. Writing, in *Edwin Drood*, shortly before these innovations, Dickens still thought reference to the Circumlocution Office relevant, in the shape of 'My Lords of the Circumlocution Department, Commandership-in-Chief of any sort, Government'.[8] That, however, was a questionable view. It was certainly becoming more inaccurate. In 1870, the civil service was opened to open competition. The 1870 Education Act required a certain level of educational provision, introducing the School Board in cases where existing parish provision was inadequate. It often was. In *Our Mutual Friend*, Lizzie, who cannot read 'real books', had felt her 'want of learning very much'.[9] The idea of the 1870 Act was to supplement private provision by filling in the gaps where it was inadequate, not replacing it. In the event, the number of denominational schools rose sharply after 1870 as both the Church of England and the Roman Catholics founded additional schools to prevent Board Schools being established. Battles between the two sectors over financing provisions continued to 1914 and heightened party conflict, notably in the localities. Moreover, the Act gave largely permissive and enabling powers to the new local authorities (School Boards where they were needed), rather than giving the central government the requisite powers. The central state provided some finance and a system of inspection for elementary schooling, but it was not attempting to control schooling directly. Nor would contemporary opinion have permitted it to do so. Compulsory schooling was not introduced until 1881.

The end of long-established distinctions, variations and privileges played a major role in the reform process. The Endowed Schools Commission established in 1870 redistributed endowments and reformed governing bodies. The legislation owed much to Nonconformist pressure: Nonconformists, an increasingly key element in Liberal support and policy, saw education as critical to their Bible-centred religious views. For Dickens, the role of Nonconformity increased his ambivalence about the Liberals, and he was never exactly an orthodox party man. Dickens never took to Nonconformity, indeed depicting most Nonconformists in his novels as hypocrites. In addition, the power of Nonconformity meant pressure for anti-drink legislation, again not a cause Dickens liked. Gladstone may have appealed to Dickens in some respects, but was a pro-ritualist High Churchman of the sort Dickens detested.

Reform was also seen elsewhere. In the army, in which Dickens had condemned conditions in 1860, peacetime flogging was abolished in 1869. The purchase of commissions was ended. Also in 1869, the Church of Ireland was disestablished.

The sense of the past as the definition of what was seen as acceptable was increasingly made problematic by the process of a consideration of alternatives within the overall context of a strong commitment to reform. Reflecting a wider sense of new economic potential, and the resulting social and political transformation, this process affected government and public alike.

Dickens himself saw much more of Britain because of his frequent public readings, after he turned professional in 1858,[10] not least the criss-crossing by rail to fulfil itineraries that were not always logical. Thus, in January 1862, he noted the economic difficulties caused by the American Civil War (1861–5). While going by rail, he was running out of steam, but the popularity of the readings gave him a sense of closeness to the public, a closeness reciprocated by the latter. Dickens focused in these readings on his early novels, notably *Pickwick Papers*, *Oliver Twist* and *David Copperfield*, as well as *A Christmas Carol*. At the same time, his energy was accompanied by increasing ill health, resulting pain, anxieties about money, an awareness of the deaths of friends and others, and a difficulty in starting another major writing project.

Meanwhile, royal recognition was an acknowledgement of his fame. George III had been very pleased to meet Dr Johnson. When Dickens met Victoria in March 1870, she asked him for a set of his works and presented him with an autographed copy of her *Leaves from the Journal of Our Life in the Highlands*. This was recognition to match that from the public.

Dickens had lost none of his sympathy for the unfortunate, nor his biting hatred for complacency. This was seen, in *Our Mutual Friend*, at Mr Podsnap's party for his daughter's eighteenth birthday, when the death from starvation of poor people in the streets was mentioned. Podsnap first disbelieves the news, and then claims that it was 'their own fault', before praising poor relief in England, and accusing the 'man of meek demeanour' who had brought up the issue of 'Centralisation. No. Never with my consent. Not English.' This was countered by this man with a denial of 'any isation'. Podsnap closed by declaring that the situation was 'the workings of Providence', and the subject an 'odious one' from which women and the young should be spared.[11] Podsnap emerges as disgusting. With lashings of sarcasm for critics of the fears of the poor, Dickens subsequently shows much sympathy when discussing the fears of Betty Higden.

In *Edwin Drood*, Dickens identified a different target in Luke Honeythunder of the Philanthropists. As with Podsnap, there was a serious lack of consideration of others, but Honeythunder's loathsome complacency was of a more active character:

a scheme he had, for making a raid on all the unemployed persons in the United Kingdom, laying them everyone by the heels in jail, and forcing them, on pain of prompt extermination, to become philanthropists ... You were to abolish war, but were to make converts by making war upon them. ... Above all things, you were to do nothing in private, or on your own account ... you were to pay up your subscription.

It need hardly be said that Honeythunder was an officious disaster at dinner.[12] The depiction was a brief prelude to George Orwell's more developed *Animal Farm* (1945) and, indeed, captured the inhumanity of a socialist totalitarianism. There was a parallel also with Slackbridge, the dishonest Socialist orator in *Hard Times*.[13] Although he referred to Cain, Abel and the Ten Commandments, Honeythunder's philanthropy, which Dickens compared to that of 'mad Malays', was more secular than spiritual.[14]

In a critique not only of the French Revolution but of all revolutions, Dickens had warned, in the dying speech of *A Tale of Two Cities*, about 'the long ranks of the new oppressors who have risen on the destruction of the old', a theme that was to be taken up by George Orwell in *Animal Farm*.[15] That was indeed becoming apparent. So also was the destructive energy of the railway that seemed in *Our Mutual Friend* to be an image of the dissolution brought by time:

Then, the train rattled among the house-tops, and among the ragged sides of houses torn down to make way for it, and over the swarming streets, and under the fruitful earth, until it shot across the river: bursting over the quiet surface like a bomb-shell, and gone again as if it had exploded in the rush of smoke and steam and glare. A little more, and again it roared across the river, a great rocket: spurning the watery turnings and doublings with ineffable contempt, and going straight to its end, as Father Time goes to his. To whom it is no matter what living waters run high or low, reflect the heavenly lights and darknesses, produce their little growth of weeds and flowers, turn here, turn there, are noisy or still, are troubled or at rest, for their course has one sure termination, though their sources and devices are many. (*Our Mutual Friend* 61)

Dickens died in Gad's Hill Place on 9 June 1870, five years after the shock of the Staplehurst railway accident. He wished to be buried in Kent, but, instead, was interred as one of the greats in Westminster Abbey. He left £90,000, an immense sum for the age. His reputation was sustained, and 'Dickensland' developed, with John Forster's *The Life of Charles Dickens* published from 1871, Dickens' letters published from 1880, and works appearing about him. A celebrity in life, he was to maintain that place after death, albeit with his reputation changing in subsequent decades, and later.[16]

14

DICKENS'S AMERICA

America was the most dynamic society in the Western world, with a booming population and an expanding economy. Indeed, in 1816, Napoleon had told the British Governor of St Helena that America was rising on the back of the follies of Europe. It certainly offered Dickens an alternative society of largely British descent, and was presented as a place of opportunity, even, as in *Great Expectations*, of 'buying a rifle and going to America, with a general purpose of compelling buffaloes to make his fortune'.[1] In *Martin Chuzzlewit*, Bill Simmons, who had never been there, was confident that 'all men are alike in the U-nited States, an't they? It makes no odds whether a man has a thousand pound, or nothing, there.'[2]

The self-confidence of America was linked to a sense of national destiny that was seen in the engagement with American landscape as sublime and morally uplifting. This view was clearly demonstrated by the enthusiastic response to the self-consciously national Hudson River school of painters. Regarded as more vigorous and unspoiled than those of Europe, the American landscape also appealed to British visitors such as Richard

Cobden, while Dickens was enthralled by the sublimity of Niagara Falls in 1842.

Similarly, transcendentalist thought, combining Romanticism and Deism and associated with writers such as Ralph Waldo Emerson and Henry David Thoreau, reflected a strong American optimism and was seen as a declaration of independence from Church control and traditionalism. Emerson presented America as a visionary poem, a country of young men who, in 1775, had fired, at Lexington on 19 April, 'the shot heard round the world'. A Romanticism of national vision affected many individual Americans, and public culture as a whole. Dickens mocked this with the 'Literary Lady': 'Mind and matter glide swift into the vortex of immensity. Howls the sublime, and softly sleeps the calm Ideal, in the whispering chambers of Imagination.'[3]

To some British progressives, Britain and America could be seen as taking part in the same advance of progressive reform, notably Catholic emancipation and the Reform Act in Britain. There was a parallel with France under Louis Philippe (r. 1830–48). Some liberals and radicals, such as Cobden, who visited America in 1835, John Bright, and the Unitarian utilitarian Harriet Martineau, who published *Society in America* (1837), saw aspects of the country as a desirable model. Yet, there were also powerful cross-currents in Anglo-American relations, notably American anti-Toryism that affected the situation when there were Tory ministries in Britain, as well as a more general dislike of Britain for not being America and for being allegedly hostile to its policies, institutions and life.[4]

Moreover, the many Irish Catholics who settled in America tended to oppose Britain, often very strongly, and to support the Jacksonians (and later the Democrats), which, in turn, encouraged the rival American Whigs, as a key element of adopting and defining the nativist cause, to criticise the Catholics. This stance encouraged the Jacksonians, in tapping the breadth of Anglophobia, to label their opponents 'British Whigs'. British commentators opposed to reform were particularly hostile to

American populists such as Andrew Jackson, President from 1829 to 1837, a theme that was subsequently taken up by Walter Bagehot.

Britons' views of America were not simply an extrapolation of their political allegiances. There was also concern about American support for slavery and racism. Captain Basil Hill wrote from Fayetteville, North Carolina in 1828, 'Democracy and Slavery a preposterous medley,' and, in 1830, published *Travels in North America in the Years 1827 and 1828*. In *Martin Chuzzlewit*, Dickens is critical of slavery. However, Thackeray returned from his second lecture tour sympathetic to slavery. Very frequently, the high degree of Anglophobia British visitors experienced first-hand coloured their views of America. Furthermore, American politicians frequently spoke on the stump about their right to Canada, which annoyed British visitors including Frances Trollope and Frederick Marryat.

Alongside contempt for a range of factors including brawling patriotism,[5] Dickens found America exciting for the same reason as Alexis de Tocqueville, a French lawyer who visited the country in 1831. In the oft-cited *De la Démocratie en Amérique* (1835), de Tocqueville described a new type of society and political culture that was different from that of Europe, a mass society organised on the basis of an equality that ignored the aristocratic ethos of honour and threatened to create conformism, but that also had great potential. At the same time, de Tocqueville regarded the real transition as that from the old to the new, with the reforming monarchies of Europe, such as France after the 1830 revolution, which were also opposed to privilege. To Dickens, America had much to offer as a society that was not run by an aristocracy.

In 1842, when he visited for the first time, diplomatic relations between the two states were contentious. There were long-standing disputes over the boundaries of Maine and Minnesota, and over the situation in Canada. Alongside the refusal of the American government to support Quebec separatists, there was a different attitude on the part of some groups. This focused in an episode straight out of a novel. In an instance of anticipatory self-defence, an American ship, the *Caroline*, gun-running to Canadian rebels, had been intercepted by loyal Canadians in 1837 on the Niagara River in American waters, and one of the Americans on board, Amos Durfee, was killed before the ship was set on fire. In November 1840, Alexander McLeod, Deputy Sheriff to the Niagara District, was arrested in New York State and charged with the murder, even though he had probably not been on the Niagara River at the moment in question, while the British government had already informed the Americans that the interception was an official act, and not one for which individuals could be held responsible. The refusal of the American government to intervene in the judicial action of New York State led to bitter complaints in the British press. The British envoy was ordered to leave if McLeod was executed, and the American envoy in London reported on the possibility of war.[6] The Oregon Question – the allocation of the modern areas of British Columbia, Oregon and Washington – was also becoming more prominent as a cause of dispute.

Dickens therefore arrived in January 1842 against a background of contention, but also an ability to handle it without war. Bluster was not matched by action, but, repeatedly, was contained. Indeed, the Peel government brought the Maine and Minnesota borders to a conciliatory close with the Ashburton–Webster Treaty signed in Washington on 9 August 1842. This was criticised by some commentators, including Palmerston, as a weak step that failed to support the balance of power in North America or guarantee Canada's security. Nevertheless, Palmerston's criticisms did not find favour with his Whig colleagues, notably Russell. Palmerston was regarded as overly bellicose.

Aside from Dickens, particularly in *Martin Chuzzlewit*, many wrote about the United States, including Anthony Trollope. Both men were widely popular in America and taken by its energy and drive, yet often shocked by its 'vulgar' (populist) politics. And so more generally. The British attitude towards America was more generally ambivalent, and vice versa. In a pattern still seen today, a standard means of criticising a politician was to accuse him of the 'Americanisation' of British politics. At the same time, there were very strong financial and economic links between the United States and Britain. The financial links were not only with the City of London but also with some provincial cities, not least Liverpool. Much of the expansion of American railroads involved British capital. These links helped to stop lurches towards war, although, in themselves, they could not prevent war.

There was indeed much downright hostility between the two countries, as over the Crimean War (1854–6), when the Americans were regarded as supporting the Russians, and the American Civil War (1861–5). The latter divided British public opinion fairly widely. The South sought to win diplomatic recognition, a step that would have legitimated secession. There was sympathy in Britain for the South, not least as a result of the economic disruption arising from the war, especially in the important Lancashire cotton manufacturing industry, alongside opposition over slavery. However, fears that recognition of Southern independence would lead to war with the Union prevented it, as did the brake on Confederate success seen with the Battle of Antietam in 1862.

It was not only power politics that led to hostility. As America was brought nearer by steamship, and then by telegraph cable, there were also cultural and economic rivalries, with Dickens keenly feeling this the case over copyright law. Dickens was hit very hard by the breaching of his copyright in the United States, where his novels were popular. This long-standing issue more particularly helped poison Dickens' relationship with the American press, leading him to some of his most vituperative writing:

> As if a man could live in the United States a month, and not see [that] the whole country is led and driven by a herd of rascals, who are the human lice of God's creation! ... I never knew

what it was to feel disgust and contempt, 'till I travelled in America.[7]

In 1848, Dickens wrote to the actor William Macready, advising him against retiring in America in a letter that also highlighted the hazard of selective quotation:

Permit me in conclusion to nail my Colors to the Mast. Stars and Stripes are so-so-showy perhaps – but my colors is

THE UNION JACK

which I am told has the remarkable property of having braved a thousand years the battle and the breeze. Likewise it is the flag of Albion – the Standard of Britain – and Britons, as I am informed, never never never-will-be-Slaves!

There is not a throat in Britain, where its lies ... and shortcomings, stick more intolerably than in mine. And, as a general principle, I have no such thing as patriotism about me. But my sentiment is: – Success to the United States as a golden campaigning ground, but blow the United States to 'ternal [eternal] smash, as an Englishman's place of residence.[8]

The reference to patriotism is striking. Dickens was a very particular sort of Liberal, but not always a very consistent one.

In the event, Macready found America even more angering than Dickens had done in 1842, and notably its actors and press. The bloody riot by nativist zealots against Macready's final performance in *Macbeth* on 10 May 1849 in New York led Dickens to reflect:

... the scene astounds even me. I know perfectly well that many things may take place in the first City of the United States which could not possibly occur in a remote nook of any other country in the World, – but the bestiality of this business, and the incredible

business of that public opinion ... I regard as a positive calamity to
the rational freedom of men.

In the same letter, New York returned as 'that damnable
jumble of false pretensions and humbugs'.[9] Dickens particularly
disliked what he saw as American cant. He wrote from a personal
experience that was affected by his continuing subsequent
personal anger over copyright. In *Martin Chuzzlewit*, the wronged
Martin resolves to go to America, and maintains that resolution
despite Tom Pinch saying, 'Don't be so dreadfully regardless
of yourself.' In practice, the ship was uncomfortable for its
passengers, but a positive environment:

> Every kind of domestic suffering that is bred in poverty, illness,
> banishment, sorrow, and long travel in bad weather, was crammed
> into the little space; and yet was there infinitely less of complaint
> and querulousness, and infinitely more of mutual assistance and
> general kindness to be found in that unwholesome ark, than in
> many brilliant ball-rooms.[10]

The American press of that period, and notably so in New York,
was notorious for inaccuracy and sensationalism, and celebrities,
often the focus of such accounts, fell victim to this process. This
was especially so if, like Dickens, they were foreigners.

A writer happiest with drawing on his own varied experience
for his work, Dickens benefited from his visits to the United
States. They provided him with a direct view of another British
society, one that had taken a different trajectory less than a
century earlier. Moreover, the high rate of British migration to
the United States in the intervening period, a rate higher than that
to any British colony, ensured that there were continuing close
links at a personal level that very much encouraged individual
reflection on similarities and contrasts. The United States
provided a different image of a counterfactual Britain, but also,
as such, offered reflections on Britain itself. There was a very

different monarch, in the shape of the President, and an élite that was less dominated by a landed interest, and certainly not by a titled hereditary aristocracy.

On the other hand, the United States was still a slave society, and this made it deeply abhorrent to Dickens, leading him to take American protestations of freedom as hypocritical, as with Mr Chollop in *Martin Chuzzlewit*.[11] Moreover, slavery was repeatedly a theme in his novels when describing unacceptable circumstances in England, as in *Dombey and Son*, where Carker presents himself and Edith as linked in 'old slavery' to Dombey, while in *Edwin Drood* there is also reference to garnishing 'the exhausted Negroes' in an account of a dark and depressing dining room, and the flying waiter is treated as 'this slave' by the immovable waiter.[12] Indeed, some Americans, for example Charles Lester, author of *The Glory and Shame of England* (1841) and a prominent abolitionist, saw the plight of the English poor as worse than that of slaves. Lester read *Oliver Twist* and cited it with approval.[13]

Aside from outrage, Dickens linked the situation in America to that in Britain in a way different to that of most abolitionists:

> I believe it is in New Orleans that the man is lying under sentence of death, who, not having the fear of God before his eyes, did not deliver up a captive slave to the torture? The largest gun in that country has not burst yet – *but it will*. Heaven help us, too, from explosions nearer home! I declare I never go into what is called 'society' that I am not aweary of it, despise it, hate it, and reject it. The more I see of its extraordinary conceit, and its stupendous ignorance of what is passing out of doors, the more certain I am that it is approaching the period when, being incapable of reforming itself, it will have to submit to be reformed by others off the face of the earth.[14]

Yet, as with many in Britain, Dickens had mixed views on the Civil War, being dubious of Northern claims, as he had earlier shown when discussing abolitionist hypocrisy in *Martin Chuzzlewit*.[15] In 1862, Dickens argued that the war was complex, writing that March:

> I take the facts of the American quarrel to stand thus. Slavery has in reality nothing on earth to do with it, in any kind of association with any generous or chivalrous sentiment on the part of the North. But the North having gradually got to itself the making of the laws and the settlement of the Tariffs, and having taxed the South most abominably for its own advantage, began to see, as the country grew, that unless it advocated the laying down of a geographical line beyond which slavery should not extend, the South would necessarily recover its old political power, and be able to help itself a little in the adjustment of commercial affairs. Every reasonable creature may know, if willing, that the North hates the Negro, and that until it was convenient to make a pretence that sympathy with him was the cause of the War, it hated the abolitionists and derided them up hill and down dale. For the rest, there is not a pin to choose between the two parties. They will both rant and lie and fight until they come to a compromise; and the slave may be thrown into that compromise or thrown out of it, just as happens.[16]

There were parallels here with Dickens' discussion of British politics in *Little Dorrit*. Three years later, he had not changed his views, which made him, as he noted, a 'Southern Sympathiser', as he did not 'believe in the Northern love of the black man, or in the Northern horror of Slavery having anything to do with the beginning of the war' except as a pretext.[17] Gladstone was also a 'Southern sympathiser'.

Dickens' sympathy with those of African descent was not confined to America, but was shown in the account of a night touring Liverpool with the police given in his 'Poor Mercantile Jack' in *The Uncommercial Traveller* (1860):

> The male dancers were all blacks, and one was an unusually powerful man of six feet three or four. The sound of their flat

feet on the floor was as unlike the sound of white feet as their faces were unlike white faces. They toed and heeled, shuffled, double-shuffled, double-double-shuffled, covered the buckle, and beat the time out, rarely, dancing with a great show of teeth, and with a childish good-humoured enjoyment that was very prepossessing. They generally kept together, these poor fellows, said Mr Superindendent, because they were at a disadvantage single, and liable to slights in the neighbouring streets. But, if I were Light Jack, I should be very slow to interfere oppressively with Dark Jack, for, whenever I have had to do with him I have found him a simple and a gentle fellow.

Dickens also presented in this account a positive view of the relationship between black men and white women. By the time of his visit to America in 1867–8, slavery had been abolished.

Although, after mentioning serious flaws, he had compared America to a Phoenix 'for its power of springing from the ashes of its faults and vices, and soaring up anew into the sky!',[18] Dickens did not warm toward American policy. After the end of the Civil War, he remarked, 'If the Americans don't embroil us in a war before long it will not be their fault. What with their swagger and bombast, what with their claims … I have strong apprehensions with a settled animosity toward the French usurper [Napoleon III], I believe him to have always been sound in his desire to divide the States against themselves, and that we were unsound and wrong in "letting I dare not wait upon I would".'[19] This was a reference to Napoleon III's unsuccessful attempt in 1862 to persuade Britain to a joint Anglo-French mediation of the war. This step would have entailed recognition of the Confederacy and war with the Union.

Yet, Dickens was cheered by the great success of his 1867–8 tour to America, where his average evening profit was close to three times as much as his Farewell Lectures brought in Britain.[20] He also found Boston and New York much changed, especially the latter. Dickens again met friendship and experienced celebrity. While remaining to a degree wary of American politics (seeing it as like 'England governed by the Marylebone vestry and the penny papers'[21]), power and intentions, Dickens, who was received by President Andrew Johnson at the White House, praised America. He did so notably at the Press Dinner held in Delmonico's in New York on 18 April 1868, an occasion that was much reported. In this speech, Dickens noted what he saw as the great improvement since his first visit.

15

BRITAIN AND THE WORLD

Mr Towlinson reserves his sentiments on this question, being rendered something gloomy by the engagement of a foreigner with whiskers (Mr Towlinson is whiskerless himself), who has been hired to accompany the happy pair to Paris, and who is busy packing the new chariot. In respect of this personage, Mr Towlinson admits, presently, that he never knew of any good that ever come of foreigners, and being charged by the ladies with prejudice, says, look at Bonaparte who was at the head of 'em, and see what *he* was always up to! Which the housemaid says is very true.[1]

In the person both of the Dombey butler, Towlinson, and of Podsnap, who 'would conclusively observe, "Not English"', Dickens, who once referred to France as 'that detestable nation', nevertheless chided the xenophobia of many of his contemporaries.[2] In practice, steam and the telegraph brought Britain and the world closer, and Dickens benefited from each.

The Calais-Dover telegraph cable was laid in 1851 and this dramatically speeded up the process by which news of abroad was spread. The public responded with engagement, but that was already well developed. Londoners' awareness of international issues was not simply abstract. Workers were angered in 1850 by the visit of Julius Haynau, an Austrian general who had played an allegedly cruel role in the suppression of the 1848–9 Hungarian revolution. Haynau was set upon by a crowd of London draymen. Conversely, when the liberal hero of the same, defeated, revolution – Lajos Kossuth – fled to England the following year, he was entertained officially by the Lord Mayor and Corporation, and thousands of Londoners cheered his procession through the city. In 1864, the visiting Italian liberal hero Giuseppe Garibaldi was similarly applauded by working-class crowds, especially by Protestants. He could not land at Portsmouth because the crowds were so large.[3] Dickens shared these values. He made clear his support for the Roman Republic and Giuseppe Mazzini against the French military imposition of papal control in 1849:

> Disgust with that detestable nation the French, and admiration of Mazzini and his friends, have divided my thoughts for the last three months. I am very anxious Mazzini should come home and not get into danger, for the world cannot well afford to lose such men.[4]

Dickens added criticism of the governor of the British colony of Malta, a Catholic, who had refused to admit Italian refugees. Italian unification remained a cause that Dickens held dear, and, in 1866, he referred accordingly to 'the God of Free Nations and just Battles'.[5] In England, as in Birkenhead in 1862, Catholics could be very hostile to favourable mention of Garibaldi.[6]

This was a world in which the British empire was a potent and growing process, but where the personal and work links of many Britons were with the Continent. Indeed, Dickens visited the United States and nearby Continental Europe, but no British colonies. In 1862, he was offered £10,000 for an eight-month tour of Australia. Despite Dickens' concern about money and his hope of experiences he could use to help his writing, he turned the offer down, but it showed what was possible. His son

Alfred indeed went to Australia in 1865 to 'get some mercantile employment'.[7] Trade as an opportunity was touched on at the start of *David Copperfield*, with David referring to an old lady who

> to the last expressed her indignation at the impiety of mariners and others, who had the presumption to go 'meandering' about the world. It was in vain to represent to her that some conveniences, tea perhaps included, resulted from this objectionable practice. She always returned, with greater emphasis and with an instinctive knowledge of the strength of her objection, 'Let us have no meandering.'[8]

The trans-oceanic world certainly offered much for the imagination. The source of such imagination is captured in *David Copperfield* in which the young David, the fictional character closest to Dickens himself,

> had a greedy relish for a few volumes of Voyages and Travels ... and for days and days I can remember to have gone about my region of our house, armed with the centre-piece out of an old set of boot-trees – the perfect realisation of Captain Somebody, of the Royal British Navy, in danger of being beset by savages, and resolved to sell his life at a great price.[9]

That perspective changes when David is ten and goes to work at Murdstone and Grinby's warehouse: 'an important branch of it was the supply of wines and spirits to certain packet ships ... some among them made voyages both to the East and West Indies.'[10]

The heroic Walter in *Dombey and Son* makes money on the China trade; although in an unspecified fashion. In *Our Mutual Friend*, Bella on the Thames imagines

> all sorts of voyages for herself and Pa. Now, Pa, in the character of owner of a lumbering square-sailed collier, was tacking away

to Newcastle, to fetch black diamonds to make his fortune with; now, Pa was going to China in that handsome three-masted ship, to bring home opium ... and to bring home silks and shawls without end for the decoration of his charming daughter ... There would embark in that troop-ship ... a mighty general ... who wouldn't hear of going to victory without his wife, and she was destined to become the idol of all the red coats and blue jackets below and aloft. And then again: you saw that ship being towed out by a steam-tug? ... She was going among the coral reefs and cocoa-nuts and all that sort of thing ... to fetch a cargo of sweet-smelling woods ... the lovely woman who had purchased her and fitted her expressly for this voyage, being married to an Indian Prince, who was a Something-or-Other, and who wore Cashmere shawls all over himself, and diamonds and emeralds blazing in his turban, and was beautifully coffee-coloured and excessively devoted, though a little too jealous.[11]

A far less encouraging account of opium is offered with death by opium overdose in *Bleak House*,[12] and, more dramatically, in the beginning of *The Mystery of Edwin Drood* with the description of a London opium den, which Dickens had researched by visiting one in Shadwell in 1869. This description also captures the role of both foreigners and natives. The bed in which the English narrator lies taking opium also holds 'Jack Chinaman' wrestling 'with one of his many Gods or Devils, perhaps' and snarling 'horribly'; a Lascar laughing and dribbling at the mouth; and a haggard woman who makes up the pipes, who 'has opium-smoked herself into a strange likeness of the Chinaman. His form of cheek, eye, and temple, and his colour, are repeated in her.'[13] This writing was very much in the style of Arthur Conan Doyle.

Returning to a more positive imagination, Herbert Pocket fantasises about trading 'to the East Indies, for silks, shawls, spices, dyes, drugs, and precious woods ... to the West Indies, for sugar, tobacco, and rum. Also to Ceylon, specially for elephants' tusks'.[14] Indeed, in London, 'half-naked shivering figures stopped to gaze at Chinese shawls and golden stuffs of India'.[15] Edwin

Drood plans to marry and 'go engineering into the East', thus 'to change the whole condition of an undeveloped country'. However, the Landless wards who arrive in Cloisterham come from Ceylon where their mother dies while they are young, leaving them to a cruel stepfather. The causes of the violent attitude of Neville Landless are possibly this, but there is also a reference to the Tropics: 'There is something of the tiger in his dark blood', and he has 'dark skin'.

Emigration attracts a number of Dickensian characters, and for different reasons. Augustus Moddle runs off to Van Dieman's Land (correctly Van Diemen's Land, from 1856 Tasmania) to escape marriage to Charity Pecksniff.[16] The feckless Tip Dorrit abandons his intended emigration to Canada at Liverpool,[17] but Clara Copperfield's neighbours, the Graypers, go to South America.[18] Micawber is encouraged to think of emigration, which is taken to mean Australia. He seeks reassurance on the grounds of climate and opportunities, being reassured on both by Betsey Trotwood: 'Mrs Micawber presently discoursed about the habits of the kangaroo!' The departure of the emigrant ship in this novel is a fine piece of writing, and it also takes with it Martha and Emily, each hopefully in Dickens' eyes to find redemption: 'Heaven bless you, you good man. You take her with you!'[19] Once in Australia, Micawber is a success.

Empire as the means to soak up those for whom there is no place at home and, less positively, to harbour the difficult was glanced at in the scene-setting of *David Copperfield* alongside an amusing instance of the propensity of those at a distance to be the cause of inaccurate reports. Betsey Trotwood's husband, separated on the grounds of his incompatibility and cruelty,

> went to India with his capital, and there, according to a wild legend in our family, he was once seen riding on an elephant, in company with a Baboon; but I think it must have been a Baboo – or a Begum. Anyhow, from India tidings of his death reached home, within ten years.[20]

Dickens' lifetime saw a major territorial expansion of the empire, and also an intensification of imperial relationships. Thus, 'emigrant ships'[21] helped link the homeland to some of the colonies. In 1815–30, a period of post-war depression and apparent overpopulation, when emigration was seen as a useful device for Britain, the majority of emigrants from the British Isles went to Canada, where most immigrants came from the British Isles. This growth was sustained by the Canada Company, a private enterprise established by John Galt and chartered in 1825. Investors provided the capital with which just over a million hectares of land were purchased, while the company laid out townships and attracted settlers. Thanks to trans-oceanic steamship services, the average ocean crossing between England and Halifax fell from forty days in 1837 to twelve days westbound in 1852. Steamships also cut the cost of migration. The size and cost of these new ships ensured a need for more emigrants.

Compared with Canada, the number of migrants was lower to far more distant Australia, which suffered from its reputation as a penal destination – a total of 158,000 convicts were sent there, and it was also a dumping ground for other unwanted groups, such as demobilised troops. However, numbers received a boost in 1829 when Britain annexed Western Australia and established its first settlement there as the centre of a free colony. Furthermore, the sale (as opposed to grant) of Crown lands was seen as a way to encourage settlement by providing funds to pay transport costs, and the establishment in 1830 of the National Colonisation Society by Edward Gibbon Wakefield was designed, at a time of growing economic expansion in Britain, to encourage more selective emigration, and thus to enhance the value of colonies. Wakefield's ideas influenced bounty policies introduced from 1832, and were taken up by the South Australian Association which founded a colony in 1836. The New Zealand Association followed in 1837. The role of convicts in imperial settlement diminished, as no more were sent to New South Wales after 1840, or to Tasmania after 1852, and although Western Australia had responded to labour shortages in 1850 by requesting convicts, none were sent after 1868.

The colonies, which were increased by major territorial expansion, provided raw materials, markets and employment, as with 'the huge piles of building belonging to the sugar refiners' mentioned by Dickens in *The Uncommercial Traveller* in 'Wapping Workhouse' (1860). Yet, not all trans-oceanic trade with the empire was in an imperial context, the United States being an important partner. That is referred to by Dickens in his piece 'Poor Mercantile Jack'. In this, criticising the plight of sailors, he asks a fundamental question about the profit motive:

> Is it unreasonable to entertain a belief that if, aboard the brig Beelzebub or the barque Bowie-knife, the first officer did half the damage to cotton that he does to men, there would presently arise from both sides of the Atlantic so vociferous an invocation of the sweet little cherub who sits calculating aloft, keeping watch on the markets that pay, that such vigilant cherub would, with a winged sword, have that gallant officer's organ of destructiveness out of his head in the space of a flash of lightning.

This was also a reference to the dependence of the trade on slavery in America.

Combined with Evangelicalism, imperial expansion encouraged a perception of Britain as at the cutting edge of civilisation. The cultural and ideological factors focused on the attraction of empire were such that imperialism became normative. This drew on a sense of mission, as well as triumphalism, racialism and cultural arrogance. All supported a belief that the West was unbeatable, and was bringing civilisation to a benighted world, not least by ending what were seen as uncivilised and un-Christian practices, such as widow-burning (*sati*), abolished in Bengal in 1829, and ritual banditry (*thuggee*) in India. Captain Swosser of the Royal Navy, a 'very distinguished officer' and Mrs Bayham Badger's first husband, contracts yellow fever on the

Africa Station,[22] where slavers were hunted. The achievements of the warships were celebrated in Britain. Thus, the capture of the slave schooner *Bolodora* by HMS *Pickle* in 1829 led to a painting by William Huggins that was engraved by Edward Duncan.

Heroic literature was produced by a number of writers, including Frederick Marryat (1792–1848). A veteran of the Napoleonic Wars, Marryat was senior naval officer at Rangoon in 1824 during the First Burmese War. He made his name with *The Naval Officer or Scenes and Adventures in the Life of Frank Mildmay* (1829), a narrative of naval exploits based on his experiences which was a tremendous literary and financial success. Other naval adventures followed, including *The King's Own* (1830) and *Peter Simple* (1834), which drew on Marryat's services in the Napoleonic Wars, as well as *Jacob Faithful* (1834), *Mr Midshipman Easy* (1836), *The Pirate, and the Three Cutters* (1836), *The Phantom Ship* (1839) and *The Privateer's Man* (1846). For children, an important market, Marryat wrote *Masterman Ready, or the Wreck of the Pacific* (1841), a tale of a marooned family.

Yet, Queen Victoria's Proclamation to the People of India of 1858 repudiated any right or desire to impose Christianity on her subjects and promised all, irrespective of religion, the rights of law; although this did not stop missionary activity, which, indeed, was generally treated (although not by Dickens) in a hagiographical fashion as in the response to the life and death of David Livingstone.[23]

Dickens was cautious about any assumption of superiority. Planning *Household Words*, he considered a piece that did not in the event appear: 'A history of savages, showing the singular respects in which all savages are like each other; and those in which civilised men, under circumstances of difficulty, soonest become like savages.'[24] Dickens could also criticise those in favour of missionary work in Africa, as in *Little Dorrit*.[25] Mrs Jellyby in *Bleak House* is one of his comically horrid philanthropists:

She has devoted herself to an extensive variety of public subjects ... and is at present (until something else attracts her) devoted to the subject of Africa; with a view to the general cultivation of the coffee berry – *and* the natives – and the happy settlement, on the banks of the African rivers, of our super-abundant home population.[26]

Mrs Jellyby is shown to be neglectful of her family, home and cooking. Mr Quale wants the natives taught 'to turn pianoforte legs and establish an export trade'. Yet, as Dickens correctly notes in *A Tale of Two Cities*, Londoners had been 'but newly released from the horror of being ogled through the windows, by the heads exposed on Temple Bar with an insensate brutality and ferocity worthy of Abyssinia or Ashantee'.[27]

Empire, moreover he shows, can be unsatisfactory and the source of unpleasant attitudes in England. David Copperfield finds 'Jack Maldon was not at all improved by India', and, instead, arrogant and callous toward the plight of others in England: 'There's an account about the people being hungry and discontented down in the North, but they are always being hungry and discontented somewhere.'[28]

Another aspect of imperial arrogance was provided by hunting, for which empire provided an unprecedented opportunity. This was taken up with relish not only by individual hunters, for whom it served to display prowess and skill, but also by a press that was keen to recount their achievements, and by writings of adventure stories, such as Robert Ballantyne in *The Gorilla Hunter* (1861). The activities of hunters, especially their 'bags', were recorded in photographs, and photography was also used to capture and classify images of imperial people. Clashes with the latter provided part of the narrative of hunters' accounts, whether in publications or in lectures.

While Dickens' collected Napier's *Peninsula War*, military glory, a key element in national survival and imperial expansion, was scarcely to the fore in his attention. Indeed, the account of the military review at Rochester exposes not only the Pickwickians, who were its eager spectators, but also, to a degree, the army to humour:

> Colonel Bulder, in full military uniform, on horseback, galloping first to one place and then to another, and backing his horse among the people, and prancing, and curvetting, and shouting in a most alarming manner, and making himself very hoarse in the voice, and very red in the face, without any assignable cause or reason whatever.[29]

In a somewhat ridiculous fashion, Micawber ends his long letter attacking Uriah Heep:

> Let it be, in justice, merely said of me, as of a gallant and eminent naval Hero, with whom I have no pretensions to cope, that what I have done, I did, in despite of mercenary and selfish objects, 'For England, home, and Beauty.'[30]

More positively, Bucket in *Bleak House* likes to hear the 'British Grenadiers' tune, and the Bagnet family provide an attractive instance of life in the aftermath of military service.[31]

The values of Dickens' childhood, when Britain was emerging victorious from the Napoleonic War, are echoed in *Edwin Drood* when the complacent auctioneer Sapsea gives the toast:

> 'When the French come over,
> May we meet them at Dover!'
> … a patriotic toast in Mr Sapsea's infancy, and he is therefore fully convinced of its being appropriate to any subsequent era.

Sapsea subsequently returns to his theme, making it 'pretty clear that Providence made a distinct mistake in originating so small a nation of hearts of oak, and so many other verminous peoples'. Dickens rejects the prejudice: 'when Mr Sapsea has once declared anything to be un-English, he considers that thing everlastingly sunk in the bottomless pit.'[32]

The values of society were commented on by Dickens when he reflected that 'while statues are erected to fighting men by sea and land, I like one to be put up now and then, in honor of that amiable Dragon, Intellect, which Saint George (in his court-dress) is rather fond of riding over'.[33] In response to the difficult and costly victory over the Sikhs at Chillianwallah, Dickens wrote in 1849: 'Indian news bad indeed. Sad things come of bloody war. If it were not for Elihu, I should be a peace and arbitration man' – Elihu Burritt being a somewhat foolish American pacifist. Dickens was not keen on some of those involved in particular causes that otherwise he viewed with some favour. Later that year, Dickens declined to join the General Peace Congress held in Paris with Victor Hugo in the chair and a number of British participants including Cobden.

Returning to his characters, Dickens sometimes showed them with few options as when David Copperfield tells his aunt that he 'must think of his future, there are few occupations to consider, soldier and sailor being two'. In *Bleak House*, Mrs Rouncewell's younger son 'ran wild, and went for a soldier, and never came back'.[34] A grimmer view was taken in 'The Great Tasmania's Cargo' (1860). The contrast then is drawn between 'the great battles of the great Indian campaign', a reference to the suppression in 1857–9 of the Indian Mutiny, and the appalling circumstances of military life. For the first, Dickens writes:

Any animated description of a modern battle, any private soldier's letter published in the newspapers, any page of the records of the Victoria Cross, will show that in the ranks of the army, there exists under all disadvantages as fine a sense of duty as is to be found in any station on earth. Who doubts that if we all did our duty as faithfully as the soldier does his, this world would be a better place?

The shocking state of sick and wounded soldiers is the focus of this powerful piece, one that was well grounded in actual circumstances and that also enabled Dickens to make broader points. He had a personal commitment to the army. In 1863, his second son, Walter, who was serving in India with the army, but a disappointment to Dickens,[35] died of an aneurism. Of his other sons, Frank was sent to join the Bengal Mounted Police, while Henry served on the Africa Station where the navy was principally involved in stopping illegal slave trading.

His imperial connections contributed to Dickens' strong response at the time of criticism in Britain of Edward Eyre, Governor of Jamaica, who, in 1865, had proclaimed martial law and very harshly suppressed the Morant Bay Rebellion. Other factors also played a role in Dickens response, including anger at what he saw as a mismatch between the response to hardship abroad and at home, as well as his view that missionaries were humbugs:

> The Jamaica insurrection is another hopeful piece of business. That platform – sympathy with the black – or the native, or the devil – afar off, and that platform indifference to our own countrymen at enormous odds in the midst of bloodshed and savagery, makes me stark wild. Only the other day, here was a meeting of jawbones of asses at Manchester, to censure the Jamaica Governor for his manner of putting down the insurrection! So we are badgered about New Zealanders and Hottentots, as if they were identical with men in clean shirts at Camberwell ... But for the blacks in Jamaica being over-impatient and before their time, the whites might have been exterminated.[36]

Drawing probably on this episode, Dickens referred to popular reports about imperial cruelty when he mocked the foolish reports about Neville Landless, the alleged murderer of Edwin Drood:

> Before coming to England he had caused to be whipped to death sundry 'Natives' – nomadic persons, encamping now in Asia, now in Africa, now in the West Indies, and now at the North Pole –

vaguely supposed in Cloisterham to be always black, always of great virtue, ... and always reading tracts of the obscurest meaning, in broken English, but always accurately understanding them in the purest mother tongue.[37]

With less force, the *thuggees* in India are mentioned in *Dombey and Son*, as is the burning of widows, and the great wealth to be obtained there.[38] In *Our Mutual Friend*, Riah, a Jew, is a positive figure, countering Fagin in *Oliver Twist*, although the evil of the latter is presented as no different from that of Monks, a Christian character. Dickens' correspondence reveals anti-Semitic comments, but, with Riah, he notes that Jews are uniquely badly treated as only with them are the bad that are in every group seen as indicative of all the group.[39]

Often seen as a quintessentially English figure, Dickens became very much an international one, his works much translated, and he with personal experience of France, Italy, Switzerland and the United States, and at a time of rapid and incessant political change and tension in all four. He also was fully aware of the culture of France. John Forster recorded of Dickens soon making himself: 'familiar in the streets of Genoa ... The ugliness of the old woman, begotten of hard work and a burning sun, with porters' knots of coarse grey hair grubbed up over wrinkled and cadaverous faces, he thought quite stupendous.'[40]

Dickens' response was an aspect of a more general engagement with the Continent, or at least at the level of the upper and middle classes. Music and intellectual life were particularly important spheres of Continental influence in British life. Thus, London was open to Continental influences in music. Johann Strauss the Elder and his orchestra came over for Victoria's coronation in 1838, and was extremely successful, and in 1847 Verdi produced his new opera, *I Masnadieri*, at Covent Garden, winning a good response. Continental pianists, such as Franz Liszt in 1827, were very popular in London.

Possibly more surprising to modern readers, accustomed to consider the classics of their own literature, was the popularity of foreign fiction. This was far from exclusively French, but French fiction was very important in the English literary world. French novels were important in terms of private purchase, and with reference to libraries and periodical reviews. There was criticism in England of this commercial and literary role, as by John Wilson Croker in the *Quarterly Review* of 1836, but French novels, mostly in translation, took an increasingly important part, one that lasted for several decades. Novelists such as Balzac, Alexandre Dumas and Eugène Sue were widely read and affected the discussion in England about the content and style of fiction as well as raising issues of cultural competition.

While the private reading of French novels concerned moralists, whose eighteenth-century predecessors had been worried about the reading of any novels, the public nature of what was available was also at issue.[41] This was significant for Dickens. On one level, English novelists, such as Dickens, can be understood as stimulated by similar drives and issues to those of many French contemporaries. He was also influenced by the writings of some of these, and knew others. At the same time, the popularity of Dickens in part arose as a response to the influence of the French novelists. The latter were perceived as rivals by some English commentators. Moreover, whatever the similarities, the French writers had less depth within English culture, society and politics. There was no comparison, for example, with Dickens' role in English political journalism, nor with his public readings.

Well read in French novels and able to depict both Paris past, in *A Tale of Two Cities*, and an attractive view of Paris's dynamism, in *Bleak House*, Dickens also greatly praised Charles Fechter, a leading French actor who presented not only French roles, such as Ruy Blas, but also Shakespearean classic parts, notably Hamlet on the London stage in 1862: 'You were never in pain for him as a foreigner.'[42] Ready to look at individual merit, rather than collective guilt, Dickens was no xenophobe. He had a positive vision for France, as in the last speech given to Sydney Carton as he faced the decapitating Terror of the French Revolution:

I see a beautiful city and a brilliant people rising from this abyss, and, in their struggles to be truly free, in their triumphs and defeats, through long years to come, I see the evil of this time and of the previous time of which this is the natural birth, gradually making expiation for itself and wearing out.[43]

Moreover, Dickens could put nationalism in the voice of the villain, as when the accused Artful Dodger declared, 'I'm an Englishman, an't I. Where are my priwileges?'[44] Individual fragments might not seem to amount to much, and have to be cited with care, but a theme in *Oliver Twist* is of the questionable superiority of English arrangements. Soon after in the story, Nancy complains about the lack of charitable feelings of 'those who claim to be God's own folks', leading to the response from Mr Brownlow:

A Turk turns his face, after washing it well, to the East, when he says his prayers; these good people, after giving their faces such a rub against the World as to take the smiles off, turn, with no less regularity, to the darkest side of Heaven. Between the Mussulman and the Pharisee, commend me to the first![45]

Given his views of English life and institutions, it is scarcely surprising that Dickens could be sceptical about any idea of automatic national superiority, as in *Edwin Drood*:

that sensitive constitution, the property of us Britons: the odd fortune of which sacred institution it is to be in exactly equal degrees croaked about, trembled for, and boasted of, whatever happens to anything, anywhere in the world.[46]

He addressed the issue of supposed superiority at great length in *Little Dorrit*, where John Baptist Cavalletto, a 'lame foreigner', proves a positive addition to the poor inhabitants of Bleeding Heart Yard. There is a sign of Dickens' views in his response: 'Solitary, weak, and scantily acquainted with the most necessary words of the only language in which he could communicate with the people about him, he went with the stream of his fortunes, in a brisk way that was new in those parts.' Dickens pressed on to consider the xenophobia of the locals:

> In the first place, they were vaguely persuaded that every foreigner had a knife about him; in the second, they held it to be a ... axiom that he ought to go home to his own country ... In the third place, they had a notion that it was a sort of Divine visitation upon a foreigner that he was not an Englishman, and that all kinds of calamities happened to his country because it did things that England did not, and did not do things that England did.
>
> ... They believed that foreigners had no independent Spirit, as never being escorted to the poll in droves by Lord Decimus Tite Barnacle, with colours flying and the tune of Rule Britannia playing.[47]

Given Dickens' strongly presented view of the Barnacles, the point is very clear. Cavalletto is totally different to Riguad in *Little Dorrit*, the very embodiment of the sinister foreigner lurking in London.

The interaction of personality and culture is separately captured with the vicious intentions of Ralph Nickleby, who wishes harm for his nephew Nicholas: 'If we were only citizens of a country where it could be safely done, I'd give good money to have him stabbed to the heart and rolled into the kennel for the dogs to tear.'[48] Ralph is English. Neither virtue nor vice was national in origin in Dickens' accounts. While patriotic, he disliked mindless patriotism.

16

DICKENS IN RETROSPECT

Ethelinda,
Reverential Wife of
Mr Thomas Sapsea,
Auctioneer, Valuer, Estate Agent, etc,
Of This City
Whose Knowledge of the World,
Though somewhat extensive,
Never brought him acquainted with
A Spirit
More capable of
Looking up to him.
Stranger, Pause
And ask thyself the Question,
Canst Thou Do Likewise?
If Not,
With A Blush Retire.[1]

The desire to impress not just the present but also the future
affects many of the pompous characters in Dickens' works. Unlike

Hardy, whose characters are often punished for morality, Dickens presented family and kindness as the best way to make a positive impression, and, while in practice finding that the former did not meet his often unreasonable expectations, was able to meet with a good response for the latter. Alongside the savagery of many of his passages, indeed an anger that helped cause a strong streak of nastiness, his writing, he argued, was a form of kindness. Greatly buoyed by the success of *Dombey and Son*, Dickens wrote in 1848:

> Although Literature as a profession has no distinct status in England, I am bound to say that what I experience of its recognition, all through Society, in my own person, is honourable, ample, and independent. I find that to make no exacting assertion of its claims, on the one hand – and steadily to take my stand by it, on the other, as a worthy calling, and my sole fortune – is to do right, and to take sufficient rank. Go where I will, in out of the way places and odd corners of the country, I always find something of personal affection in people whom I have never seen, mixed up with my public reputation. This is the best part of it, and it makes me very happy.[2]

Understandably, there are many difficulties in Dickens' vision of England. Thus, the ambiguity of change was captured from the outset. 'Scotland Yard', which appeared in the *Morning Chronicle* on 4 October 1836, satirised the idea of the discovery of primitive people in its account of the transformation of part of London. More generally, Dickens was clearly interested in using exploration in order to make points about England. In *Little Dorrit*, he referred to Mrs Clennam after her Calvinistic denunciation of sin:

> she still abided by her old impiety – still reversed the order of Creation, and breathed her own breath into a clay image of her Creator. Verily, verily, travellers have seen many monstrous idols in many countries; but no human eyes have ever seen more daring, gross, and shocking images of the Divine nature, than we creatures of the dust make in our own likenesses, of our own bad passions.[3]

Change is presented in 'Scotland Yard' as both restlessness and innovation, and the fading away of 'the ancient simplicity of its inhabitants' is regretted. The reference to 'the ancient simplicity' suggests a tendency, frequently seen in Dickens, to lapse into thinking about 'noble savages', although that attitude does not extend in his case to rebellion by the lower classes or by Blacks.

In England, the setting of life was indeed being changed. Townscapes were being transformed in the name of utility, propriety, convenience and reform, with timber and thatch seen as dated, unattractive, non-utilitarian and, increasingly, non-urban. Markets were removed from town streets to purposely built market houses, as in Tiverton in 1830 and Crediton in 1836.

More generally, Dickens' view of the past was scarcely rosy. In *Great Expectations*, Magwitch may have 'pondered over the question whether he might have been a better man under better circumstances. But he never justified himself by a hint tending that way, or tried to bend the past out of its eternal shape.'[4] In 'Refreshments for Travellers' (1860), his grim account of the terrible nature of the food available in the modern age of rail, Dickens avoided looking back with nostalgia:

> Take the old-established Bull's Head with its old-established knife-boxes on its old-established sideboards, its old-established flue under its old-established four-post bedsteads in its old-established airless rooms, its old-established frouziness up-stairs and down-stairs, its old-established cookery, and its old-established principles of plunder. Count up your injuries, in its side-dishes of ailing sweetbreads in white poultices … stringy fowls …

Soon after, in *Great Expectations*, Pip stays in a London hotel, the Hummums in Covent Garden, being lit there with a candle:

> As I had asked for a night-light, the chamberlain had brought me in, before he left me, the good old constitutional rush-light of those

virtuous days – an object like the ghost of a walking-cane, which instantly broke its back if it were touched, which nothing could ever be lighted at ... this foolish Argus.[5]

In *Martin Chuzzlewit*, conservatism was satirised in the views of the elderly denizens of the taverns near Todgers in London:

These gentry were much opposed to steam and all new-fangled ways, and held ballooning to be sinful, and deplored the degeneracy of the times; which that particular member of each little club who kept the keys of the nearest church professionally, always attributed to the prevalence of dissent and irreligion: though the major part of the company inclined to the belief that virtue went out with hair-powder, and that Old England's greatness had decayed amain with barbers.[6]

At the start of *A Christmas Carol*, Dickens mocks the standard conservatism, and applies that brilliantly to the use of language:

Old Marley was as dead as a door-nail. Mind! I don't mean to say that I know, of my own knowledge, what there is particularly dead about a door-nail. I might have been inclined, myself, to regard a coffin-nail as the deadest piece of ironmongery in the trade. But the wisdom of our ancestors is in the simile; and my unhallowed hands shall not disturb it, or the Country's done for. You will therefore permit me to repeat, emphatically, that Marley was as dead as a door-nail.

A particular setting of continuity was offered by Dickens' accounts of churches and churchyards. The wistful nostalgia for ruins of so many authors and painters over the previous century frequently, but not invariably, becomes, instead, with Dickens a hostility to decay and to the sentimentalisation of ruins, which he took as evidence of decay. Moreover, the coldness of many of the churches he depicts is a physical expression of what he sees as the institution's lack of warmth and true charity. Yet, in an historical sense, Dickens could also use churches to depict the inroads on the nation's past, and to do so in a fashion that challenged attempts to present it as exemplary. In *The Chimes*, the battered nature of history was captured by the old chimes in the church where the story begins:

> Centuries ago, these Bells had been baptised by bishops: so many centuries ago, that the register of their baptism was lost long, long before the memory of man: and no one knew their names. They had had their Godfathers and Godmothers, these Bells ... and had had their silver mugs no doubt, besides. But Time had mowed down their sponsors, and Henry the Eighth had melted down their mugs: and they now hung, nameless and mugless, in the church tower. Not speechless, though. Far from it.

In his *Child's History of England* (1853), Dickens described Henry VIII as 'a most intolerable ruffian' and 'a blot of blood and grease upon the History of England'. Jane Austen's closest work, although written while she was a child, was less colloquial.

Continuity is offered in the focus for a portion of *The Old Curiosity Shop* on an ancient Shropshire church with a benign schoolmaster and sexton, focus reminiscent of the close of H. V. Morton's *In Search of England* (1935), with its similar sense of a national identity away from the cities. There is a sentimentalisation of old rural churches, an aspect of Dickens' inconsistency in his estimation of the relativities of past and present. The schoolmaster in Dickens' novel, his only one in which he was positively influenced by the Gothic Revival before he started reacting against it quite forcefully, seeks to preserve the memory of the church from learned antiquaries who would 'strip fair Truth of every little shadowy vestment in which time and teeming fancies love to array her'. Moreover,

> when the aforesaid antiquaries did argue and contend that a certain secret vault was not the tomb of a grey-haired lady who had been

hanged and drawn and quartered by glorious Queen Bess for succouring a wretched priest who fainted of thirst and hunger at her door, the bachelor did solemnly maintain against all comers that the church was hallowed by the said poor lady's ashes; that her remains had been collected ... and there deposited ... and the bachelor did further (being highly excited at such times) deny the glory of Queen Bess, and assert the immeasurably greater glory of the meanest woman in her realm who had a merciful and tender heart.[7]

In *Oliver Twist*, the theme of falseness clouding true quality, until virtue brings forth the latter, is brought out alongside a village church, at the close of the happy ending, when Harry Maylie declares to Rose:

I left you with a firm determination to level all fancied barriers between yourself and me; resolved that if my world could not be yours, I would make yours mine; that no pride of birth should curl the lip at you, for I would turn from it. This I have done. Those who have shrunk from me because of this, have shrunk from you, and proved you so far right. Such power and patronage: such relatives of influence and rank: as smiled upon me then, look coldly now; but there are smiling fields and waving trees in England's richest county; and by one village church – mine, Rose, my own! – there stands a rustic dwelling which you can make me prouder of, than all the hopes I have renounced, measured a thousandfold. This is *my* rank and station now, and here I lay it down![8]

The reference, as so often in the novel, is to tarnished virtue, as with Charles Bates, once removed from a world of crime, becoming 'the merriest young grazier in Northamptonshire'.[9]

Dickens had a strong sense of the continuity of English culture,[10] and felt that the country around Gad's Hill was 'very little changed since Shakespeare's time',[11] the exact opposite to the situation in London. This sense of continuity, as well as the wonder of literature, and notably for children, was captured in *David Copperfield*. Oppressed by the education imposed by the Murdstones and their 'gloomy theology', David finds a solace:

> My father had left a small collection of books ... From that blessed little room, Roderick Random, Peregrine Pickle, Humphrew Clinker, Tom Jones, the Vicar of Wakefield, Don Quixote, Gil Blas, and Robinson Crusoe, came out, a glorious host, to keep me company. They kept alive my fancy, and my hope of something beyond that place and time, – they, and the Arabian Nights, and the Tales of the Genii, – and did me no harm; ... impersonating my favourite characters in them – as I did – and by putting Mr and Miss Murdstone into all the bad ones – which I did too. I have been Tom Jones (a child's Tom Jones, a harmless creature) for a week together. I have sustained my own idea of Roderick Random for a month at a stretch.

Robinson Crusoe is a subsequent point of reference for his experience.[12] Dickens' father indeed had such a collection of books, and Dickens' passage captures his admiration for the autodidact.

The 1841 preface to *Oliver Twist* includes a discussion of John Gay's *The Beggar's Opera* (1728), and made reference to Fielding, Defoe, Goldsmith, Smollett, Richardson, Mackenzie and Hogarth. In 1849, Dickens referred to Oliver Goldsmith's *The Vicar of Wakefield* (1766) as 'a book of which I think it is not too much to say that it has perhaps done more good in the world, and instructed more kinds of people in virtue, than any other fiction ever written'.[13] George Lillo's play *The London Merchant* (1731), the moralistic account of the fall of a young apprentice, George Barnwell, seduced by Sarah Millwood, a prostitute, was cited by Dickens in *Martin Chuzzlewit* with reference to the murder of an uncle.[14] Dickens also enjoyed the views of eighteenth-century literary sites in Peter Cunningham's *A Handbook for London, Past and Present* (1849).[15] In *Our Mutual Friend*, he refers to Ann Radcliffe's Gothic novel *The Mysteries of Udolpho* (1794), while, in *Hard Times*, the workers of

Coketown read Defoe and Goldsmith.[16] There was a comparison with Robinson Crusoe in *Hard Times*.[17]

Nevertheless, the novelists of the previous century, read by Dickens as a child,[18] and used as a source of names for his sons,[19] had, in part, faded from attention by the 1860s, with his own 1847 plan for an edition of them coming to nothing. It was difficult then to believe that a similar lack of interest would not happen to another generation of writers.

Dickens, perhaps always a journalist by nature, was adept at picking up movements and episodes from the times. Now we often think of him as the originator of what was really the currency of the day. Moreover, by addressing the condition of the people as a topic, and doing so through the prism of individual circumstances and personality, and in a way that offered much to those of very differing background and experience, Dickens ensured a continuing relevance, even if the particular issues of concern dated or became irrelevant. Dickens indeed presented himself as responding to the changing exigencies of the period. In 1849, he observed: 'I hope David Copperfield will "do", for your good correspondent. The world would not take another Pickwick from me, now; but we can be cheerful and merry I hope, notwithstanding, and with a little more purpose in us.'[20]

One form of resonance and relevance was offered by the extent to which the lived environment of much of urban England long remained what was seen as 'Dickensian'. Thus, W. Stanley Sykes, in his much reprinted *The Missing Money-Lender* (1931), referred to Barhaven, a fictional English manufacturing town where rapid, unplanned growth in the nineteenth century had left

dingy back-to-back houses crowded into courts and alleys of incredible ugliness with a complete disregard for light and air; noisy, smoky and odorous factories scattered at random among the residential parts of the town – all lay under a perpetual pall of smoke from the maze of chimney-pots.

George Orwell's *The Road to Wigan Pier* (1937) is in the same tradition.

Dickens' ability to personalise circumstances even more helped maintain relevance. In doing so, there was a continual risk of sentimentality, but the engagement with individuals, however poorly realised in some cases, provided a far more humane as well as imaginative account of society than that offered by those who dwelt on groups and trends. Dickens used imaginative literature as material for understanding and depicting historical events and peoples, selecting historical events, with the Gordon Riots (*Barnaby Rudge*) and the French Revolution (*A Tale of Two Cities*), that he can shape into effective tales. Dickens was also very conscious that he was a kind of contemporary historian, interpreting the extraordinary past he lived through His focus is on getting to grips with and understanding nineteenth-century people.

Taking an increasingly dim view of life and times, Dickens has been used as evidence to support the pessimist case of socio-economic change, and notably with *Hard Times* (1854) which was based on his 1854 visit to Preston where a strike to raise wages was totally unsuccessful. This pessimist case presents victims of early industrialisation with falling real wages and bad working conditions. There is also alleged middle-class indifference to domestic horrors and a greater focus on slavery and overseas problems, as in Mrs Jellyby in *Bleak House*. The optimist case replies that, although employees lost out for a time as producers, they gained as consumers of the cheap, mass-produced goods that industrialisation made possible, and from cheaper food. In practice, the critique of industrial towns was not original to Dickens, and he was not the foremost purveyor of it. In fact, the critique was a bandwagon onto which Dickens jumped. In part, *Hard Times* was his response to the commercial success of 1840s works about industrial towns, of which Gaskell's *Mary Barton* was the most celebrated.

With Dickens, there was the danger of being misleading. The most prominent financier is Merdle, a gigantic fraud, as are the Americans in *Martin Chuzzlewit* pushing sales in property in the town of Eden.[21] There were indeed fraudulent financiers in the period, such as Samuel Peto, while Anthony Trollope was to present the more memorable Augustus Melmotte in *The Way We Live Now* (1874–5), a more vital figure than Merdle who, instead, displays banality. Yet, this depiction by Dickens and Trollope underplayed the more positive role of finance. Financial services indeed developed in Dickens' lifetime as a major force for effective investment, and thus for economic growth; and, as he commented in 1866, when Overend, Gurney [and Company], the leading private bank failed, it would 'play the deuce with all public gaieties and with all the Arts'.[22] Moreover, while in the end, Peto's companies collapsed in 1866, he had been a builder, notably of railways and of major buildings in London, on a massive scale, one of the world's biggest. There was much more to Peto than a mere fraud, unlike the Merdles and Melmottes. His financing was dodgy, but his achievements real.

Yet, as also with the workhouses, a critical approach, then or now, on the basis of accuracy is only justified if it is assumed that the novels should be analyses of social conditions without imaginative painting, which was clearly not the case. Indeed, in November 1865, Dickens replied to criticism of *Our Mutual Friend* from a friend and fellow novelist, Bulwer Lytton:

> I work slowly and with great care, and never give way to my invention recklessly, but constantly restrain it; and that I think it is my infirmity to fancy or perceive relations in things which are not apparent generally. Also, I have such an inexpressible enjoyment of what I see in a droll light, that I dare say I pet it as if it were a spoilt child.[23]

Social context indeed takes on its power for Dickens as the provision of plot for moral accounts of virtue and vice, salvation and retribution:[24] 'The eyes again!' cries Sikes 'in an unearthly screech' as he falls to his death.[25] Evil is punished, which provides a reason for optimism.

'One must have a heart of stone to read the death of Little Nell without laughing.' The verdict of Oscar Wilde captures a critical reaction to Dickens, and yet pays unwilling tribute to his continuing popularity. Wilde in practice had not read *The Old Curiosity Shop*, in which Little Nell's death is not in fact described. The sentimentality he derided continues to attract, and helps sugar the pill offered by an imaginative engagement with the frequently grim and miserable nature of life. The latter was an inherent aspect of Dickens' focus on moral as well as political and social injustices. He achieved this focus by broadening the sympathies of his readers and listeners. This was an aspect of the responsibility to his audiences that Dickens saw as crucial to his purposes.

These sympathies were inherently problematized by the role in individual plight of the issues posed by background and upbringing.[26] The crises of response to these issues provide key elements of continuity, as in *Dombey and Son*. Dickens, indeed, was concerned with far more than truth as a measure of society. Indeed, with the original concept of an omnipresent shadow,[27] *Household Words* was advertised as intended 'to help in the discussion of the most important social questions of the time'. However, in his novels, the imaginative dimension was more to the fore. Advising William Snow not to focus on fiction, Dickens observed:

Whether the substance of your book be true or fictitious, is nothing to the purpose. If you cannot grace truth in the narration, and have not the faculty of telling it in writing, you should either leave it untold, or leave it to the chance of being told by some one else. If it were a reason for writing, that what is written is true, surely there is nothing to prevent the whole civilised world from becoming authors, in as much as every man, woman, and child, has some truthful experience, and might, on such a plea, rush into print with it.[28]

Dickens, in contrast, was a master of image and word-painting, as in his comment on Mr Morfin playing his violoncello and thinking of Harriet:

> By degrees, the violoncello, in unison with his own frame of mind, glided melodiously into the 'Harmonious Blacksmith,' which he played over and over again, until his ruddy and serene face gleamed like true metal on the anvil of a veritable blacksmith. In fire, the violoncello and the empty chair were the companions of his bachelorhood until nearly midnight; and when he took his supper, the violoncello, set up on end in the sofa corner, big with the latent harmony of a whole foundry full of harmonious blacksmiths, seemed to ogle the empty chair out of its crooked eyes, with unutterable intelligence.[29]

Writing eighteen years later, to praise Bulwer Lytton's 'The Secret Way' from *Lost Tales of Miletus* (1866), Dickens again focused on the pictorial quality of the prose:

> the narrative itself, the painting in it, the distinctness attained, the glowing force of it, the imagination in it, and yet the terseness and closeness of it, these *astonish* me! … quite apart from its winning tenderness and grace. Of Death and Sisyphus at table – again – I have as dear and vivid a picture as if I had looked in at the window and seen them together.[30]

Dickens' own narrative structure, perforce, had to be different. He preferred to make his characters 'play out the play' and wrote of the need to set the major scenes so as to impress them on the memory of the readers.[31] Drama, frequently of a melodramatic, even Neo-Gothic type, was also a key element, as in 'No Thoroughfare', which he proposed to Wilkie Collins

> to culminate in a wintry flight and pursuit across the Alps. Let us be obliged to go over – say the Simplon Pass – under lonely circumstances, and against warnings … There we can get Ghostly

interest, picturesque interest, breathless interest of time and
circumstance, and force the design up to any powerful climax we
please ... we shall get a very Avalanche of power out of it, and
thunder it down on the readers' heads.[32]

Dickens was not alone in generating such tension. Written by
Hardy in 1872 and serialised in *Tinsley's Magazine*, *A Pair of
Blue Eyes* was a love triangle between Elfride Swancourt and
two suitors. At the end of an episode, one of her suitors, Henry
Knight, is left hanging on a cliff edge and the readers do not
know whether he will survive. At the start of the next episode,
he is rescued by a rope made of Elfride's underwear and lives to
continue the romantic tension. This is the original use of the idea
of a cliff-hanger ending.

The frenetic journeys of guilty figures provide drama in
Dickens, as in *Martin Chuzzlewit* and *Dombey and Son*; while a
fantastic, imaginative, opium-induced dream begins *The Mystery
of Edwin Drood*. The journey of life brings in justice repeatedly
and vividly in Dickens' novels, a justice distinct from that of
human law. Thus, Ralph Nickleby hangs himself 'on an iron
hook immediately below the trap-door in the ceiling – in the
very place to which the eyes of his son, a lonely, desolate, little
creature, had so often been directed in childish terror, fourteen
years before'.[33]

Dickens addresses the universal human condition. He tackles
in part historical events, some of which happened thirty years
before. Reform and change had worked their effect, as in
the closure of the Marshalsea Prison. Yet, not only do these
and other institutions seem to be contemporary, to belong
to Dickens' own times, but they also point forward to ours.
Class, social opportunity (or the lack of it), frustration with
the organs of government, and the debate on money and
its corrosive impact on those who have it as well as those
who have not, all seem very fresh. Dickens employed fiction
to awaken attention to the state of the nation and, more
particularly, of the poor and the precarious. He believed that

the people should work for a better future, and be steady and sure accordingly.

Much of the engagement of readers is because of the genius of Dickens' writing. This is exemplified by how he gives life to inanimate objects. Thus, not only is the railway a revolutionary form of transport, but it also seems to have a life of its own: powerful, alarming, exciting, even destructive. It can kill people, yet it can offer new horizons to their lives. Far from being simply comically sad about failings, notably selfishness, and voyeuristic about crime, fraud and misery, Dickens also offered hope through the redemptive power of goodness.

SELECTED FURTHER READING

Claire Tomalin's is the best among a number of fine biographies. The Pilgrim edition of his letters is crucial. The following is a selective list. Earlier works can be pursued through their bibliographies.

Ackroyd, P., *Dickens' London. An Imaginative Vision* (1987).

Ackroyd, P., *Dickens* (1990).

Belchem, J., *Popular Radicalism in Nineteenth-Century Britain* (1995).

Biagini, E., *Gladstone* (1999).

Bills, M. (ed.), *Dickens and the Artists* (2012).

Black, J., *The English Press. A History* (2001).

Collins, P., *Dickens and Crime* (1962).

Collins, P., *Dickens and Education* (1963).

Collins, P., *Dickens: The Public Readings* (1975).

Davis, J., *The Great Exhibition* (1999).

Dentith, S., *Society and Cultural Forms in Nineteenth-Century England* (1999).

Englander, D., *Landlord and Tenant in Urban Britain, 1838-1978* (1983).

Fielding, K. J. (ed.), *The Speeches of Charles Dickens* (1988).

Forster, J., *The Life of Charles Dickens* (1872-4).

Fox, C. (ed.), *London: World City, 1800-1840* (1992).

Foxell, S., *Mapping London: Making Sense of the City* (2007).

Freeman, M. J., and Aldcroft, D. H. (eds), *Transport in Victorian Britain* (1988).

Goodway, D., *London Chartism, 1834-1848* (1982).

Halliday, S., *The Great Stink of London: Sir Joseph Bazalgette and the Cleansing of the Victorian Metropolis* (1999).

Hartley, J., *Charles Dickens and the House of Fallen Women* (2008).

Hirst, D., *Welfare and Society 1832-1991* (1991).

Hunt, T., *Building Jerusalem: The Rise and Fall of the Victorian City* (2005).

Jenkins, T., *Sir Robert Peel* (1999).

Kidd, A., *Society and the Poor in Nineteenth-Century England* (1999).

Koven, S., *Slumming: Sexual and Social Politics in Victorian London* (2004).

Macaskill, H., *Charles Dickens At Home* (2011).

McCalman, I., *Radical Underworld: Prophets, Revolutionaries and Pornographers in London, 1795-1850* (1988).

McWilliam, R., *Popular Politics in Nineteenth-Century England* (1998).

Mingay, G. E., *Land and Society in England 1850-1914* (1996).

Mokyr, J., *The Enlightened Economy: An Economic History of Britain, 1700-1850* (2009).

Mullan, J., *The Artful Dickens: The Tricks and Ploys of the Great Novelist* (2020).

Porter, A., *The Oxford History of the British Empire. III. The Nineteenth Century* (1999).

Ridley, J., *The Young Disraeli* (1995).

Ridley, J., *Victoria, 1837-1901* (2015).

Schlicke, P., *Dickens and Popular Entertainment* (1985).

Schlicke, P., *Oxford Reader's Companion to Dickens* (1999).

Smith, P. T., *Policing Victorian London. Political Policing, Public Order, and the Metropolitan Police* (1984).

Stephens, W. D., *Education in Britain, 1750-1914* (1999).

Taylor, D., *Crime, Policing and Punishment in England 1750-1914* (1998).

Tillotson, K. and Butt, J., *Dickens at Work* (1957).

Tomalin, C., *Charles Dickens. A Life* (2011).

Tosh, J., *A Man's Place: Masculinity and the Middle-class Home in Victorian England* (1999).

Tyack, G., *Sir James Pennethorne and the Making of Victorian London* (1992).

White, J., *London in the Nineteenth Century: 'A Human Awful Wonder of God'* (2009).

Wilson, A. N., *The Mystery of Charles Dickens* (2020).

NOTES

Numbers after abbreviations in footnotes relate to chapter numbers.

BH   *Bleak House*, 1852–83

BR   *Barnaby Rudge*, 1841

DC   *David Copperfield*, 1849–50

DS   *Dombey and Son*, 1846–8

GE   *Great Expectations*, 1860–1

LD   *Little Dorritt*, 1855–7

MC   *Martin Chuzzlewit*, 1843–4

MED   *The Mystery of Edwin Drood*, 1870

NN   *Nicholas Nickleby*, 1838–9

OCS   *Old Curiosity Shop*, 1840–1

OT   *Oliver Twist*, 1838–9

OMF   *Our Mutual Friend*, 1864–5

PP   *Pickwick Papers*, 1836–7

TTC   *Tale of Two Cities*, 1859

Preface

1. *LD* 3, 6, 7.
2. *DC* 11.
3. *ED* 6.
4. *NN* 28.

1 London: The Stage of All

1. *MC* 40.
2. W. Thom, *Pedestrianism; or, an account of the performances of celebrated pedestrians during the last and present century* (Aberdeen, 1813).
3. *LD* 46.
4. *MC* 36.
5. *OCS* 40; *OMF* 2.
6. J. Baker, *The Business of Satirical Prints in Late-Georgian England* (Basingstoke, 2017).
7. *NN* 21.
8. *Letters* VII, 2.
9. *OMF* 3.
10. *DC* 36.
11. *OMF* 12.
12. *NN* 32.
13. E. W. Marrs Jr. (ed.), *The Letters of Charles and Mary Anne Lamb* III (1978), p. 96.
14. *BH* 22.
15. *DC* 5.
16. See also, for example, the death of Barkis, *DC* 30.
17. *OT* 8.
18. *Letters* X, 53.
19. *LD* 70.
20. *MC* 27.
21. *BH* 26.
22. D. R. Thorpe (ed.), *Who's In. Who's Out. The Journals of Kenneth Rose I, 1944–1979* (London, 2018), p. 415.
23. *LD* 3.

24. P. J. Waller, *Town, City, and Nation: England 1850-1914* (Oxford, 1980).
25. 'Poor Mercantile Jack.' For details including for the nineteenth century, I. C. Taylor, 'The Court and Cellar Dwelling: The Eighteenth Century Origin of the Liverpool Slum', *Transactions of the Historic Society of Lancashire and Cheshire*, 122 (1971), pp. 67–90.
26. OCS 8.
27. DS 47.
28. GE 54.
29. OCS 5.
30. DC 47.
31. OMF 12; GE 20–1; ED 11.
32. LD 3.
33. NN 19.
34. HT 10; Letters XI, 325.
35. DC 47.
36. DS 4.
37. DS 33.
38. OMF 4.
39. GE 25.
40. *Haunted Man* 1.
41. OT 21.
42. GE 20.
43. OCS 1.
44. *Letters* V, 642-5.
45. *Letters* V, 648.
46. NN 62; BH 11.
47. BH 16.
48. *Letters* V, 554.
49. *Letters* V, 618.
50. BH 22.
51. *Letters* IV, 92.
52. *Letters* V, 342.
53. LD 3.

54. B. Weinstein, *Liberalism and Local Government in Early Victorian London* (Woodbridge, 2011).
55. S. Jenkins, *A Short History of London. The Creation of a World Capital* (London, 2019), p. 161.
56. V. Kelley, *Cheap Street. London's Street Markets and the Cultures of Informality, c. 1850–1939* (Manchester, 2019).
57. OCS 24; DC 17; GE 27.

2 The Condition of the People

1. *Letters* XI, 152.
2. *HT* 18.
3. H. I. Dutton and J.E. King, '"A Fallacy, A Delusion, and A Snare": arbitration and conciliation in the Preston strike, 1853-4', *Transactions of the Historic Society of Lancashire and Cheshire*, 131 (1981), p. 65.
4. *OT* 23.
5. *OT* 2, 4.
6. *OMF* 16.
7. *OMF* 31; R. Richardson, *Dickens and the Workhouse. Oliver Twist and the London Poor* (Oxford, 2012).
8. *DS* 55.
9. *Letters* III, p. 312.
10. *Letters* XI, 165.
11. *MC* 5.
12. *PP* 6; GE 42; DC 1, 13.
13. *DS* 58.
14. *OT* 26.
15. *NN* 17.
16. *BH* 7.
17. *Letters* X, 37.
18. *Letters* I, 51.
19. H. Barker, *Family and Business during the Industrial Revolution* (Oxford, 2017).
20. *DS* 1.

21. *ED* 1.
22. *Letters* II, 10.
23. *OMF* 4, 10, 33.
24. *MC* 29-30.
25. *ED* 3-4.
26. *DS* 60.
27. *DS* 5.
28. *Letters* XI, 269.
29. *HT* 5.
30. *MC* 2.
31. *MC* 11, 36.
32. *DS* 34.
33. *OCS* 8.
34. *OMF* 3.
35. *OMF* 20.
36. *GE* 56.
37. *GE* 23.
38. *GE* 42.
39. *OT* 5.
40. *MC* 9.

3 The World of Steam

1. *BH* 28.
2. *MC* 40.
3. *Letters* V, II, 30.
4. *BH* 55.
5. *ED* 6.
6. *BH* 27.
7. *DS* 6.
8. *PP* 8.
9. *GE* 7.
10. *Letters* X, 1–2.
11. *Letters* XI, 56–7.
12. *Letters* XI, 61–2.
13. *Letters* XI, 306–7, 313–14.
14. *DS* 2.

15. *Letters* V, 378.
16. *Letters* V, 65, cf. 350.
17. *Letters* XI, 68, cf. 116.
18. *DC* 61.
19. *OT* 42; *LD* 13.
20. *Letters* XI, 79, 137.
21. *Letters* V, 514.
22. *HT* 12.
23. *HT* 27.
24. *OCS* 43.
25. *OCS* 44.
26. *OCS,* 44.
27. *OCS* 45.
28. *Letters* 7, pp. 4, 6.
29. *BH* 63.
30. *ED* 13.
31. *DC* 17.
32. *BH* 7, 28.
33. *DS* 4.
34. *MC* 28.
35. *LD* 66; *NN* 1.
36. *OT* 26.
37. *MC* 36.

4 Crime and the Press

1. *Letters* V, 159.
2. *BH* 54.
3. *MC* 36–7.
4. *DS* 3
5. *Letters* XI, 371, 394.
6. *OMF* 3.
7. *OMF* 4, 16.
8. *GE* 18.
9. *OT* 50; *MC* 48.
10. *NN* 50.
11. *Letters* V, 473–4.

12. *Letters* V, 650.
13. *DC* 36.
14. *DS* 53.
15. *OT* 11.
16. *MC* 16.
17. *OT* 23.
18. *NN* 16.
19. *Letters* III, 262–3, 265–7.
20. *OT* 3, 5, 17, 42.
21. *MC* 8, 11, 18.
22. *BH* 11, 29; *LD* 20.
23. *NN* 32, 38, 46.
24. *Letters* XI, 160.
25. *NN* 16.

5 Government

1. *Letters* XI, 141.
2. *Letters* VII, 400.
3. *HT* 2.
4. *Letters* XI, 116.
5. *GE* 21.
6. *MC* 1.
7. *Letters*, IV, 7.
8. *DS* 4.
9. *NN* 2.
10. *HT* 17.
11. J. Aitkenhead, *Census of Religious Worship, 1851: Returns for Worcester* (Worcester, 2000).
12. *BH* 12.
13. *ED* 23.
14. *Letters*, V, 251.
15. *HT* 15. See also K. Levitan, 'Literature the City and the Census: examining the social body in Victorian Britain', *Gaskell Society Journal*, 20 (2006), pp. 68–71.
16. N. Russell, *The Novelist and Mammon: Literary Responses to the World of Commerce in the Nineteenth century* (Oxford, 1986).

17. E. Freedgood, *Victorian Writing about Risk: Imagining a Safe England in a Dangerous World* (Cambridge, 2000).
18. NN 1; GE 22.
19. MC 27; OMF 1.
20. MC 34.
21. MC 27.
22. OMF 10.
23. *Letters* XI, 144.

6 Public Order and Pressure for Change

1. *Letters* IV, 1.
2. GE 16.
3. OT 31.
4. OCS 16.
5. OT 10–11.
6. NN 2.
7. *Letters* II, 281.
8. MC 51.
9. OT 9.
10. TTC 1.
11. GE 21.
12. GE 28.
13. NN 46.
14. *Letters* III, 329–30.
15. OT 19.
16. *Letters* VII, 110.
17. *Letters* IV, 31.
18. *Letters* V, 156.
19. *Letters* XI, 43.
20. OT 6.
21. TTC 13.
22. *Letters* V, 488.
23. MC 31.
24. *Letters* XI, 278–9.
25. *Letters* XI, 283.
26. OT 51.

27. MC 3.
28. MC 13.
29. NN 46.

7 Culture

1. PP 7.
2. NN 24.
3. LD 17.
4. P. Humfrey, *The Stafford Gallery. The Greatest Art Collection of Regency London* (London, 2019).
5. *Letters* III, p. 299.
6. *Letters* V, 622.
7. T. Richards, *The commodity culture of Victorian England: advertising and spectacle, 1851–1914* (Stanford, CA, 1990).
8. LD 48.
9. OT 30.
10. *Battle of Life* 2.
11. M. Wheeler, *English Fiction of the Victorian Period, 1830–1890* (London, 1985).
12. OMF 8.
13. *Letters* X, 30.
14. MC 5.
15. K. Flint, *The Victorians and the Visual Imagination* (Cambridge, 2000).
16. HT 3.
17. OMF 8.
18. L. Bending, *The Representation of Bodily Pain in Late Nineteenth-Century English Culture* (Oxford, 2000).
19. *Letters* IV, 108, 114, V, 7.
20. *Letters* XI, 48.
21. M. Wheeler, *Heaven, Hell and the Victorians* (Cambridge, 1994).
22. *Letters* V, 184.
23. OT 40.
24. *Letters* V, 45.
25. *Letters* V, 45–6.

26. ED 6.
27. *Letters* V, 158, cf. 194.
28. *Letters* V, 194 cf. 613.
29. *All The Year Round*, 8 March 1862.
30. S. Orwell and I. Angus (eds), G. Orwell, *Collected Essays I* (London, 1970), p. 471.
31. *Letters* XI, 157.
32. *DS* 5.
33. *LD* 3.
34. *DC* 26.
35. *OT* 5, 18.
36. *ED* 2, 7.
37. *Letters* V, 20.
38. *Letters* V, 541.
39. *BR* 82.
40. *DS* 46.
41. *OT* 26.
42. *NN* 23.
43. *Letters* III, 325–6.
44. *MC* 5, 30.
45. *Letters* V, 162–3.
46. *Letters* V, 640.

8 The 1810s

1. Exeter, Devon County Record Office, Sidmouth Papers, 152 M, correspondence 1815 OH 3, 8.
2. *DC* 26.
3. W. Hay, *Lord Liverpool: A Political Life* (Woodbridge, 2018).
4. R. Poole, *Peterloo. The English Uprising* (Oxford, 2019).
5. *GE* 20.

9 The 1820s

1. *GE* 2.
2. *DC* 47.
3. E. A. Smith, *George IV* (New Haven, Conn., 1999).

4. T. Paul, *The Poverty of Disaster. Debt and Insecurity in Eighteenth-Century Britain* (Cambridge, 2019); C. Allen, *Charles Dickens and the Blacking Factory* (Oxford, 2011).

10 The 1830s

1. MC 31.
2. BH 7.
3. *Letters* 1, 6.
4. OT 49.
5. *Letters* 1, 53.
6. OT 27.
7. Shakespeare, *King Lear*, Act IV, scene 6.
8. *Letters* 1, 106–7.
9. LD 48.
10. NN 16.
11. NN 18.
12. DC 48; A. Sparrow, *Obscure Scribblers: A History of Parliamentary Journalism* (London, 2003), pp. 24, 37–9, 42.

11 The 1840s

1. *Letters* III, p. 291.
2. D. Read, *Peel and the Victorians* (Oxford, 1987).
3. DC 27.
4. *Letters* V, p. 149.
5. MC 35.
6. ED 4.
7. DS 61.
8. *Letters* V, 486.
9. *Letters* V, 580.
10. 'Travelling Abroad' (1860).
11. *Letters* XI, 42.
12. *Letters* II, 23-7.
13. *Letters* II, 16-17, X, 54.
14. *Letters* IV, 254, 259.
15. NN 64.
16. *Letters* V, 342, 602–3.

17. *Letters* II, 100.
18. J. Sutherland, *Victorian Fiction. Writers, Publishers, Readers* (Basingstoke, 1995), pp. 87–94.
19. *Letters* II, 176.
20. *Letters* II, 201.

12 The 1850s

1. *HT* 11.
2. *HT* 4.
3. *HT* 7.
4. W. L. Burn, *The Age of Equipoise: A Study of the Mid-Victorian Generation* (London, 1964).
5. *BH* 2.
6. *BH* 7, 9.
7. *Letters* V, 43.
8. *Letters* XI, 109.
9. *BH* 12.
10. *BH* 40.
11. *Letters* VII, 571.
12. *LD* 58.
13. *Letters* VII, 715–16.
14. *LD* 26.
15. *Letters* VIII, 6, 10.
16. *LD* 10.
17. *Letters* VII, 587-8.
18. *TTC* 7.
19. *Letters* VII, 599.

13 The 1860s

1. *Letters* XI, 3.
2. *OMF* 20, 26, 33.
3. *Letters* XI, 184.
4. *Letters* XI, 69.
5. *Letters* XI, 73.
6. *Letters* XI, 292-3.

7. M. R. D. Foot and H. C. G. Matthew (eds), *The Gladstone Diaries* III (Oxford, 1974), p. 226, see also 314.
8. *ED* 11.
9. *OMF* 3.
10. P. Collins, *Charles Dickens. The Public Readings* (Oxford, 1975), p. xx.
11. *OMF* 11.
12. *ED* 6.
13. *HT* 20.
14. *ED* 17.
15. *TTC* 45.
16. P. J. Waller, *Writers, Readers, and Reputations: Literary Life in Britain 1870–1918* (Oxford, 2003).

14 Dickens's America

1. *GE* 34.
2. *MC* 13.
3. *MC* 34.
4. *MC* 34.
5. *MC* 16, 33–4.
6. K. R. Stevens, *Border Diplomacy: The Caroline and McLeod Affairs in Anglo-American-Canadian Relations, 1837-1842* (Tuscaloosa, Al., 1989).
7. *Letters* IV, p. 11.
8. *Letters* V, 396.
9. *Letters* V, 548–9.
10. *MC* 12, 15.
11. *MC* 21, 33.
12. *DS* 54, 31; *ED* 11.
13. *Letters* II, 102–7.
14. *Letters* IV, 74.
15. *MC* 17.
16. *Letters* X, 53–4.
17. *Letters* XI, 21.
18. *MC* 34.
19. *Letters* XI, 115.

20. Collins, *Readings*, p. xxix.
21. *Letters* XII, 13.

15 Britain and the World

1. *DS* 31.
2. *DS* 35, *OMF* 11.
3. J. Davis, 'Garibaldi and England', *History Today*, 32/12 (1982).
4. *Letters* V, 579.
5. *Letters* XI, 218, 226, 231.
6. F. Neal, 'The Birkenhead Garibaldi Riots of 1862', *Transactions of the Historic Society of Lancashire and Cheshire*, 131 (1981), pp. 87–111.
7. *Letters* XI, 40.
8. *DC* 1.
9. *DC* 4.
10. *DC* 11.
11. *OMF* 25.
12. *BH* 10–11.
13. *ED* 1.
14. *GE* 22.
15. *NN* 32.
16. *ED* 2-3, 7–8; *MC* 54.
17. *LD* 7.
18. *DC* 22.
19. *DC* 52, 57.
20. *DC* 1.
21. *GE* 54.
22. *BH* 13.
23. J. Lewis, *Empire of Sentiment: The Death of Livingstone and the Myth of Victorian Imperialism* (Cambridge, 2018).
24. *Letters* V, 622.
25. *LD* 21.
26. *BH* 4.
27. *TTC* 7.

28. *DC* 36.
29. *PP* 4.
30. *DC* 52.
31. *BH* 49.
32. *ED* 4, 12, 14.
33. *Letters* IV, 77.
34. *BH* 7.
35. *Letters* X, 53.
36. *Letters* XI, 115–16. In 2020, the Dickens Museum in Kent was defaced with graffiti calling the author racist: https://www.telegraph.co.uk/news/2020/06/29/charles-dickens-museum-defaced-graffiti-calling-author-racist/.
37. *ED* 16.
38. *DS* 41, 44.
39. *Letters* II, 92.
40. Forster, *Life of Charles Dickens*, II, 100–2. See also M. Hollington, 'Dickens and Italy', *Journal of Anglo-Italian Studies*, 1 (1991), pp. 126–36.
41. J. Atkinson, *French Novels and the Victorians* (Oxford, 2017).
42. *Letters* X, 53.
43. *TTC* 45.
44. *OT* 43.
45. *OT* 46.
46. *ED* 11.
47. *LD* 25.
48. *NN* 38.

16 Dickens in Retrospect

1. *ED* 4.
2. *Letters* V, 341.
3. *LD* 66.
4. *GE* 56.
5. *GE* 45.
6. *MC* 9.
7. *OCS* 54.
8. *OT* 51.

9. OT 53.

10. *Letters* V, 163.

11. *Letters* XI, 449.

12. *DC* 4-5, 26.

13. *Letters* V, 517.

14. *MC* 9.

15. *Letters* V, 555.

16. *OMF* 32; *HT* 8.

17. *HT* 27.

18. *Letters* V, 158.

19. *Letters* V, 483.

20. *Letters* V, 527.

21. *MC* 23.

22. *Letters* XI, 293, 200.

23. *Letters* XI, 113.

24. J. R. Reed, *Dickens and Thackeray: Punishment and Forgiveness* (Athens, Ohio, 1995).

25. OT 50.

26. A. Sadrin, *Parentage and Inheritance in the Novels of Charles Dickens* (Cambridge, 1994).

27. Letters *V*, 622–3.

28. *Letters* V, 160. See also 163–4. Snow followed his advice.

29. *DS* 58.

30. *Letters* XI, 135-6.

31. *Letters* XI, 160-1.

32. *Letters* XI, 413.

33. *NN* 62.

THE STREETS ARE COLOURED ACCORDING TO THE

Lowest class. Vicious, semi-criminal.   Very poor, casual. Chronic want.   Poor. 18s. to 21s. a week for a moderate family.

A combination of colours—an dark blue and black, or pink and red—indicates that th

Charles Booth's map of London poverty, 1889. (Courtesy of the Wellcome Collection)

arts of St. George's Hanover Square, Westminster, Strand, Holborn and Islington; the whole of St. Giles's and
d most of St. Pancras.

: GENERAL CONDITION OF THE INHABITANTS, AS UNDER:—

Mixed. Some comfortable, others poor.   Fairly comfortable. Good ordinary earnings.   Middle class. Well-to-do.   Upper-middle and Upper classes.
Wealthy.

he street contains a fair proportion of each of the classes represented by the respective colours.

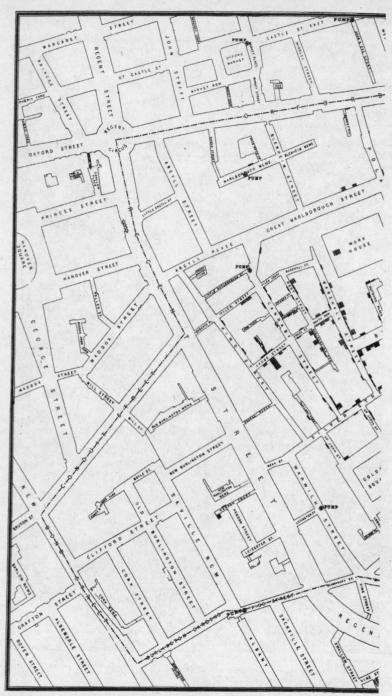

John Snow's map of cholera cases in the London epidemic of 1854, drawn by Charles Cheffins. (Courtesy of the Wellcome Collection)

PLATE I.

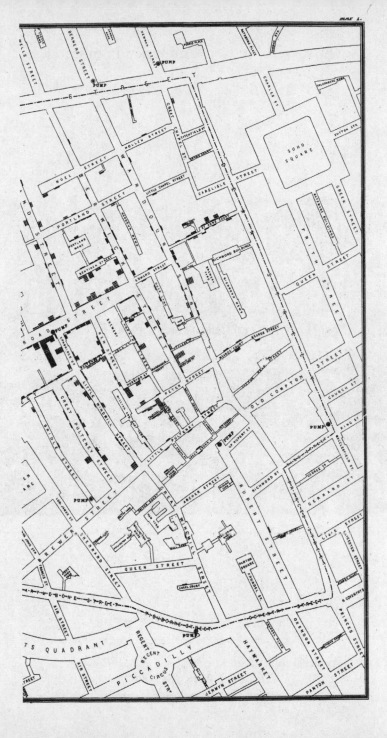

Also available from Amberley Publishing

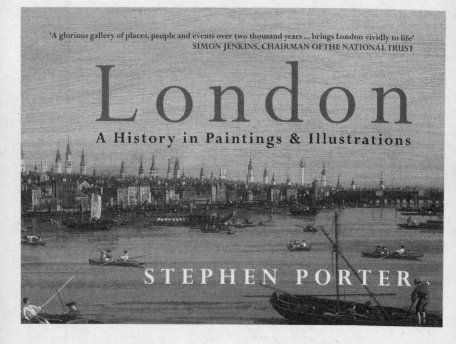

'A glorious gallery of places, people and events over two thousand years ... brings London vividly to life'
SIMON JENKINS, CHAIRMAN OF THE NATIONAL TRUST

London

A History in Paintings & Illustrations

STEPHEN PORTER